The Mediating Nation

The Mediating Nation

Late American Realism, Globalization, and the Progressive State

NATHANIEL CADLE

The University of North Carolina Press *Chapel Hill*

Cover illustration: George Luks (1867–1933). *Armistice Night* (detail), 1918. Oil on canvas,
37 × 68⅜ in. (94 × 173.7 cm). Whitney Museum of American Art, New York; gift of an
anonymous donor 54.58. Digital image © Whitney Museum of American Art.

Library of Congress Cataloging-in-Publication Data
Cadle, Nathaniel, author.
The mediating nation : late American realism, globalization, and the progressive state /
Nathaniel Cadle.
pages cm
Includes bibliographical references and index.
ISBN 978-1-4696-1845-6 (pbk : alk. paper) — ISBN 978-1-4696-1846-3 (ebook)
1. American literature—20th century—History and criticism. 2. Realism in literature.
3. Progressivism in literature. 4. Multiculturalism in literature. 5. Literature and
transnationalism. 6. Modernism (Literature)—United States. I. Title.
PS228.R38C33 2014
810.9'12—dc23
2014008429

Portions of this work have appeared previously as "America as 'World-Salvation':
Josiah Strong, W. E. B. Du Bois, and the Global Rhetoric of American Exceptionalism,"
in *American Exceptionalisms: From Winthrop to Winfrey,* ed. Sylvia Söderlind and James
Taylor Carson (Albany: State University of New York Press, 2011), 125–46, and are reprinted
here with permission of the publisher.

18 17 16 15 14   5 4 3 2 1

THIS BOOK WAS DIGITALLY PRINTED.

To my mother and my father

Contents

Acknowledgments

One of the chief pleasures of undertaking research is having the opportunity to share ideas with—and allow those ideas to take shape in conversation with—colleagues, both near and far. I am fortunate that my most enthusiastic interlocutors are also the nearest: those I see on an almost daily basis at Florida International University. I am particularly grateful for the discerning comments and questions of Steven Blevins and Jason Pearl, who between them have read nearly every part of this book as it was being written. I am also grateful to Vernon Dickson, Paul Feigenbaum, Michael Gillespie, Bruce Harvey, Ana Luszczynska, Phillip Marcus, Asher Milbauer, Carmela Pinto McIntire, Meri-Jane Rochelson, Heather Russell, and Andrew Strycharski for their willingness to respond to requests for all sorts of advice, ranging from the conceptual to the mundane. Across town, at the University of Miami, John Funchion, Joel Nickels, and Tim Watson have served as sounding-boards on multiple occasions, providing valuable feedback at important junctures in this project's history. Farther afield, Carrie Tirado Bramen, James Taylor Carson, Keri Holt, Johannes Lang, David Luis-Brown, Walter Benn Michaels, Donald Pease, Yvette Piggush, and Sylvia Söderlind have helped me to articulate the aims and claims of this book more clearly by asking thoughtful questions or by making judicious recommendations. I appreciate their generosity and goodwill.

For providing material support for my research in the form of a Summer Faculty Development Award, I thank FIU's College of Arts and Sciences. I also thank James Sutton, my department's chairperson, for his unwavering support of my research, which has manifested itself in a course release and in steady funding for travel to conferences as well as in his general commitment to advocating for junior faculty.

I continue to owe a debt of gratitude—I always shall—to my mentors at the University of North Carolina at Chapel Hill for modeling the kind and quality of scholarship and teaching that I strive to achieve. Jane Thrailkill in particular inspires me not only because of her knowledge, professionalism, and scholarly acumen, but also because of her long-term investment in each of her students. I am the beneficiary of such an investment. And while it has taken several years for the ideas to gestate fully, I can trace my thinking about some of the problems that this book explores back to specific conversations with Tyler Curtain, Michael Hunt, Joy Kasson, Timothy Marr, and John McGowan.

Working with the University of North Carolina Press has been an extremely rewarding experience. Mark Simpson-Vos is as patient, perceptive, and encouraging an editor as any author could hope for, and he has a knack for providing the right sort of guidance at exactly the right time. Cait Bell-Butterfield, Susan Garrett, Ron Maner, and John Wilson have carefully and cheerfully shepherded my manuscript through its later stages. The finished book also benefits greatly from the insightful and practical recommendations of two anonymous but very engaged readers.

Portions of chapter 1 appeared in an earlier form in the edited collection *American Exceptionalisms: From Winthrop to Winfrey* (2011); I am grateful to SUNY Press for permission to reprint that material here. I am also grateful to the Bridgeman Art Library for helping me obtain the illustration that appears in chapter 4 and to International Publishers for assisting me with information about the introduction's epigraph.

I reserve my deepest appreciation for my family and friends, who have provided the less tangible but no less crucial emotional support that has sustained me throughout this project. My parents, Bill and Connie Cadle, instilled in me a love for the printed word, and they remain a welcome and encouraging presence in my life. My brothers, Neil Cadle and Patrick Cadle, are informed readers who are almost as fascinated by the period I study as I am. Some of their astute observations have made their way into this book, and their good humor has helped to keep me grounded. More than anyone else, however, it is Dulce María Escobio who has lived the longest with *The Mediating Nation* and who has been its most ardent champion. Her faith in this project—and in me—has been the strongest motivation and the most meaningful reward for completing it.

The Mediating Nation

Transnational Circulation in the Age of Realism and Progressivism

World history did not always exist; history as world history is a result.
—*Karl Marx, "Introduction to a Critique of Political Economy" (1857)*

On April 20, 1915, as the First World War continued to divide most European nations into armed camps, Woodrow Wilson justified his administration's commitment to U.S. neutrality in a speech delivered at the annual Associated Press luncheon at the Waldorf-Astoria. The power of his audience, with its ability to disseminate his words throughout the world, was apparently not lost upon Wilson. In its account of the speech, the *New York Times* noted, "The importance attached to his clear statement of the neutrality policy of his Administration was reflected in a request . . . that all newspaper reports of the President's speech be based on the verbatim copy to be taken by a stenographer and supplied to all of the newspapers and news-gathering associations represented."[1] Such care in ensuring that the press had access to an accurate transcription of his speech was perhaps due to a fine distinction Wilson makes about the purpose of U.S. neutrality. For Wilson, isolationism is not desirable in itself; however, remaining disentangled from the war allows the United States to continue improving its domestic affairs and thus to be in a stronger position to help Europe arbitrate peace and rebuild once the war ends.

Wilson also seems to have wanted his audience to pick up on the subtle polysemy that serves as the principal rhetorical strategy of the speech. He refers to the United States as "the mediating Nation" three times, attaching new and increasingly complex meanings to the phrase each time. At first, he uses it to emphasize the nation's growing economic power: "We shall some day have to assist in reconstructing the processes of peace [because] we are more and more becoming by the force of circumstances the mediating Nation of the world in respect to its finance."[2] Then, briefly staking out a role for the United States as an international arbiter, which a double negative halfheartedly disavows, he explains his vision more fully:

> We are the mediating Nation of the world. I do not mean that we undertake not to mind our own business and to mediate where other people are quarreling. I mean the word in a broader sense. We are compounded of the nations of the world; we mediate their blood, we mediate their traditions, we mediate their sentiments, their tastes, their passions; we are ourselves compounded of those things. We are, therefore, able to understand all nations; we are able to understand them in the compound, not separately, as partisans, but unitedly as knowing and comprehending and embodying them all. It is in that sense that I mean that America is a mediating Nation.[3]

At its most basic level, this argument rests upon the illusory notion of the period that the United States was a "melting pot" where the racial and ethnic tensions that led to war elsewhere could resolve themselves and serve instead to produce complementary frames of reference for understanding the world. According to Wilson, the United States is unique among the community of nations because its population and culture are "compounded" of all other nations, by which he is almost certainly referring to the physical presence of various ethnic groups and their diverse cultural practices within U.S. borders. This concern for the corporeality of the body politic and the affective ties of nationhood is reflected in the speaker's choice of words. Instead of casting the United States' relationship with other countries in terms of economic interests, alliances, or trade routes, as his first, economic definition of "mediating" would lead one to expect, Wilson talks primarily about "blood," "traditions," "sentiments," "passions," and "tastes." In other words, he offers an idealistic definition of American identity as something that is ethnically and culturally composite.

The historical contradictions are obvious. For one thing, events would force Wilson to change his rhetoric and foreign policy. Anti-German sentiment was already strong, and less than a month after Wilson delivered this speech, the German submarine *U-20* torpedoed the *Lusitania*, killing over one hundred Americans and helping to elicit greater public support for France and Great Britain. More troublingly, Wilson's vision stands in stark contrast to his own dismal record on civil rights. Even as he proclaimed the United States' ability to "embody" all the peoples of the world, his administration was pushing for ever more stringent Jim Crow legislation. Several of Wilson's appointees actively segregated their offices, and Wilson himself approved a new requirement that all applicants for federal jobs submit photographs of themselves with their applications.[4] In short, Wilson helped federalize Jim Crow.

Rather than echo the work of other scholars who have exposed how these sorts of contradictions are central, ongoing problems in American cultural history and not just examples of personal hypocrisy or brief contests over who is allowed to represent the nation at particular moments in time, I wish to suggest that Wilson's concept of the mediating nation signifies less a concern with fixing a static, utopian definition of American identity than with constructing a more dynamic narrative of the United States' role in world affairs, one that exploits various modes of circulation.[5] The multiple meanings of "mediating" draw repeated attention to the existence of a closely integrated system of nation-states in which the United States occupies a unique place—simultaneously "mediating" and being "compounded of" the entire system. For Wilson, the mediating nation is one that, successively, oversees worldwide financial transactions, settles international disputes, and connects people from different parts of the world together. The fourth and perhaps most important meaning remains implicit, emerging only when Wilson's audience of journalists is taken into account: the concept of the mediating nation also produces a better understanding of what the world is or could be (determined through the "compounding" of peoples in the social laboratory of the United States) and then represents and transmits that understanding back to the world. Here, Wilson's language is even more suggestive because he uses four times as many words associated with culture and affect ("traditions," "sentiments," "tastes," "passions") as he does words associated with race or ethnicity ("blood").

What finally emerges is a predominantly aesthetic conceptualization of the nation that is characterized by polyvocality, the ability to give expression to other nations' "sentiments" and "passions." Wilson envisions the United States not only as a microcosm that can literally embody all the earth's peoples but also as a globalizing force of representation that can literarily speak for all other nations and cultures. This assertion of America's role in the world, however, depends upon the United States exploiting the modes of transnational circulation to which Wilson's polysemy draws attention: financial transaction, diplomatic arbitration, human migration, and dissemination of information. By definition, "the mediating Nation of the world" occupies a position of centrality because it is the means whereby all transactions (economic, social, and cultural) are completed. Without extensively engaging the rest of the world through these various means, Wilson implies, the United States cannot fulfill its obligations or its promise.

I have opened with Wilson's speech because I contend that it provides a remarkably articulate and sophisticated illustration of how some Americans at the turn of the twentieth century attempted to come to terms with what we now understand to be the historical emergence of globalization, and I have taken Wilson's polysemantic phrase as the title for this book because, with its canny concatenation of economic, diplomatic, relational, and cultural meanings, "the mediating Nation" offers a powerful formula for understanding how those same Americans explained and exploited the United States' growing global power. Wilson's concept of the United States as a mediating nation therefore stands in for a much wider, though by no means universal, effort by politicians, authors, and intellectuals from the mid-1880s onwards to articulate dynamic narratives of the role of U.S. economic, political, and cultural power in the world. This book examines several exemplary figures who anticipated, shared, elaborated upon, or otherwise responded to Wilson's vision, including such major American realists as William Dean Howells, Henry James, Abraham Cahan, and Jack London, as well as such seemingly peripheral writers as Lafcadio Hearn and Knut Hamsun and such intellectuals and activists as Jane Addams, W. E. B. Du Bois, Louis Brandeis, and Randolph Bourne. Through a series of thematic readings, the following chapters argue, first, that realism in what I am calling its late form emerged as a literary mode particularly suited to representing the increasingly global currents of U.S. society and culture in the late nineteenth and early twentieth centuries and, second, that these literary efforts were embedded in and sometimes contributed to broader political and social efforts to negotiate and control those global conditions.

By no means did all of these figures attempt to tell the same story of U.S. international power or the U.S. body politic that Wilson does—Du Bois and Bourne actively wrote against Wilson in order to correct what they viewed as his omissions, for instance—but even in their critiques, they acknowledged and sought to direct (or redirect) the growing authority that the United States exercised over other nations. More to the point, the particular writers and intellectuals this book examines often achieved prominence by drawing attention to and exploiting the modes of transnational circulation that preoccupy Wilson in his April 20 speech. Subsequent chapters, for instance, assess Henry James's widely acknowledged reputation as the most cosmopolitan author of his generation, William Dean Howells's self-appointed role of America's gatekeeper of world literature, and even Knut Hamsun's canny use of his experiences as an immigrant in the United States to build a literary career for himself in his native Norway. Their efforts at mastering these newly emergent modes of transnational circulation disclose an important transnational turn in late realism that, in its insistence upon the centrality of the United States to a global system of migration and economic and cultural exchange, intersects with the transnational logic that a number of historians have recently identified at work in the thinking of many Progressives, including Wilson. Looking back on this period from near the end of her life, Jane Addams, to name just one intellectual who figures prominently in many histories of Progressivism, identified a "nascent world consciousness" as "the unique contribution" of her generation.[6] This book traces a particular genealogy of this "world consciousness," focusing primarily on those figures who deployed the powerful—but sometimes surprisingly malleable—narrative of the mediating nation in order to help define or redefine the United States' role in the world.

Methodologically, then, *The Mediating Nation* employs the techniques of literary analysis, including extended close readings of particular texts written by the figures named above, in order to supplement and qualify existing accounts of the age of realism and Progressivism. This approach has long been a staple of the kind of scholarship generally labeled American studies. In his introduction to the influential 1991 essay collection *The New American Studies*, Philip Fisher identified a scholarly shift toward what he called "rhetorics," which manifested critical interest in "the place where language is engaged in cultural work" and in "the action potential of language and images, not just their power or contrivance to move an audience but also the location of words, formulas, images, and ideological units of meaning within politics."[7] Even as the New American Studies has itself been subjected to critique in recent years by scholars who have faulted it for, among other things, not attending to the role of the state and the relationship of the United States to other states (Fisher closed his introduction by celebrating "the lack of what might be called, in the European sense, the state in American experience"), a general commitment to analyzing literature alongside other texts in order to achieve a richer understanding of U.S. culture and history remains strong.[8] Gretchen Murphy, whose work exemplifies the turn toward transnational circulation as much as any scholar's, recently affirmed the ability of "cultural forms like novels and poems [to] construct narratives that limit or expand readers' sense of social possibility" as well as the importance of continuing to pair those "cultural forms" with "historically concurrent print culture as evidence for literature's perceived and actual potential to shape and contest popular notions of U.S. global power."[9] *The Mediating Nation* continues this practice of situating particular literary works within their wider social context in order to clarify that "sense of social possibility."

In identifying Progressivism as its social context, *The Mediating Nation* also takes part in a very long tradition in American literary studies of associating important shifts in realism with the rise of Progressivism. In order to establish this historical context more fully, subsequent chapters will engage the work of a number of recent historians who have identified important transnational dimensions to U.S. Progressivism.[10] Far from attempting to replicate this kind of historical scholarship, however, *The Mediating Nation* seeks to initiate dialogue between two fields of inquiry that have been similarly reshaped by their growing interest in modes of transnational circulation. This effort at initiating such dialogue will appear most prominently in the first chapter, where I examine the relationship between shifting notions of literary cosmopolitanism and emerging discourse about internationalism, but several key Progressives, including Brandeis and Bourne, continue to figure in subsequent chapters as a means of illuminating the more ambitious interventions that such realists as James and Cahan sought to make. Moreover, these particular Progressives' insistence upon the *cultural* dimensions of the mediating nation puts them in direct conversation with James, Cahan, and other realists. As already noted, Wilson's vision of America as the mediating nation is primarily aesthetic, with his speech focusing on such cultural rather than economic currencies as "traditions" and "tastes," and as chapters 3 and 4 make clear, Brandeis and Bourne presented their solutions to the respective problems of finance capitalism and immigration in similarly cultural terms. Through literary analysis of their writings, *The Mediating Nation* demonstrates an epistemological disposition that a number of important and influential realists and Progressives shared.

Thus while, broadly speaking, *The Mediating Nation* presents an account of the globalization of America—in the sense that the United States became fully integrated into the world economy in the late nineteenth century and emerged as the chief force of further westernization in the twentieth—it argues more particularly for the importance of understanding how those processes of globalization were conceived by some of the most articulate writers and intellectuals of the period. After all, if Jane Addams could identify an abstract "world consciousness" rather than any number of concrete political or social achievements as "the unique contribution" of her time, then her and her peers' efforts at conceptualizing globalization demands extensive interrogation, both for what they add to our understanding of the history of globalization and for how they might present forgotten or alternative ways of thinking through the problems and possibilities of globalization. What is perhaps most surprising about the concept of globalization that emerges from close study of their writings, as I emphasize throughout this book, is their unwillingness to separate the state and, in the case of the realists, the ideological state apparatus of American literature from the processes that were increasingly interconnecting their world.[11] While both literary scholars and historians have begun explaining the diversification of the U.S. publishing industry and the expansion of state institutions at the turn of the twentieth century in terms of the global movements of people, goods, and ideas, I propose that these and other material developments, such as financial regulation, immigration control, and international copyright protection, can be productively reexamined in light of a conceptual reorientation toward the state as a means of empowering Americans to harness emerging modes of transnational circulation. Through textual analysis of exemplary expressions of this idea of the state, *The Mediating Nation* makes a case for reconsidering the relationship between the state and the transnational imaginary.

The transfer of global hegemony from Europe to North America, I therefore argue, was made legible by the efforts—and capacities—of Americans like Wilson, Addams, and the other figures I examine here to articulate it. In constructing narratives of a more active role for the United States in world affairs, these Americans both reflected and commented upon existing material realities and actively directed the future negotiation and management of those realities. Crucially, their narratives only make sense in a truly global context, where the impact of decisions made or actions taken in the United States upon events occurring elsewhere (and vice versa) can be anticipated, evaluated, and regulated. This global interpenetration is what I mean when I invoke the term "globalization," and it is these writers' and intellectuals' awareness of and engagement with the modes of circulation that produce this interpenetration between the domestic and the international that I contend characterizes the transnational concept of the mediating nation and distinguishes its deployment at the turn of the twentieth century from more nativist and protectionist imaginings of the United States both before and after.

To be sure, in its impossible idealism and outright hypocrisy, the phrase "the mediating Nation" is uniquely Wilson's and peculiar to the political context of April 1915, but the fact that both the phrase and the ideals to which it aspired were widely embraced by the public, including commentators who disagreed with the official U.S. policy of neutrality, indicates the appeal of Wilson's rhetoric and the degree to which he was attuned to Americans' attitudes about their relationship with the rest of the world. On the same day that it reported the speech, the *New York Times* printed a separate editorial in which its anonymous author supported both neutrality and Wilson's choice of words: "We are naturally the mediating nation of the world."[12] In the days that followed, additional articles demonstrated that Wilson's speech had indeed been circulated around the world, though these responses often indicated that the modes of circulation Wilson sought to control and exploit also enabled important forms of resistance to assertions of U.S. hegemony. On April 24, the *Times* translated a response from Paris's *Le Temps* in which a French commentator agreed that "America is, as President Wilson says, the mediating nation of the world" but warned that "no mediation can hope for success unless a final decision is first reached on the battlefield," and an April 28 article claimed that a senior German politician "did not take kindly to the desire America seemed to have for a mediating role in the settlement of the war."[13] In the years that followed, even after the United States entered the war, the speech was widely reprinted—sometimes as a representative historical example of U.S. neutrality while it lasted, but also as an emblem of American aspirations.[14] As I demonstrate in subsequent discussions of Randolph Bourne and W. E. B. Du Bois, even when other intellectuals and writers did not employ Wilson's terminology, they often directly responded to the ideas articulated in this speech. My central point, however, is that the concept of the mediating nation can stand in for a widespread effort, across political and ethnic lines, to empower the United States through embracing and exploiting emerging modes of transnational circulation.

One final, direct response to Wilson's speech proves the extent to which his turn of phrase both represented the increasingly global perspectives and ambitions of his American contemporaries, including those who disagreed with his policies, and illustrated a more general development in the history of globalization itself. In an essay entitled "The Crux of the Peace Problem" and published in the April 1916 issue of *Atlantic Monthly*, William Jewett Tucker, a former president of Dartmouth College and an early advocate for war against Germany, identified Wilson's speech as the strongest possible justification for neutrality but ultimately rejected Wilson's conclusions. Tucker's rationalization for war anticipated Wilson's own the following year: that the United

States' entry into the war would ensure the success of democracy and, consequently, a more lasting peace. Tucker evidently found it impossible to deny the appeal of the concept of the mediating nation. He observes, "This [phrase] is a noble and commanding conception of the duty attending the increase and expansion of the nation."[15] Only two paragraphs later, however, Tucker's anti-German sentiments appear and reveal his true concern: that a German victory would threaten U.S. geopolitical interests. "In the event of the final victory of Germany," he reasons, "we have the definite prospect of the consolidation of the Teutonic nations, with the inclusion of the tributary races of Southeastern Europe, and with the incorporation of the Turk. . . . No one can fail to understand the part which this combination would play in the continued struggle between absolutism and democracy. . . . The party of aggression has the most to gain and the least to lose."[16]

While Tucker's racial anxieties are readily apparent (Teutonic consolidation, conquest of the Slavs, and alliance with the Turks), his association of the United States and Germany with oppositional—and highly charged—abstract values also indicates awareness of what Immanuel Wallerstein and Giovanni Arrighi have identified as a historical struggle for hegemony between those two nations after Great Britain's economic decline toward the end of the nineteenth century. Both Wallerstein and Arrighi have argued that only Germany and the United States were geographically and economically capable of replacing Great Britain as the center of the world economy.[17] Within this context, Tucker's desire to guarantee American global supremacy explains his vilification of the Germans and willingness to go to war, if necessary, in a way that his racial anxieties alone do not. Wilson's reluctance to wage war to achieve those same ends also makes sense if Arrighi is correct and the United States' supremacy had been secured already by those very qualities that define Wilson's mediating nation. According to Arrighi, "The policy consistently followed by [the U.S.] government of keeping the doors of the domestic market closed to foreign products but open to foreign capital, labor, and enterprise [meant that] the U.S. domestic economy was well on its way to being the new center of the world-economy."[18] In other words, Wilson's present-tense declaration that the United States already *is* "the mediating Nation of the world" renders Tucker's concerns irrelevant because that economic, diplomatic, and cultural hegemony was already assured by the nation's increasing control over various forms of transnational circulation.

In the remainder of this introduction, I will explain what I mean by "the history of globalization," "late realism," and "Progressivism"; how they fit into the specific narrative I am telling; and what general contributions they offer American literary studies. First, however, I wish to clarify how I will be employing perhaps the most contentious term of all: "globalization."

That there has been a widespread explosion of interest in globalization in recent years cannot be denied; however, inconsistent use of the term has rendered it both ambiguous and ambivalent. Hence David Harvey's suggestion that the language of globalization is "to be rejected": "Acceptance of the globalization language is disempowering for all anti-capitalist and even moderately social democratic movements. It denies any relative autonomy . . . and makes it impossible to envision the modification, transgression or disruption of the trajectory of capitalist globalization."[19] While Harvey is specifically referring to the degree to which neoliberals have hijacked the rhetoric of cosmopolitanism in order to mask or justify the spread of economic inequalities that accompanies the expansion of free-market politics, rejecting the term altogether would be akin to throwing out the baby with the bathwater. The problem with the definitions provided by Harvey and other critics of globalization is that, in their own way, they are as limited as those offered by neoliberals, in the sense that both sets of definitions are predetermined by their users' ideological commitments. Just as appeals to cosmopolitanism and internationalism often obscure the power relations that serve as the grounds for participation in or exclusion from the international stage, equating globalization with imperialism (even in Lenin's broad sense) likewise elides the forms of resistance and mobility that the disenfranchised create for themselves out of the very same technologies and modes of circulation that frequently exploit them.[20] Similarly, one can acknowledge that the world economy is a force that simultaneously results from and further enables globalization while still maintaining that the world economy is not globalization itself. If the term "globalization" is to denote any meanings besides explicitly ideological ones or to provide the means for generating new knowledge that cannot be obtained otherwise, then globalization must serve as its own object of analysis and mode of inquiry—distinct from other concepts or processes, such as imperialism and the world economy, that intersect with globalization in complex and meaningful ways but remain their own objects of analysis.

The Mediating Nation approaches globalization as a conceptual problem. How have the processes by which the world has become interconnected, as well as the results of that interconnection, been conceived? (By "conceived," I purposely invoke both meanings of the word: origination and imagination.) In this respect, I return to the early and relatively broad definitions provided by Anthony Giddens and Roland Robertson. According to Giddens, "Globalisation can thus be defined as the intensification of worldwide social relations which link distant localities in such a way that local happenings are shaped by events occurring many miles away and vice versa."[21] For Robertson, "Globalization as a concept refers both to the compression of the world and the intensification of consciousness of the world as a whole."[22] What I find most useful about these definitions is the extent to which both Giddens and Robertson draw attention to conceptual issues. Without ignoring the historical and material conditions of globalization ("events" and "the compression of the world"), they point to the crucial role of perception and conception in globalization. This acknowledgement is most clear in the second part of Robertson's definition ("consciousness of the world as a whole"), but it is also implicit in Giddens's assumption that the interconnections he describes can be perceived and studied.

In focusing on networks and forms of compression, Robertson and Giddens offer a mode of analysis that is not ideologically driven but still leaves room for taking uneven power relations and both positive and negative outcomes into account. They acknowledge the essential dynamism of globalization as a set of processes and threads of connection rather than reducing it to a monolithic entity that subsumes individual states' interests. Instead of Wallerstein's famous world-system, with its unidirectional historical development, what Giddens and Robertson ultimately offer is a mode of analysis that attempts to understand the transformation that occurs within a society, culture, or nation when it comes into sustained contact not just with another society, but seemingly with *all* other societies at once. In following their lead throughout this project, I consistently emphasize those modes of circulation, including weblike networks of cultural and economic exchange and various routes of physical and material movement, that produce such transformative contact.

The Mediating Nation is not alone in returning to the conceptual problems of globalization. In their recent *After Globalization*, Eric Cazdyn and Imre Szeman note:

Globalization was and remains a messy concept. Though it is now used without comment in journalism and in academic literature— as if to suggest that it is a term that has accrued a fixed definition about which there is general agreement—it is best to think about it as a concept that conjures up a set of associations. The topics, issues, and themes one associates with globalization are not limited to "real" world developments, systems, and processes, but also include desires, hopes, and beliefs.[23]

For Cazdyn and Szeman, globalization is a construct, "a discourse [that] has come into being and continues to operate precisely to cover and obscure the system that *does* operate, namely capitalism."[24] While *The Mediating Nation* does not go this far—as I argue below, the "relations" created by the processes of globalization, which Cazdyn and Szeman dismiss as a "system of nothing," constitute our reality as much as the more concrete effects of technology do—Cazdyn and Szeman's insistence upon the constructedness of globalization offers a means of identifying more clearly the role of the state, which supposedly had been rendered moribund, in the work of globalization: "Globalization was the name for a novel assertion of economic, cultural, and political power that wanted desperately to hide behind the veil of its claims to have identified, in almost scientific fashion, an actually existing phenomenon. At its core was an extension and expansion of U.S. power."[25] Wilson's concept of the mediating nation illustrates the longstanding nature of this relationship between globalization and the state: the power and influence that Wilson attributes to—and thus also seeks to bestow upon—the United States only makes sense within a network of nation-states. As the mediating nation of the world, the United States occupies the central position in a complex web of economic, cultural, and political transactions.

Moreover, Cazdyn and Szeman's goal of imagining an *after* to globalization—what they call "an alternative presentness and futurity"—can itself be historicized in productive ways.[26] Alternatives to what we now take to be globalization can be located in its history, including not just failed movements and forgotten or suppressed critiques, but also proposed solutions to problems that continue to bedevil the twenty-first century. In Louis Brandeis's praise of credit unions as a viable alternative to investment banks or in Randolph Bourne's suggestion of dual citizenship as a palliative for nativist resentment of immigrants, for example, *The Mediating Nation* locates an American tradition of conceiving interventions in globalization's development.

THE HISTORY OF GLOBALIZATION

In insisting on globalization's status as a longstanding conceptual question, this book categorically rejects the notion that globalization is only a recent phenomenon and therefore an unsuitable lens for examining U.S. cultural or literary production before the 1960s. Certainly, "globalization" has emerged as a crucial twenty-first-century keyword, in Raymond Williams's sense of that term, dominating recent academic discourse, political rhetoric, and mass media punditry alike.[27] Yet while several noted theorists, such as Wallerstein and Robertson, have called attention to the historical processes of globalization, the relatively recent currency of the term itself presents the twin risks of anachronism and presentism to scholars interested in applying global theory to historical contexts before the 1960s, when Marshall McLuhan's *The Gutenberg Galaxy* (1962) popularized the concept of the "global village."[28] Arguing that globalization has emerged out of the interplay of material processes and cultural and discursive practices, *The Mediating Nation* foregrounds the conceptual implications of globalization and its history in order to avoid these risks. More importantly, the chapters that follow focus on how earlier writers sought to explain and respond to emerging modes of circulation and thereby helped to shape our current understanding of globalization. Our concept of "transnational," for instance, remains more or less the same as Randolph Bourne's in the 1916 essay that popularized the term, "Trans-National America."[29] The word "imperialism" likewise accrued most of its present meanings in the United States during the 1890s.[30]

The "history of globalization" that I wish to invoke in this section therefore involves the historical processes that, as Karl Marx puts it in the epigraph that heads this introduction, "result" in something that we can conceive of as "world history." Thus while there are also histories to the term "globalization" itself and to the intellectual traditions that have given rise to global theory, my focus will be on those historical processes that helped propel the United States into its position of global power, particularly those processes that Americans at the turn of the twentieth century already recognized as taking place and sought to understand and manage.[31]

Most historians of globalization associate its origins with several key developments of the mid-fifteenth through mid-seventeenth centuries, including the rise of capitalism in Europe, the "discovery" and then exploitation of non-European societies, and the creation of the modern nation-state system.[32] Virtually all these historians agree, however, that the nineteenth century, and the latter half of the nineteenth century in particular, marked a decisive transition in the development of globalization. Eric Hobsbawm has argued that three principal developments produced a truly global economy during the "long nineteenth century": the creation of the bourgeois state as a result of the French and Industrial revolutions; the unification of disparate regional and national markets into an interdependent world economy through new technologies of travel and communication; and the emergence of imperialism, by which Hobsbawm means not only the division of the undeveloped world by the developed nations into dependent and semi-dependent colonies but also the wider consolidation of economic power by the developed nations through corporatization and the international division of labor.[33] Despite his focus on earlier periods, even Wallerstein has noted that, "by the late nineteenth century, *for the first time ever*, there existed only one historical system on the globe" (emphasis added).[34] Roland Robertson has even more precisely labeled the period between 1870 and 1925, which corresponds roughly to the chronology of *The Mediating Nation*, "the crucial take-off period of globalization," and he lists a number of specific developments as evidence: the "inclusion of a number of non-European societies [such as Japan] in 'international society'"; a "very sharp increase in number and speed of global forms of communication [such as radio and motion pictures]"; the "implementation of world time"; and the "development of global competitions—for example the Olympics and Nobel prizes."[35] These historical developments form the conditions of possibility for Wilson's conceptualization of the mediating nation.

A number of historians have identified a brief slowdown in the processes of globalization between the First and Second World Wars, and this slowdown marks the end of the specific stage in the globalization of the United States that *The Mediating Nation* examines. Kevin H. O'Rourke and Jeffrey G. Williamson have labeled this slowdown a "backlash": "The interwar decades saw a return to autarkic trade policies, the breakdown of international capital markets, and an end to mass migration."[36] This "backlash" was partly a reaction against the perceived threat to the security of the nation-state that the processes of globalization sometimes posed. After all, the global conflagration of 1914–18 resulted not only in the proliferation of several new nation-states (thus reinscribing that particular form of social organization) but also in the disappearance of others, and the clampdown on immigration in many countries often resulted from the fear that the Soviets might disseminate their own brand of internationalism through immigrants. These concerns were only exacerbated by the economic downturn following the crisis of 1929.[37]

Following the Second World War and especially since the 1970s, these reverses have themselves been reversed, and the processes of globalization have been accelerated by financial deregulation, the proliferation of multinational corporations, and the adoption of the ideology of neoliberalism by most mainstream political parties in what were once referred to as "first-world" nations. U.S. foreign policy works from the assumption that, together, democratization and the expansion of the free market can solve existing political and economic problems.[38] Nevertheless, in focusing on historical conceptualizations of globalization, *The Mediating Nation* reminds readers that this current form, in which the state has largely renounced responsibility for controlling globalization, is not and has not been inevitable. In highlighting what was ultimately a failed "global moment," this book employs the techniques of literary analysis to uncover alternative ways of thinking about globalization.

In the chapters that follow, *The Mediating Nation* examines those conceptualizations of globalization that coalesced in American culture during the late nineteenth and early twentieth centuries, Robertson's "take-off period." One such intellectual formulation that provides a particularly useful illustration of Americans' efforts to come to terms with new modes of circulation and connection is the relational thinking advocated by William James in "A World of Pure Experience" (1904) and his other later writings on radical empiricism. James's repeated emphasis on the meanings produced *through* relations is an idea, I contend, that helps us understand other writers' attempts at making sense of their own transnational experiences, even if they were not always capable of giving an adequate account of James's philosophy. Specifically, in "A World of Pure Experience," James identifies two "kind[s] of thing experienced": "terms" (facts or otherwise concrete things) and "relations" (less tangible lived experiences that nevertheless "must be accounted as 'real' as anything else in the system").[39] James's refusal to count relations as less "real" than terms represents a refusal to privilege material over perceived experiences.

James goes even further, arguing that facts and our experiences of those facts are not independent of one another but that our "reality" emerges only through the interaction between the two. "In radical empiricism," he writes, "there is no bedding; it is as if the pieces clung together by their edges, the transitions experienced between them forming their cement. . . . Life is in the transitions as much as in the terms connected. . . . These relations of continuous transition experienced are what make our experiences cognitive."[40] While we may highlight particular "facts," isolating them from the context of their relations for the sake of convenience, there is no qualitative difference between terms and relations, between facts and our experiences of them. The relations that we perceive to exist between two terms (objects, people, places, etc.) produce meanings that are not simply inherent to the terms themselves. Furthermore, in his discussion of "conjunctive" and "disjunctive" relations, James claims that new meanings emerge when existing "terms" are thrown into new "relation" with one another or with new terms.[41]

On a basic level, James's radical empiricism offers a means of bypassing the question of whether a particular writer helped constitute or merely reflected the ongoing processes of globalization. To think about—or, as Roland Robertson puts it, to demonstrate "consciousness" of—globalization is to contribute to its development by imagining and attempting to negotiate that development. More importantly, however, radical empiricism offers a way of thinking about globalization itself: as a reformulation of relations, whereby an event, a new technology, or a new mode of circulation creates a network that brings people and cultures into contact with each other. This radical empiricist approach thus poses globalization as a web of interconnection (i.e., relations between terms) and focuses upon how newly formed connections or relations alter both the material conditions of life at one point in the web and the perceptions of those people who live there about their own location and its relationship to other locations. Fully realized, then, globalization is about much more than just "international exchange" because it is about the increase in the total number of possible relations. Globalization is about what happens when a particular society or culture seems to come into simultaneous contact with all other societies or cultures.

In subsequent chapters, I examine how the transnational circulation of authors, their texts, and their ideas produced such reformulations of relations and forced them to conceptualize and articulate their new experiences. A brief illustration, however, can be found in one of Mark Twain's attempts to create humor out of the recent "implementation of world time," which Robertson lists as an important development in the late-nineteenth-century consolidation of globalization. In 1883, sponsored by the major U.S. railroad companies, the General Time Convention established time zones in North America, and in 1884, the International Meridian Conference designated the meridian that passes through Greenwich as the prime meridian for the purposes of both timekeeping and geographic longitude. Historian Frank Ninkovich calls the International Meridian Conference "an epochal event" because it changed people's relationship with time itself.[42] In order to coordinate transportation and communication more effectively, local time everywhere after 1884 depended upon local time at Greenwich rather than when the sun appeared overhead. In producing a newly global temporality, nineteenth-century scientists, politicians, and entrepreneurs managed to reshape the everyday aspects of people's lives by constructing new relations between otherwise seemingly disconnected communities.

Published only ten years after the International Meridian Conference, Twain's *Tom Sawyer Abroad* (1894) begins with Tom, Huck, and Jim boarding a giant balloon that eventually transports them to Africa. As they travel eastward, they notice that the town clocks they pass over do not match their own watches. The following exchange reveals the growing frustration of Tom, who understands the principles of world time, as he attempts to explain the reason for the discrepancy to the increasingly perplexed and disturbed Jim:

> [Tom:] "We've covered about fifteen degrees of longitude since we left St. Louis yesterday afternoon, and them clocks are *right*." . . .
> Jim was working his mind, and studying. Pretty soon he says—
> "Mars Tom, did you say dem clocks uz right?"
> "Yes, they're right."
> "Ain't yo watch right, too?"
> "She's right for St. Louis, but she's an hour wrong for here."
> "Mars Tom, is you tryin' to let on dat de time ain't de *same* everywheres?"
> "No, it ain't the same everywheres, by a long shot."
> Jim looked distressed, and says—
> "It grieve me to hear you talk like dat, Mars Tom; I's right down 'shamed to hear you talk like dat, arter de way you's been raised. Yas-sir, it 'd break yo' Aunt Polly's heart to hear you." (original emphasis)[43]

Eventually, Jim concludes that, if Tom is right and it can be Monday evening in North America and Tuesday morning in Europe, there cannot be a literal Last Day, in the biblical or eschatological sense. At least temporarily, Jim's encounter with one aspect of nineteenth-century globalization shakes his religious faith.

LATE REALISM AND RELATIONAL THINKING

Twain's humorous treatment of world time in *Tom Sawyer Abroad* is only one instance of late realism's extensive engagement with transnational circulation and the emergence of globalization. By "late realism," I refer most obviously to the emergence of such second-generation realists, or naturalists, as Hamlin Garland, Frank Norris, and Jack London, who were particularly concerned with the question of how economic conditions determine a character's identity, behavior, and ultimate fate. Their emergence coincided with—and may have accelerated—a shift in the fiction-writing and literary criticism of the major first-generation realists, especially Henry James, William Dean Howells, and Twain. For example, from the late-1880s onwards, Howells's literary criticism became less nationalistic in tone and more interested in foreign authors and international literary movements, including the rise of naturalism and the romantic revival. Likewise, the fiction of Howells, James, and Twain became more politicized during the second half of the 1880s and exhibited a shift in focus from the primarily moral conflicts experienced by individual characters in, say, *The Portrait of a Lady* (1881), *The Rise of Silas Lapham* (1885), and *The Adventures of Huckleberry Finn* (1885) to a more overt engagement with the broader social implications of unequal political representation and economic access in *The Tragic Muse* (1890), *A Hazard of New Fortunes* (1890), and *A Connecticut Yankee in King Arthur's Court* (1889), among other works.

Many literary critics have argued that these shifts in the content and style of American realism were due to an impulse that the realists themselves felt to intervene in the social conditions that were also drawing the attention of Progressive reformers. Thus critics ranging from Vernon Parrington and Alfred Kazin to Larzer Ziff and Amy Kaplan have emphasized a relationship between literary production and social reform and have identified such turning points as the Haymarket affair's impact on Howells's growing politicization in 1886 and 1887 and the symbolic significance of his move shortly thereafter from Boston to New York, where he increased his contact with younger writers and became more aware of the power of the advertising and journalism industries.[44] *The Mediating Nation* concurs with the general thrust of this line of argument, but just as recent historians have argued that Progressivism was a political and social response to the increasingly complex international relations of the United States, as I note below, I maintain that this transition in American realism in the late-1880s was an aesthetic response to the accelerating processes of globalization and the resulting increase in American wealth and power. *The Mediating Nation* broadens recent efforts to trace the international routes of intellectual exchange out of which conceptions of the aesthetic took shape among American writers. Building off of the work of Tom Lutz, Russ Castronovo, and other scholars, I examine the transnational networks of intellectual and aesthetic exchange that shaped the production and consumption of late American realism.[45] More specifically, I contend that authors, critics, and even readers eagerly cultivated a set of aesthetic strategies for representing as much of the world as possible in their fiction and nonfiction—sometimes to the point of enabling and promoting foreign writers who critiqued American culture and political interests.

What unified these various practitioners of what I am calling late American realism was not so much a *particular* aesthetic style or set of political beliefs as a general commitment to the relational thinking I described in the preceding section. (As has been frequently observed, realism is a notoriously difficult literary movement to pin down, and the most common characteristic that virtually all American realists shared was their connection to Howells, who tirelessly promoted their work.) Perhaps the most famous example of this relational thinking informing an individual author's aesthetic sensibility is Henry James's famous metaphor of "a kind of huge spider-web" that catches "every air-borne particle in its tissue" in his 1884 essay "The Art of Fiction."[46] James's advice that an author must be open to every possible experience, that no topic can be foreclosed because of a presumed lack of first-hand knowledge, is a conception of literature, I suggest, that could exist only in a mind where the world's interconnectedness is taken for granted. Hence James's example of "an English novelist, a woman of genius," whose momentary glimpse of a group of young Parisian Protestants at a meal enabled her to capture "the nature and way of life of the French Protestant youth": "She had got her impression, and she evolved her type. She knew what youth was, and what Protestantism; she also had the advantage of having seen what it was to be French; so that she converted these ideas into a concrete image and produced a reality."[47] That this "reality" can be produced *across* national boundaries, that an "English novelist" can give voice to "French Protestant youth," speaks to the globalizing aspirations of realist fiction as well as to its own transnational production and circulation. James's vision in 1884 may lack the overt geopolitical ambitions of Woodrow Wilson's concept of the mediating nation, but James's effort to develop a transnational aesthetic clearly anticipates the amalgamation of political, economic, relational, and symbolic meanings we find in Wilson's use of the word "mediating." That sort of literary work is the primary subject of *The Mediating Nation*.

PROGRESSIVISM AND THE WORLD

That literary critics from Parrington and Kazin to Kaplan and Castronovo have drawn attention to the relationship between the shifts in realism and the increased social unrest of the late nineteenth century suggests that late realism cannot be understood without reference to Progressivism. It is partly for this reason that *The Mediating Nation* focuses extensively on the late realists' nonfictional writings, which, apart from representing a logical extension of the realist impulse to catalogue and describe empirical reality, often reveal the authors' own efforts at intervening in wider public discourse. (As I demonstrate in subsequent chapters, such works of nonfiction as Henry James's *The American Scene* [1907] and Jack London's Russo-Japanese war correspondence [1904] sometimes possess their own literary merit and frequently shed important light on their authors' fiction, too.) Because Progressivism serves as the broader social and political context in which late realism was embedded, I engage existing historical scholarship in order to establish both the longstanding appreciation of the Progressives' faith in the state and a much more recent recognition of the transnational currents of U.S. Progressivism. This approach will become clearer in the first chapter, where I describe several important intersections in the transnational thinking of realists and Progressives, but a brief summary of the particular understanding of Progressivism that guides my use of the term in subsequent chapters is in order here.

Like realism, the Progressive movement was filled with contradictions, as Wilson's speech, with its celebration of diversity at a time when Jim Crow was spreading, amply illustrates. The fact that Progressivism not only was bipartisan, achieving important objectives under both Theodore Roosevelt's Republican and Wilson's Democratic administrations, but encompassed a wide spectrum of political positions (agrarian populism, pro- and anti-imperialism, woman suffrage, the social gospel, etc.) helps account for its internal inconsistencies. Progressivism sought to address a dizzying array of challenging social conditions that were transforming the material realities of everyday life in the United States. Urbanization, mass immigration, increased economic disparity, and the perceived threat of socialism—Progressive thinkers expended considerable effort to make sense of these changes to the social fabric. The popularity and influence of *Our Country: Its Possible Future and Its Present Crisis* (1885) were undoubtedly due to the way in which its author, Josiah Strong, found connections among these seemingly disparate "perils" to American culture. Thus Progressivism is perhaps best understood as an effort to find an adequately encompassing response to the radical reconfiguration and expansion of American society during the late nineteenth century. What ultimately unified these disparate groups was their willingness to turn to the state itself: to empower the state to resolve those social, economic, and political problems.

The Progressives' efforts to authorize the federal government to regulate what they perceived to be the excessive wealth and power of newly corporatized business combinations is a common theme in histories of the period, but the study of Progressivism has experienced its own transnational turn in recent years. Classic accounts of the Progressive era, such as Richard Hofstadter's *The Age of Reform*, frequently ignored or deemphasized the international perspectives and implications of Progressivism.[48] Even William Appleman Williams, who pioneered the study of how Americans' political and economic ambitions overseas have helped shape U.S. foreign policy, inadvertently reinforced the view that Progressivism was a movement focused almost exclusively on domestic concerns by arguing that the imperialist ideologues surrounding William McKinley and Theodore Roosevelt appropriated Progressive arguments in favor of social change in the domestic sphere and redirected them toward foreign policy.[49] By contrast, more recent scholars, such as James T. Kloppenberg and Daniel T. Rodgers, have demonstrated the extent to which American reformers thought of themselves as taking part in an international movement, even going so far as to model their efforts in the United States upon similar reform movements in Germany, Britain, France, and New Zealand.[50] While Kloppenberg, Rodgers, and other historians continue to agree with Hofstadter that Progressivism represented an effort to empower the state, they now contend that this effort took shape transnationally.

Rather than seeking to replicate or reinvent this kind of historical scholarship, *The Mediating Nation* continues drawing attention to the intersection between late realism and Progressivism that other literary scholars have already highlighted and identifies an underlying reason for this intersection: a shared commitment among several leading realists and Progressives to imagining and articulating narratives of a state strong enough to respond to pressing social, political, and economic problems whose causes and solutions lay in complex transnational networks. My readings of Louis D. Brandeis's *Other People's Money* (1914) in chapter 3 and of Randolph Bourne's "Trans-National Nation" in chapter 4 therefore serve to underscore the larger issues at stake in Henry James's and Abraham Cahan's fictional treatments of finance capitalism and immigration, respectively. Simultaneously, the solutions that Bourne and Brandeis locate transnationally—dual citizenship for Bourne and cooperative organizations for Brandeis—also gain in meaning and resonance when viewed as part of a much wider discourse in which even immigrant writers could participate, giving voice to their own experiences and desires. These readings—and the cultural meanings they disclose—can enrich our understanding of the range and depth of responses to the emergence of globalization and thereby supplement existing historical accounts of the period.

Thus the Progressive writings that *The Mediating Nation* examines are approached primarily as texts that, when read from a literary perspective, exhibit the same transnational and relational concerns that characterize the novels of Henry James, William Dean Howells, and Abraham Cahan. For instance, in his 1889 analysis of the depression of 1873–96, David Ames Wells, an influential American economist of the era, opined that "its most noteworthy peculiarity has been its universality; affecting nations that have been involved in war as well as those which have maintained peace; those which have a stable currency, based on gold, and those which have an unstable currency . . . ; those which live under a system of free exchange of commodities, and those whose exchanges are more or less restricted."[51] As a result, Wells claims that,

> in order that there may be intelligent and comprehensive discussion of the situation, and more especially that there may be wise remedial legislation for any economic or social evils that may exist, it is requisite that there should be a clear and full recognition of . . . the causes and extent of the industrial and social changes and accompanying disturbances which have especially characterized the last fifteen or twenty years of the world's history.[52]

The point here is that Wells's desire to improve social conditions is inextricably bound up with his desire to understand and master the international relations that have produced them. Wells's relational thinking enables him to recognize and respond to the interpenetration of foreign and domestic concerns, and his attentiveness to the modes of circulation that were interconnecting the world's economies connects his Progressivism to the transnational thinking that structures the late realism of James, Howells, and Cahan.

GLOBAL THEORY, THE STATE, AND TRANSNATIONAL AMERICAN (LITERARY) STUDIES

Already primed by the work of Benedict Anderson, Homi Bhabha, and Paul Gilroy to question the stability of the nation-state as the primary organizing principle of cultural production and consumption, literary scholars have exhibited little reluctance in embracing global theory and transnational methodologies.[53] Thanks in part to special issues of notable journals, such as *PMLA*'s "Globalizing Literary Studies" (January 2001) and *ESQ*'s "American Literary Globalism" (2004), the discipline as a whole has demonstrated a willingness to engage the topic and terminology of globalization and thereby legitimize their usefulness to literary studies.[54] In the case of American studies more specifically, Donald E. Pease has noted that "the 'transnational turn' in American studies has effected the most significant reimagining of the field . . . since its inception, [changing] the way Americanist scholars imagine their relationship to their work, their objects of study, and their disciplinary protocols."[55] The assumption that American culture is not only imbricated in—and shaped by—a larger global network but is also a major force of globalization has begun to supplement empire as one of the key starting-points in American studies, as indicated by the inclusion of "Globalization" in *Keywords for American Cultural Studies* (2007).[56]

Despite—or perhaps because of—this impact upon the field, several important scholars have voiced concern over what they perceive to be the uncritical adoption of transnational approaches that celebrate rather than interrogate neoliberal notions of cosmopolitan movement and exchange of ideas. Perhaps the most notable scholar to articulate this critique is Winfried Fluck, whose status as one of the most prominent Americanists in Europe makes him particularly sensitive to the wider political and cultural implications of such methodological shifts. In a 2011 essay entitled "A New Beginning? Transnationalisms," Fluck notes that celebratory accounts of the transnational dimensions of cultural production and reception often obscure the continued power of nation-states as well as the exploitative economic practices that globalization exacerbates. As Fluck puts it, "There is . . . in current transnational American studies very little acknowledgement that a rhetoric of flow and transnational communities may mirror and reinforce a neoliberal ideology. It is striking to what extent this transnationalism avoids references to globalization as a new world order that may also undermine visions of a happy postnational communality."[57] In this respect, Fluck echoes the concerns of David Harvey and other early global theorists. Such concerns remain as valid as ever, and Fluck's warning holds particular relevance for literary scholars who might otherwise unwittingly articulate new expressions of American exceptionalism. "The global dominance of American culture," Fluck observes, "can now be attributed to the fact that American culture is already in itself constituted by diversity and has thus anticipated an international trend toward cosmopolitanism" that has "not been possible to the same extent in other, less multicultural nations."[58]

The logic that Fluck ascribes to less self-reflexive adopters of the transnational lens bears an uncanny resemblance to Woodrow Wilson's notion of the mediating nation. In both cases, U.S. global authority is cast as an outgrowth of the nation's own (exceptional) multiculturalism and rendered benign through its characterization in predominantly cultural terms. In a sense, Fluck's concerns underscore the continuing appeal of the narrative of the mediating nation that emerged at the turn of the twentieth century. *The Mediating Nation* works to disclose the historical and cultural roots of the very problem that Fluck identifies in the thinking of a number of U.S. Americanists today: the celebration of American diversity that simultaneously serves to reinscribe U.S. cultural and political power. Moreover, as indicated in my earlier discussion of Eric Cazdyn and Imre Szeman's *After Globalization*, which seeks to reintroduce the state to the study of globalization, I share Fluck's view that "the transnational [cannot] be separated from the national from which it takes its point of departure."[59]

Finally, *The Mediating Nation* builds on the work of two scholars who have explicitly invoked global theory in their own studies of the production and reception of American literary realism: Thomas Peyser, in *Utopia and Cosmopolis* (1998), and Russ Castronovo, in *Beautiful Democracy* (2007).[60] For both Peyser and Castronovo, appealing to the history of globalization serves to decenter the nation as the primary means of understanding literary production and to challenge traditional realist canons. Peyser argues that late-nineteenth-century realism and utopian fiction, far from being oppositional genres, emerged out of the same Progressive ferment that sought to reimagine and revise the nation but that, in so doing, also destabilized the nation-state by drawing attention to its constructedness and by appealing to transcending cosmopolitan values. Castronovo identifies a globalizing impulse in aesthetic discourse of fin de siècle America that both borrowed from European philosophical traditions and appealed to universal standards of beauty but also sought to contain foreign political ideologies that might challenge the expansionist tendencies of U.S. democracy. For both, the "global" helps to construct national consciousness by serving as a sort of "other" against which U.S. democracy is positioned. Peyser highlights "the mutually constitutive aspect of nation and globe": "only when an acute consciousness of different cultures has arisen will one feel impelled to catalogue or cultivate those traits that allegedly distinguish one's own national culture from all others."[61] The global, however, simultaneously disrupts that consciousness by introducing a far greater cultural heterogeneity than any nation or aesthetic formulation could ever assimilate—what Castronovo refers to as "the anarchic brio of global culture."[62]

The Mediating Nation seeks to expand these efforts even further. Indeed, attentiveness to the transnational circulations of writers and their texts can potentially reconfigure the American canon altogether. To be sure, adopting a global lens serves to solidify the positions of some major figures, such as Henry James and William Dean Howells, but it also increases the prominence of others who have been largely forgotten, such as Lafcadio Hearn. Reconstructing Americans' understanding of globalization during this period thus necessitates compiling not just a nonliterary archive, including political speeches, journalism, and philosophical essays, but even a non-American one. My second and fourth chapters, where I take seriously what Howells read and reviewed and what perhaps the most notable "failed" immigrant wrote about his experiences in the United States, extend "American" literature far enough beyond U.S. borders to encompass select writings of two of the most prominent authors from other national canons: the Filipino José Rizal and the Norwegian Knut Hamsun. Rather than suggest that such globalization of American literature merely extends its homogenization of the world, however, my inclusion or Rizal and Hamsun underscores the existence of global routes of resistance to U.S. political and cultural expansion that often overlapped the circulation of American literature itself.

This last methodological detail draws attention to two points where my conclusions diverge significantly from those of Peyser and Castronovo. First, while both of them emphasize the ways in which the global participates in the construction of the national, each seems to work from the assumption that globalization ultimately supplants the state and produces a *postnational* consciousness.[63] By contrast, *The Mediating Nation*, even while focusing on the transnational production of American culture, reintroduces the state as a vital force in the historical processes of globalization. For this reason, I consistently employ the term "transnational" instead. Globalization is not a phenomenon that exists outside of the state but instead develops in part through the actions and interactions of independent states. In this respect, I follow the lead of David Lloyd and Paul Thomas, who have identified the crucial role that "cultural (or aesthetic) formation comes gradually to play" in "forming citizens for the modern state."[64] For Lloyd and Thomas, the nineteenth-century institutions of cultural production and dissemination, such as schools and presses, provided an arena wherein "a certain *idea* of the state" could be articulated, contested, and revised (original emphasis).[65] *The Mediating Nation* more or less picks up where Lloyd and Thomas leave off: toward the end of the nineteenth century, when broader participation in this discourse about the state—broad enough, for instance, to include even the socialist Eugene V. Debs, who ran successively impressive presidential campaigns between 1900 and 1920—produced widespread investment in the state as the most effective unit of social organization. *The Mediating Nation* also explores the increasingly transnational dimensions of cultural production and dissemination, including their impact on the way in which the "idea of the state" was articulated.

Second, in reducing globalization to such abstractions as cosmopolitanism or imperialism, Peyser and Castronovo sometimes fail to account for the dynamism and multidirectionality of globalization, which enables the spread of a homogenous mass culture but also its "indigenization" by local peoples and facilitates both a universalizing cosmopolitanism and a sometimes splintering multiculturalism.[66] I contend that the aesthetics of late American realism placed value on polyvocality and different points of view, sometimes to the extent of undermining the imperial designs of the United States. *The Mediating Nation* therefore embraces a variety of global theorists in order to provide a more adequate account of the multiple and sometimes contradictory tendencies of globalization. At times, this variety may result in a somewhat more optimistic treatment of globalization in individual chapters than my alignment with Fluck and Pease might suggest. My aim is not to portray the turn of the twentieth century as a kind golden age, when American political life was characterized by transformative bipartisanship and when American authors meditated extensively on their nation's responsibilities to the rest of the world. Rather, this book is offered in the hope that, through the examination of its past instances, we can relocate lost and alternative answers to the problems and possibilities of globalization.

The following chapters continue to present the transition into late realism at the turn of the twentieth century as an aesthetic response to the historical emergence of the United States as an economic and political world power. This transition was embedded in the larger culture of Progressivism, which was itself a set of social and political responses to the same historical conditions that late realism was engaging. Foregrounding the language of relational thinking and the modes of transnational circulation that many Americans sought to exploit, *The Mediating Nation* focuses on how late realism worked to empower the Progressive state and ideological state apparatuses in such a way that the United States could harness the processes of globalization for social change. The first two chapters examine the conceptual and aesthetic vocabularies that enabled Americans to articulate these goals. The first chapter analyzes the interrelated use of three terms ("cosmopolitanism," "internationalism," and "world-salvation") in order to illustrate the intellectual and literary efforts at articulating the role of the state in an increasingly globalized society. Concentrating primarily on how these words were deployed by elite writers and intellectuals, such as William James and W. E. B. Du Bois, I approach the three terms as keywords in order to position their literary use within a wider social and political context. The second chapter explains in more detail how literary realism provided a means for American literature to play a more vital role in world literature by exploring William Dean Howells's late fiction and criticism, in which he made a concerted effort to reposition realism as a transnational project.

Each of the three remaining chapters focuses on the role literature played in one of the more prominent and controversial processes of globalization at the turn of the twentieth century: the rise of finance capitalism, the movement of immigrants, and the widespread adoption of the European model of overseas imperialism. Simultaneously, these chapters draw closer attention to three of the modes of transnational circulation at work in Woodrow Wilson's depiction of the mediating nation: financial transaction, migration, and diplomatic arbitration. The middle chapter explores the transformation in Henry James's understanding of America's relationship to Europe by analyzing his extensive revisions of his early novel *The American* in light of his return to the United States after a twenty-year absence, as recounted in *The American Scene*. Through those revisions, James transformed a straightforward satire of Gilded Age investment bankers into a stinging critique of finance capitalism and an investigation into the global cultural economy that aligned Europe's and America's cultural commitments and economic interests.

My fourth chapter focuses on immigration as a process of circulation rather than absorption, involving not just one-way trips to the United States but also physical and cultural returns to the homeland. Analyzing the transnational circulation of American money, products, and culture that Abraham Cahan portrays in *The Rise of David Levinksy* as well as the descriptions of U.S. society that Norwegian Nobel-laureate Knut Hamsun published upon his return to Europe after his own failed immigrant years, I suggest that the routes of physical and material movement created and maintained by migrant communities helped to lay the foundation for U.S. cultural hegemony but also provided a means for resisting and critiquing that same cultural imperialism.

The final chapter addresses the history of U.S. overseas expansion by focusing on the unique relationship between the United States and Japan, two nations that rose to international prominence at the same time and on mutually agreeable terms. Jack London's Russo-Japanese War correspondence and Lafcadio Hearn's nonfiction books about Japan reveal that London and Hearn found in Japan an example of what the philosopher Charles Taylor terms "alternative modernities," the existence of modernized but nonwesternized societies. Finally, the coda considers the legacy of "the mediating Nation" during the modernist era and beyond.

CHAPTER ONE

From Cosmopolitanism to World-Salvation

The Transnational Imaginary and the Idea of
the Progressive State

Between 1900 and 1910, the *Atlantic Monthly*, a magazine that was widely regarded as the epitome of cultural authority in the United States, published eleven articles that, in one way or another, explicitly invoked the concept of cosmopolitanism.[1] Of these eleven articles, seven are, broadly speaking, works of literary criticism, and three specifically name Henry James as the leading exponent of cosmopolitanism in American literature. James's perceived status as the most cosmopolitan American author of his era comes as no surprise, especially not in a magazine that had once serialized *The American* (1876–77), *The Portrait of a Lady* (1880–81), and several of James's other "international" novels. What is surprising, however, is the relatively ambivalent attitude toward cosmopolitanism that emerges collectively from these articles. In a January 1903 essay entitled "Number 4 Park Street," Bliss Perry, the magazine's editor at the time, offered a self-reflective meditation on the *Atlantic Monthly*'s continued national and international reputation, despite not having relocated from Boston to New York, and he satirized "the publishers of many periodicals [who] have reasoned that the readiest way of acquiring the air of cosmopolitanism was to give their magazine the imprint of the commercial capital of the country."[2] This ambivalence over cosmopolitan pretentions extends even to the magazine's treatment of James. In an April 1905 retrospective overview of James's career, W. C. Brownell praised James's fiction because it was "penetrated with the spirit of cosmopolitanism": "Out of his familiarity with contemporary society in America, England, France, and Italy, grew a series of novels and tales that were full of vigor, piquancy, truth, and significance."[3] Yet only twelve months earlier, in his entry for the column "Books New and Old," H. W. Boynton took issue with James's characterization of Thoreau as "provincial" and poked fun at "Mr. James's cosmopolitanism," in which "absenteeism would come to be held actually as a state of grace."[4]

The seemingly contradictory nature of Brownell's and Boynton's comments on James's cosmopolitanism may, of course, reveal certain anxieties that were unique to Perry and his regular contributors, who had seen New York displace Boston as the publishing center of the United States. William Dean Howells, who had edited the *Atlantic Monthly* during the 1870s and whose criticism had helped to define high U.S. literary culture, had moved to New York in the late 1880s in order to work for *Atlantic Monthly*'s rival *Harper's*, a move that carried symbolic significance at the time (and that the next chapter examines in more detail). Thus Perry's assertion that, while "the Atlantic has always been peculiarly identified with Boston," the magazine's "provincialism is of that honest kind which is rooted in the soil, and hence is truly representative of and contributory to the national life," may serve as tacit acknowledgement that the *Atlantic Monthly* faced the possibility of becoming marginalized by the magazines that were headquartered in New York.[5] In claiming to value "provincialism" as an alternative to "cosmopolitanism," Perry and his contributors were justifying their own commitment to keeping the *Atlantic Monthly* in Boston instead of moving it to "the commercial capital of the country."

This possible anxiety on Perry's part over the location of the *Atlantic Monthly*, however, does not explain similarly ambivalent statements about the value of cosmopolitanism that other writers in significantly different contexts also made at the turn of the twentieth century. In 1901, William P. Trent, who had just accepted a professorship of English at New York's Columbia University and who would go on to serve as editor-in-chief of the influential *Cambridge History of American Literature* (1917–21), decried "the so-called cosmopolitanism that has afflicted a small portion of our population, that has rendered them unsympathetic with their countrymen, and has driven them to spend their lives abroad."[6] Trent's "so-called cosmopolitanism" would seem to refer to expatriate artists and writers like Henry James, who had already been absent from the United States for nearly twenty years, but Trent immediately and somewhat unexpectedly makes an "exception" for "a few people of artistic temperaments," including no doubt James himself.[7] Moreover, against this "so-called cosmopolitanism," Trent positions what he calls "true cosmopolitanism," which ends up sounding much like Perry's notion of "provincialism": "We shall do our duty to the [human] race, and so prove ourselves to be true cosmopolitans all the better, by doing our intimate, our local, our national duties to the best of our abilities in the land of our birth. Shakespe[a]re is not a whit less cosmopolitan because he was a thoroughgoing Englishman of the Elizabethan period."[8]

In fact, the comments of Perry and Trent represent part of a much wider effort among American authors and intellectuals at the turn of the twentieth century to rethink and, in some cases, redefine the concept of cosmopolitanism and the forms of high art, such as literature, that were perceived to express it most fully. The paradoxes at work in the thinking of both Perry and Trent—that "true" cosmopolitanism somehow arose out of local affiliations and that this locally rooted cosmopolitanism simultaneously benefitted the nation—also characterize contemporaneous discussions of world literature, as I show later in this chapter, and of the use of local color in late realism, which I explore in the next chapter. Importantly, this discourse about cosmopolitanism, which was often though not exclusively literary in nature, sometimes overlapped or intersected with Progressive discourse about the role of the state itself and the relationship of the United States to the rest of the world. These intersections enabled literary figures to participate—and attempt to intervene—in discussions about the state that had overtly social and political implications. In some rare cases, such as Edward Bellamy's phenomenally popular novel *Looking Backward, 2000–1887* (1888), these literary interventions were very successful at shaping wider public opinion. More often, their influence was restricted to a relatively elite audience of educated readers. Nevertheless, as historian Frank Ninkovich points out in his study of the growth of internationalism in late nineteenth-century American periodicals, "a relatively small readership should not be equated with modest influence. . . . The nation's educated elites . . . at the very least framed issues for discussion, even if they did not necessarily decide them."[9] The invocations of cosmopolitanism made by Bliss Perry, William P. Trent, and other prominent writers and intellectuals served to remind readers of the important role literature could play in imagining a national identity and circulating that conception abroad. After all, the degree of Henry James's cosmopolitanism mattered because his ability to represent American literature abroad, meeting and engaging foreign authors on their own terms, might raise the international profile of American literature. At the same time, his lack of engagement with his own national culture also might, as Trent put it, "render [him] unsympathetic with [his] countrymen" and therefore unable to represent his nation adequately abroad.

This chapter examines how the ambivalent deployment of the language of cosmopolitanism at the turn of the twentieth century reflected a certain dissatisfaction with a particular notion of cosmopolitanism among a small but influential group of cultural authorities, including literary writers, critics, and intellectuals. These cultural authorities were aware of the United States' growing political and economic power and were eager to reframe the concept of cosmopolitanism, particularly as it applied to U.S. literary production, so that it bore more relevance to the emerging discourse of internationalism and world-salvation that Progressives were engaging in their attempt to empower the state within an increasingly global context. In reframing the concept of cosmopolitanism itself, these cultural authorities were suggesting that American literature could work alongside of—and, in some cases, resist—other state institutions and ideological state apparatuses in negotiating the newly global currents of U.S. society and in positioning the United States in global affairs. Thus the literary discourse about cosmopolitanism, which frequently identified the late realism of Henry James as its representative example, constitutes an important "cultural (or aesthetic) formation" that, David Lloyd and Paul Thomas claim, helps to articulate or revise "a certain *idea* of the state" (original emphasis).[10] That idea—what I am calling the idea of the Progressive state—called for a deep investment in the state itself as the primary locus of cultural as well as social and political aspirations, despite the increased opportunities that economic globalization and various transnational movements provided for turning away from the nation-state to identify alternative forms of social organization. In other words, the transnational imaginary that was emerging and, as subsequent chapters demonstrate through readings of some of its major practitioners, taking shape as late realism continued to hold onto the nation-state as the most practical means of organizing society and cultural production even as it explored the modes of circulation and exchange that were making cosmopolitanism an increasingly viable form of identification.

The paradoxical nature of cosmopolitanism—somehow emerging out of the tension between local (or national) and international affiliations—has been noted by numerous literary critics, sociologists, and philosophers over the years. Ulf Hannerz traces the "cosmopolitan-local distinction" at least as far back as sociologist Robert Merton's work during the 1950s and concludes that "there can be no cosmopolitans without locals."[11] In his oft-cited essay "Cosmopolitan Patriots," Kwame Anthony Appiah phrases the paradox as a question: "Where . . . would all the diversity we cosmopolitans celebrate come from in a world where there were only cosmopolitans?"[12] For Appiah, the answer is "straightforward" because the tension that produces this paradox is precisely what his "cosmopolitan patriots" celebrate: being "attached to a home of one's own, with its own cultural particularities, but taking pleasure from the presence of other, different places that are home to other, different people."[13] In valorizing cosmopolitanism as an end in itself, however, Appiah risks obscuring the fact that many other writers have historically deployed the language of cosmopolitanism for particular ends, including the consolidation of a sense of national identity and status and its projection outward onto the world. It is clearly such a nationalist logic that informs Trent's conception of "true cosmopolitanism," with its appeals to "national duties" and "the land of our birth." In a slightly different register, this logic also informs Woodrow Wilson's vision of the mediating nation: although his April 1915 speech does not contain the word "cosmopolitanism," Wilson's assertion that the United States can mediate the world, its various nations and peoples, and their forms of expression because the United States has already achieved a cosmopolitan commingling of ethnicities and voices within its own borders serves to reinforce the geopolitical importance of the United States, not to subsume the nation into a more transcendent category.

Thus while there is a large—and growing—body of literature on cosmopolitanism, internationalism, and various related terms and concepts, my focus in this chapter will be on their historical deployment and the shifts in meaning that that deployment produced in American attitudes toward the role of literature during the late nineteenth and early twentieth centuries.[14] My discussion centers primarily on three words that seem to have enabled the emerging transnational imaginary to link cultural matters, such as literary production and circulation, to political debates about the role of the state: "cosmopolitanism," a word with an already rich history; "internationalism," a neologism that seems to have helped prompt a reconsideration of cosmopolitanism; and "world-salvation," a much rarer term that nonetheless occupied a surprising number of prominent writers and intellectuals and that, based on its presence in two of the best-selling books of the period, seems to have struck a chord with Americans invested in rethinking the United States' relationship to the rest of the world. I treat these three terms as keywords, in Raymond Williams's sense of words "of capital importance" that "acquired new and important meanings."[15] It is therefore the shifts in—and contestations of—these words' meanings that matter rather than their abstract meanings or the consistency of their use. As Williams points out, the cultural work that keywords perform—what he characterizes as the "important social and historical processes [that] occur *within* language" (original emphasis)—depends to some extent upon their dynamic usage or, to be more precise, the ways in which particularly powerful deployments of these words shape their meanings and their perceived relevance to social, economic, and political questions.[16]

In approaching these three terms as keywords, I do not mean to discount or supplant the work of recent historians who have offered persuasive evidence of the important role that various notions of cosmopolitanism and internationalism played in fin de siècle Americans' conceptions of themselves and their place in the world. On the contrary, the next section of this chapter provides a brief survey of this important historical scholarship in order to establish a clearer sense of the particular understanding of U.S. Progressivism I am invoking here as the political and social context in which late realism was embedded and sought to intervene. Nevertheless, in characterizing his own methodology as a commitment "to the study of actual language[,] that is to say, to the words and sequences of words which particular men and women have used in trying to give meaning to their experience," Williams points to the value of subjecting "what we are in the habit of calling the known facts" to the kind of close scrutiny that the techniques of literary analysis routinely perform.[17] What attending to the writings of a select group of authors and intellectuals may sacrifice in terms of breadth, it makes up for in nuance by disclosing surprising connections between seemingly incompatible ideas or people that might otherwise go unnoticed. In this way, literary analysis can clarify or complicate existing historical accounts.

One such connection that I explore at the end of this chapter is that between Josiah Strong, one of the most influential advocates for U.S. overseas expansion during the late nineteenth century, and W. E. B. Du Bois, whose civil rights activism and commitment to Pan-Africanism led him to critique much of what Strong stood for. Despite their opposing worldviews, the concept of world-salvation, which each admittedly employs for different purposes, brings them together. Indeed, the fact that the term "world-salvation" was mainly employed in its secular sense by such elite writers and intellectuals as Strong, Edward Bellamy, and William James suggests that Du Bois may have consciously used it as a subtle assertion of his right and ability to engage them in dialogue. As I argue below, however, Du Bois's deployment of the language of world-salvation in order to expose just how short of its ideals U.S. society fell still reveals an ideological commitment to the state as the only reliable means of ensuring resolution and redress for people of color, both domestically and around the world. In Du Bois's formulation, which grows out of his vision of African Americans' potential contributions to Pan-Africanism, the "divided impulses" toward both cosmopolitanism and messianism that one noted historian locates in

Progressive thinking converge in "world-salvation," indicating that at least some astute observers of the period were already aware of these "inconsistencies" and may even have viewed them as two sides of the same coin.[18]

Finally, the subtlety of Du Bois's own writing—the "meaning" he makes, in Williams's sense—suggests the extent to which prominent activists and intellectuals joined critics and novelists in employing literary ways of thinking in order to address real-world problems. Like Woodrow Wilson, whose concept of the mediating nation emerges out of the purposeful use of polysemy in his speech, many of the most famous intellectuals and activists of the Progressive era, including William James, Jane Addams, and Du Bois, were careful writers who valued literary language, and Du Bois himself edited a magazine (*The Crisis*) that, as an early venue for members of the Harlem Renaissance, would become as influential in its own way as Bliss Perry's *Atlantic Monthly* had been. For these elite figures, the belief that appreciation for the literary use of language could help Americans make sense of their world was a working assumption. Hence despite Jane Addams's concern that the acquisition of "culture" might "set its possessor aside in a class with others like himself" and thereby render him unfit to find practical solutions to social problems (a concern voiced more than once in *Twenty Years at Hull-House* [1910]), she remained committed to the idea that cultivating an appreciation for literature in the immigrants she aided not only would "connect [them] with all sorts of people by [their] ability to understand them as well as by [their] power to supplement their present surroundings with historic background," but also help them "express in the newly acquired tongue some of [their] hopes and longings."[19] In other words, these Americans valued literary expression as a means of framing problems and imagining solutions. It seems important, therefore, to examine in some detail how they themselves exploited the dynamic language of cosmopolitanism, internationalism, and world-salvation in order to shape their readers' thinking. Following the brief survey of recent transnational accounts of the rise of U.S. Progressivism, the remainder of this chapter examines the ways of thinking about cosmopolitanism, internationalism, and world-salvation that opened up a space for literary writers, namely the late realists I examine in subsequent chapters, to participate in this wider discourse.

THE TRANSNATIONAL ACCOUNT OF PROGRESSIVISM

As noted in the introduction, the study of late nineteenth- and early twentieth-century U.S. history has experienced a significant transnational turn of its own in recent years. Several notable studies of the Gilded Age and the Progressive era have demonstrated the extent to which American reformers thought of themselves as taking part in an international movement, even going so far as to model their efforts in the United States upon similar reform movements in Germany, Britain, France, New Zealand, and elsewhere. In his 1986 study *Uncertain Victory*, James T. Kloppenberg located the intellectual foundations of Progressivism equally in Europe and North America. Explicitly eschewing the sort of comparative methodologies that emphasized national differences, Kloppenberg argued that the movement to create "the German, French, English, and American welfare states" at the end of the nineteenth century developed "within a transatlantic community of discourse rather than a parochial national frame of reference."[20] Daniel T. Rodgers's *Atlantic Crossings* (1998) similarly focused on the "North Atlantic economy" that gave rise to "an intense, transnational traffic in reform ideas, policies, and legislative devices."[21] Rodgers went on to characterize "the years between the 1870s and the Second World War" as "the Atlantic era in social politics" in which "American politics was peculiarly open to foreign models and important ideas."[22] For both Kloppenberg and Rodgers, the rise of Progressivism was an Atlantic, not just a uniquely American, phenomenon that arose out of a vibrant crosspollination of ideas between leading intellectuals and reformers in several industrialized nations.

Even more recently, however, historians have presented Progressivism as a truly global endeavor and the strengthening of state institutions in the United States and elsewhere as the result of structural changes to society the world over. In his book *A Nation among Nations* (2006), for example, Thomas Bender points to "the growth of giant cities . . . worldwide," which was "driven by industrial capitalism" and produced similar "industrial landscapes" and urban problems on virtually every continent.[23] According to Bender:

> The report of the Tenement House Committee of the New York State Legislature in 1894, for example, included summaries of housing policies in different nations and compared density, health indicators, and rents for New York City and big cities around the world— not only in western Europe but also in India, Japan, Russia, and the Austro-Hungarian Empire. The National Conference on Industrial Conciliation cast its survey nearly as wide for its investigation of labor-management issues in 1902, including data from England, Canada, France, Germany, Belgium, Italy, and Turkey.[24]

Identifying a direct connection between domestic reform and U.S. foreign policy, Ian Tyrrell goes even further in *Transnational Nation* (2007), claiming that "the growth of the *nation-state* fusing nationalism and state structures coincided with international competition over resources and political influence from the 1880s and in response to transnational economic and cultural pressures such as immigration. . . . The American state was transnationally produced" (original emphasis).[25] Thus the rise of passport regulation in the early 1900s, "an important indication of these hardening state boundaries," began when other nations, especially Italy, began to respond to "American anxieties about anarchists, socialists, and transient immigrants."[26] In short, while these current historians continue to agree with their predecessors that the Progressive movement served to empower the state, they now view this movement as taking shape transnationally, both intellectually and practically.[27]

Several historians have drawn a direct connection between the Progressive impulse to reform society and Americans' growing tendency to view themselves as cosmopolitan. Pointing to such activists as Jane Addams, who viewed her efforts at promoting world peace as a direct outgrowth of her work at helping immigrants of various ethnicities integrate themselves into U.S. society, Alan Dawley makes the claim in *Changing the World* (2003) that Progressives "were the most cosmopolitan generation of reformers to appear thus far in American history": "the dual quest for improvement at home and abroad was at the heart of what it meant to be a progressive."[28] Exactly how their desire to "improve" the world outside U.S. borders should play out—"whether internationalism called for solidarity across national borders or for keeping hands off"—remained uncertain, as Dawley notes when contrasting Woodrow Wilson's efforts at maintaining neutrality during the First World War with his willingness to invade Veracruz during the Mexican Revolution.[29] Nevertheless, Dawley contends, "it was still possible for progressives to believe that social reform and the new internationalism could march hand in hand toward a better future, and that they could be both good citizens of the United States and cosmopolitan citizens of the world."[30] It is precisely this ability to view the United States' engagement with the rest of the world as a means of strengthening the nation that, as I argue below, deployment of the language of internationalism, world-salvation, and cosmopolitanism worked to realize.

Kristin L. Hoganson extends this analysis of late nineteenth- and early twentieth-century cosmopolitanism even further in *Consumers' Imperium* (2007), where she argues that cosmopolitanism was not just a set of geopolitical aspirations that occupied the elite politicians and intellectuals who often dominate discussions of the Progressive era, but also a consumable experience for many Americans with disposable incomes. Thanks to the spread of global commerce and the United States' new position at the center of the world economy, American consumers, including even the middle-class wives and mothers who were responsible for decorating their families' homes, had access to "a collection of goods" from around the world that enabled them to display, quite literally, their appreciation for—and appropriation of—various foreign cultures: "Through their households, these women strove to convey a cosmopolitan ethos—meaning a geographically expansive outlook that demonstrated a familiarity with the wider world. Their cosmopolitanism implied an appreciation of other people's artistic productions."[31] At the same time, these patterns of everyday consumption were never far removed from the geopolitical concerns of government leaders who occupied the seats of power. "Not only did [this cosmopolitanism] emerge from U.S. commercial and political expansion," Hoganson avers, "but it helped promote it. This was a cosmopolitanism that celebrated empire, on the part of both the United States and the European powers."[32] As I discuss more fully in the third chapter, Henry James's fiction, with its attention to such matters as purchasing power and status, frequently identifies and explores just this relationship between patterns of consumption and what Hoganson calls "the globalization of the United States" itself.[33]

In *Global Dawn* (2009), Frank Ninkovich even more directly links cultural activities, such as the discussions of what constituted "civilization" that appeared in leading periodicals of the Gilded Age, to the "growth of internationalism" in U.S. foreign relations.[34] In these periodicals, Ninkovich contends, "educated Americans of the Gilded Age displayed an extraordinary degree of interest in events abroad. Indeed, many Americans took . . . interest in international relations by seeking to define the nation from a global perspective in which the United States was an active and important participant."[35] Ninkovich is quick to note that internationalism did not flourish as a dominant political philosophy until after 1890—he characterizes the Gilded Age as a kind of learning process during which American began to "think about global developments and their nation's place in history"—but he also observes that such terms as *Americanization* had begun to appear by the late-1860s as "image[s] of the nation's prowess."[36] Moreover, in his survey of the efforts to enact international copyright protection for U.S. authors—legislation that did not exist until the

1890s—Ninkovich suggests that engaging "a global literary community was . . . necessary to identity formation" because "American highbrows of the day saw culture as a universal phenomenon."[37] As noted in my opening discussion of Bliss Perry and the *Atlantic Monthly*, I contend that the perceived tension between literature's ability to produce or convey a sense of national identity and its ability to transcend national borders informed a much broader effort at renegotiating the meaning of cosmopolitanism at the turn of the twentieth century and making it more relevant to the United States' increasingly international orientations.

Finally, in highlighting the important role that language and literature played in producing what he calls "a discursive network" that enabled concerned Americans to work out the kind of roles they envisioned the United States playing in the world, Ninkovich identifies a potentially very productive common ground for historians of U.S. Progressivism and literary scholars of American realism.[38] It is this common ground that *The Mediating Nation* seeks to explore by drawing attention to the intersections in the transnational imaginings of the state that both late realists and Progressives articulated. More specifically, the next section of this chapter examines how American cultural authorities sought to reframe cosmopolitanism in light of growing Progressive discourse about internationalism.

COSMOPOLITANISM, INTERNATIONALISM, AND THE ROLE OF AMERICAN LITERATURE IN THE WORLD

In recent years, it has become common to treat the words "cosmopolitanism" and "internationalism" as synonyms. Kwame Anthony Appiah, for instance, explicitly equates their meanings in his book *Cosmopolitanism* (2006), and Alan Dawley treats them interchangeably in *Changing the World*.[39] At the turn of the twentieth century, however, these words seem to have carried divergent meanings for many Americans, and they did not appear together regularly in print.[40] Perhaps the clearest articulation of the perceived incompatibility of these words—and of the ideologies for which they stood—appears in a published dissertation entitled *The Rise of Internationalism* (1915). The author, a doctoral student in the political science department at Columbia University named John Culbert Faries, sought in his opening chapter to distance the political theory of internationalism, which he claimed arose "quite rapidly during the second half of the nineteenth century," from the longstanding philosophical concept of cosmopolitanism:

Internationalism is not the same as cosmopolitanism which has a detachedness about it that makes it seem in a degree unnatural. The man "unwept, unhonored and unsung," who drew the scorn of Sir Walter Scott, was the man without attachment for his native land. . . . There is nothing unattached or vagrant about internationalism. Its native soil is the life of the smallest human group. Those things which one social group has found it expedient and advantageous to do in advancing its economic or moral welfare have some relationship to the progress of any other group similarly circumstanced. . . . When there is conscious effort to realize the larger life of the group by action which is in harmonious adjustment to the efforts of the other group we have the essence of coöperation which, when it exists between nations, we call internationalism.[41]

By characterizing cosmopolitanism as "unnatural," Faries implies that commitment to a nation-state, the only "social group" he is able to envision as serving as the basis for internationalism, is natural, desirable, and as his quotation of Scott suggests, honorable. In other words, Faries's study of internationalism strives to reinscribe the sovereign and culturally distinct state as the primary unit of the world order.

Faries's study, which one group of historians has recently characterized as "a valuable introduction to the multilayered activities labelled as internationalism before World War I," seems broadly indicative of the political discourse of internationalism, which more or less sought to reify the state.[42] That is to say, internationalism emerged as a political philosophy that reaffirmed the role of the state in a world where interconnection had made Immanuel Kant's vision of "a universal cosmopolitan existence" increasingly feasible but also where the continued affective power of nationalism had made the destruction of the First World War part of that global "existence."[43] The language of internationalism thus offered American intellectuals and politicians a means of conceptualizing a middle ground between Herderian nationalism and the principle of national sovereignty, on one hand, and cosmopolitanism and the economic and cultural benefits of dissolving arbitrary borders, on the other. As Paul Samuel Reinsch, a political scientist who was eventually appointed U.S. minister to China, put it in 1911, "In its attempt to create a new basis for human life [cosmopolitanism] cast aside and spurned all the relations and institutions in which our national and communal life has had its being. . . . Effectual internationalism respects political and ethnic entities as essential forms of social organization within their proper limits, just as the modern state respects the autonomy of towns, provinces, and member states."[44]

What is perhaps most remarkable about the history of the word "internationalism" is how quickly it came to carry these meanings, despite its early associations with socialism. As Raymond Williams's study of keywords indicates, however, neologisms are sometimes more malleable than words with longer histories, and this malleability may explain why so many American politicians and intellectuals felt comfortable forgetting the nineteenth-century connotations of "internationalism" and embracing the word after 1900. The word did not appear in print until the 1860s and did not appear regularly in mainstream American publications until the late 1890s.[45] The first major dictionary to include the term is the American *Century Dictionary and Cyclopedia* (1889–91), where it is wholly associated with the International Workingmen's Association (the First International): "The principles, doctrine, or theory advocated by Internationalists."[46] This definition lends credence to Russ Castronovo's claim that, during the nineteenth century, the concept of internationalism was frequently associated with the threat of European socialism; however, the commentary that the *Century* adds to its entry on the First International recounts that organization's perceived loss of relevance: "By 1867 the International had become a powerful organization, though strenuously opposed by the continental European governments; but its manifestation in 1872 of sympathy with the doings of the Paris Commune in the preceding year, and internal dissensions, caused a great loss of reputation and strength."[47] Thus it seems that, by the 1890s, the word was gradually losing this association.

By the 1910s, in fact, Progressives had effectively made the language of internationalism their own, reframing it as a political theory that was designed to strengthen the United States domestically and to secure its global economic and political supremacy through cooperative engagement with the international community. Progressive reformer Frederic C. Howe employed the word this way as early as November 1902 when, in an article for the *Atlantic Monthly*, he identified friendly trade relations with other countries as a necessary precondition of the United States' own economic well-being: "The press bears constant witness to the fact that internationalism is the keynote of present day politics. We have come to think on a world scale. . . . To-day, the commercial arena is that of the world itself. It has passed national boundaries. And the future tariff policy of the United States must be governed by the size of the bargain table; not more by home than by foreign conditions."[48] Herbert Croly, cofounder of the *New Republic* and one of the major intellectual architects of U.S. Progressivism, dedicated an entire chapter of his influential book *The Promise of American Life* (1909) to what he paradoxically called "A National Foreign Policy" and "An American International System," in which he outlined his "conception of the place of a democratic nation in relation to other civilized nations" and claimed that the United States "must assume a more definite and a more responsible place in the international system."[49] According to Croly, authorizing the state to participate more actively in international affairs—through cultivating closer relationships with Canada and Mexico, using the recently acquired Philippines as a means of engaging Americans' interests in Asian politics, and counteracting European infusions of capital and labor into South America—would ultimately serve to improve domestic conditions:

> The work of internal reconstruction and amelioration, so far from being opposed to that of the vigorous assertion of a valid foreign policy, is really correlative and supplementary thereto; and it is entirely possible that hereafter the United States will be forced into the adoption of a really national domestic policy because of the dangers and duties incurred through her relations with foreign countries. The increasingly strenuous nature of international competition and the constantly higher standards of international economic, technical, and political efficiency prescribe a constantly improving domestic political and economic organization.[50]

For Howe and Croly, the viability of Progressive reform was inextricably tied to Americans' willingness to exploit global routes of exchange that might otherwise bypass the United States.

In contrasting internationalism with cosmopolitanism, then, Faries and Reinsch were simply making the logic of Howe and Croly explicit: that, in an increasingly interconnected world, the nation-state remained the most viable means of mediating between the domestic and the international and that the United States was uniquely positioned to exploit these interconnections and should be empowered to do so. "As international advantages are essential to the citizen," Reinsch argued, "so the state remains necessary to the achievement of internationalism."[51] Likewise, for all his attempts at objectivity, Faries ended up extolling the United States as "the 'melting pot' of the world" and concluding that "the American citizen should, of all men, be the most deeply interested in the growth of internationalism, as he is the most deeply concerned."[52] Faries's suggestion that the United States has the most to contribute to—and the most to gain from—the cause of internationalism more or less coincides with the logic of the mediating nation that Woodrow Wilson spelled out the same year. For Wilson, Faries, and the rest, internationalism was not incompatible with the continued growth of U.S. power and prestige; rather, adhering to the principles of internationalism directly benefitted the United States.

In the short term, of course, these writers' efforts at advocating internationalism met with limited success. The U.S. Congress eventually rejected the Versailles Treaty and the League of Nations, and Wilson's political opponents attempted to link the word "internationalism" back to Bolshevism. John Sharp Williams, one of Wilson's supporters in the Senate, was forced to make a distinction between "the so-called internationalism of Bolshevism" and "the right sort of internationalism . . . made up of treaties of peace between nations, each retaining its own sovereignty and surrendering nothing except by its own consent."[53] Indeed, the most significant legacy of this political discourse about internationalism may be its negative effect on the perceived value of cosmopolitanism, with its assumptions that humans would eventually transcend both the affective ties of nationalism and the political differences of individual nation-states. The negative connotations of cosmopolitanism register in the 1933 edition of the *Oxford English Dictionary (OED)*. Whereas earlier definitions, such as those found in Noah Webster's *American Dictionary* (1828), the British *Imperial Dictionary* (1847–50), and the American *Century Dictionary and Cyclopedia* (1889–91), had emphasized the sense of being "a citizen of the world" and achieving freedom "from local, provincial, or national ideas, prejudices, or attachments," the *OED* noted that the language of cosmopolitanism was "often contrasted with *patriot*, and so either reproachful or complimentary."[54] Hence Thomas Wentworth Higginson's "reproachful" dismissal of "the cant of cosmopolitanism" in 1897, which finds its modern-day echo in Gertrude Himmelfarb's dismissal of cosmopolitanism as an "illusion."[55]

Rather than displacing the word "cosmopolitanism," however, the growing usage of "internationalism" in political discourse served to relegate "cosmopolitanism" to the more abstract domain of culture, as indicated by the primarily literary contexts in which it appeared in the *Atlantic Monthly* during the 1900s, for example. It is no accident that Faries appealed to literature in order to make his point about cosmopolitanism (though he seems to have missed the irony that, in citing a Scottish author's "attachment for his native land," he was reinforcing literature's cosmopolitan value), and Reinsch dismissively observed that "cosmopolitanism is still current in much of our literature, although in practical affairs we have almost entirely outlived it."[56] Perhaps the most notable dismissal of this sort turns up in Theodore Roosevelt's essay "True Americanism," which first appeared in the April 1894 issue of the reform-oriented magazine *Forum* and was reprinted in several collections of Roosevelt's writings thereafter. Forwarding an argument in favor of the complete assimilation of immigrants, Roosevelt positioned what he called "Americanism," the full identification of U.S. citizens with their nation's interests, against both an "unwholesome parochial spirit" and "that flaccid habit of mind which its possessors style cosmopolitanism."[57] Roosevelt's condemnation of cosmopolitanism leads directly into a lengthy diatribe against "the man who becomes Europeanized" because he prides himself on his "standing in the world of art and letters."[58] Roosevelt may very well have had Henry James in mind when he characterized such a "Europeanized" writer as "over-civilized, over-sensitive, [and] over-refined."[59] At any rate, Roosevelt apparently considered the appeal of literary cosmopolitanism dangerous enough to his vision of a distinct and uniform American culture that he calls into question the masculinity of writers who subscribe to cosmopolitanism. "With his delicate, effeminate sensitiveness," he continued, the "Europeanized" writer "finds that he cannot play a man's part among men. . . . This *émigré* may write graceful and pretty verses, essays, novels; but he will never do work to compare with that of his brother, who is strong enough to stand on his own feet, and do his work as an American."[60]

Cultural authorities, including authors and critics, responded in kind, reframing cosmopolitanism so that it more closely resembled the internationalism that Reinsch and Faries extolled. Like "the right sort of internationalism" that John Sharp Williams claimed respected individual nations' "sovereignty," William P. Trent's "true cosmopolitanism" involves respecting and attending to "local [and] national duties." From this perspective, national literatures, just like nations themselves, matter more than any sort of transcendent category. Here, too, one can trace the legacy of this logic to more recent efforts at engaging the language of cosmopolitanism. In Appiah's "Cosmopolitan Patriots," for instance, cosmopolitanism plays out largely in terms of how fully one appreciates "cultural particularities," and Appiah's expanded argument, which appears in *Cosmopolitanism*, resembles the internationalism of Faries and Reinsch: "The primary mechanism for ensuring these entitlements [to basic human rights] remains the nation-state. . . . Accepting the nation-state means accepting that we have a special responsibility for the life and the justice of our own; but we still have to play our part in ensuring that all states respect the rights and meet the needs of their citizens."[61]

During the first two decades of the twentieth century in particular, critics and authors tended to depict literature as the only sphere where cosmopolitanism could find its fullest expression. Invoking the names of Goethe, who coined the term *Weltliteratur*, and Matthew Arnold, such critics as Brander Matthews and Henry Dwight Sedgwick maintained that cosmopolitanism was largely a matter of "stepping across the confines of language" and that, through reading works of literature from diverse cultures, "the reader acquires a larger view of life [and] imagines for a season that men are brothers."[62] For Matthews and Sedgwick, literature instilled a cosmopolitan perspective in readers precisely because individual works of literature remained inextricably tied to the local cultural and linguistic contexts in which they were produced. Hence Sedgwick asserts, "Everywhere the power that carries literary fame throughout the world must be sought in some national trait."[63] Within the context of world literature, then, individual literary works derive their power from their foreignness, and only through exposure to this foreignness can readers achieve a more cosmopolitan understanding of the world. Thomas Peyser has characterized these sorts of discussions about literary cosmopolitanism as "fashionably open-minded" expressions of "a 'liberated' readership," but there were unmistakable political implications, too.[64]

As David Damrosch points out, this conception of literary cosmopolitanism, which valorizes an a priori perception of difference and then seeks to assimilate that difference through strategic selection and translation, often serves as the basis for both "self-confirming narcissism" and "imperial acquisitiveness."[65] Damrosch does not go so far as to suggest that these discussions of literary cosmopolitanism underwrote or retroactively justified the newly aggressive geopolitical stance of the U.S. government after the Spanish-American War of 1898—he instead finds "a higher form of nativism" at work in the efforts of Henry Cabot Lodge and others to present important literary works from the past as mere precursors to U.S. democratic culture—but critics who argued in favor of literary cosmopolitanism sometimes employed the language of overseas expansion.[66] Writing in 1907, Brander Matthews offers the following revision to Goethe's thinking: "With all his wisdom Goethe failed to perceive that cosmopolitanism is a sorry thing when it is not the final expression of patriotism. . . . The cosmopolitanism of this growing century is revealed mainly in a similarity of the external forms of literature, while it is the national spirit which supplies the essential inspiration that gives life."[67] The expansiveness of Matthews's vision discloses itself in his sense of belonging to a "growing" century. Even more strikingly, however, he argues that similarity of "forms" rather than difference of content assumes the primary precondition of literary cosmopolitanism—a paradox that the next chapter's discussion of local color examines more fully. Matthews clearly views literary cosmopolitanism as an assertion of power. He implies that only through conforming to aesthetic standards determined and imposed by those at the center of the publishing world, which was increasingly becoming Matthews's own hometown of New York, could authors from more marginal cultures become legible and, consequently, their work worthy of circulation. Becoming more identifiable with an abstract cosmopolitan literary standard—say, through the production of a Henry James—meant that the United States could lay claim to more authority in determining what else qualified as cosmopolitan literature.

Frank Ninkovich locates the roots for this understanding of literary cosmopolitanism in the post–Civil War arguments for international copyright: "To cosmopolitan intellectuals, a major cause of the nation's cultural inferiority was the absence of international copyright protection for American authors."[68] Ninkovich goes on to note that, by the time the United States finally began addressing the problem, advocates for international copyright had adopted unapologetically nationalist rhetoric: "By this logic, promoting American authors was . . . a way of promoting an international literature—and vice versa."[69] In 1885, for instance, George William Curtis, a literary critic who preceded William Dean Howells as author of the "Editor's Easy Chair" column for *Harper's Monthly*, argued that international copyright protection would guarantee the ascendancy of American literature. Curtis referred to a "realm of language" that seemed to operate, like Pascale Casanova's "world republic of letters," as a transnational space that somehow still intersected with the interests of individual nations and their national literatures.[70] "As the literary guild in the United States constantly adds illustrious names to its roll," Curtis contended, "the distinctive literary interest of the country is becoming more important and powerful, and it will assert its demands more imperatively, and with increasing success."[71] Thus far from being just "fashionably open-minded," literary cosmopolitanism was often framed as a means of bringing additional prestige to American literature, with critics and authors positioning American literature as an ideological state apparatus that served the global interests of the United States and therefore deserved protection from the state through international copyright agreements.

By the early-twentieth century, both of those objectives—international copyright protection for American authors and increased standing of

American authors abroad—had been reached, and literary critics had begun to take note of the newly transnational inflections of American literature. In 1908, Henry Mills Alden, the longtime editor of *Harper's*, declared that American literary realism had achieved a "world sense of the imagination."[72] For Alden, this "world sense" was the direct result of the aesthetics that late realism—what Alden called "the new realism"—embraced: "Realism is spoken of as if it were confined to the near view of life and things, as if, indeed, it were simply the result of close observation and of a feeling for local color, . . . but we lose sight of its chief distinction if we ignore the light of its seeing and the charm of its feeling due to the sense of and knowledge of far away things—the cosmopolitanism which makes it always widely and wisely human."[73] The next chapter explores the relationship between late realism's attention to the local and particular and its "sense of and knowledge of far away things" in the fiction and criticism of Alden's most notable employee at *Harper's*, William Dean Howells. For now, it is worth noting that, like his rivals at the *Atlantic Monthly*, Alden identified Henry James most closely with this cosmopolitanism: "If our readers want a positive example of the extreme advance in fiction, they will find it in Henry James's stories."[74] For Alden, however, James's cosmopolitanism rendered the "provincialism" that Bliss Perry advocated irrelevant. In a world where Henry James had proved that being American and being cosmopolitan could mean the same thing, "what used to be called, in a peculiar sense, our Americanism," as Alden puts it, "is no longer a sought-for distinction."[75]

AMERICA AS WORLD-SALVATION

Brander Matthews's references to Goethe's concept of *Weltliteratur* and other American critics' adoption of its English translation point to an unusual lexicographical development toward the end of the nineteenth century: the rise of compound nouns using the word "world" as a prefix. While the creation of abstract compound nouns is fairly common in German, it is less so in English. The novelty of using "world" as a prefix for such compound nouns is underscored by the nineteenth-century practice of hyphenating these terms before they became commonplace, as in William Morris's discussion of a "world-market" in *News from Nowhere* (1890).[76] So novel were these compounds, in fact, that the practice goes unrecorded in the *American*, *Imperial*, and *Century* dictionaries, though the *Century* lists "world-language" as a separate entry. (The 2010 edition of the *OED* cites William Dwight Whitney, the editor-in-chief of the *Century*, as one of the first people to predict that English would become a "world-language.")[77]) The 1909 supplement to the *Century* adds several more examples, including "world-map" and "world-power"; however, the first dictionary to acknowledge the wider practice was the 1933 *OED*, which dates it to the 1830s and appends the following comment: "Orig. translating or modelled on G[erman] compounds, as *welt-handel* world-commerce, *weltkrieg* world-war, *weltmacht* world-power, *weltreich* world-empire."[78] That Thomas Carlyle, who was a scholar and translator of German literature, is cited as the original source for several of these terms, including "world-famous," "world history," and "world literature," attests to the degree to which British writers consciously modeled these compound nouns on German linguistic practices.

In one conspicuous exception to this pattern, however, the 1933 *OED* attributes first usage of the term "world-power" in its political rather than religious sense to former U.S. president Benjamin Harrison. In a February 1901 essay for the *North American Review*, Harrison offers a lengthy discussion of what a "World Power" is and, in a display of rather tortured logic, categorically rejects the assertion that the United States has become a "World Power" if being one involves "having the purpose to take over so much of the world as it can by any means . . . and having with this appetite for dominion military strength enough to compel other nations having the same appetite to allow or divide the spoils."[79] Harrison then attempts to cast annexation of the Philippines in a favorable light, but his argument is undercut considerably by the fact that one of the era's most damning condemnations of U.S. imperialism, Mark Twain's "To the Person Sitting in Darkness," immediately precedes Harrison's essay in the very same issue of the *North American Review*. Twain's satiric article, with its closing image of "our usual flag, with the white stripes painted black and the stars replaced by the skull and cross-bones," flying over the Philippines, belies Harrison's denial of the United States' status as a world power and all that that designation implies.[80]

Harrison's discussion of "world power," just like Brander Matthews's revision of the cosmopolitanism underpinning Goethe's concept of "world literature," indicates the extent to which Americans in the early twentieth century had quite literally "come to think on a world scale," as Frederic C. Howe put it. Rather than examine these "world-" compounds collectively, however, I end this chapter by discussing only one: "world-salvation." Although this term does not appear in print as frequently as "internationalism" and "cosmopolitanism" do, usage of "world-salvation" exhibits a similar malleability of—and contestation over—meaning, revealing the same desire on the part of American intellectuals to position the United States as a central actor on the international stage. Even more significantly, the language of world-salvation was employed by some of the most prominent and influential intellectuals in the United States at the time, including Josiah Strong, Edward Bellamy, William James, Jane Addams, and W. E. B. Du Bois. These writers skillfully exploited both the global and religious implications of the term, imparting a sense of urgency to their own particular efforts at Progressive reform. In so doing, they take the shifting discourse of internationalism and cosmopolitanism to its logical conclusion and designate the United States not just as a powerful or integral part of the international community, but as the site of hope for the whole world's future.

The optimistic belief in the possibility of the world's salvation, which originates in the late eighteenth-century theology of Christian Universalism, is cosmic in nature: all human souls will eventually achieve reconciliation with God. By the mid-nineteenth century, American Congregational theologians and ministers had enthusiastically adopted the rhetoric of world-salvation in order to justify and elicit support for their missionary activities abroad. In the pages of the *Universalist Union*, a weekly periodical that was published in New York between 1836 and 1847, and in Enoch Pond's treatise *The World's Salvation* (1845), they argued that God had charged them to ensure the world's salvation through the spread of Protestant Christianity around the world. While the term "world-salvation" never completely dropped this religious inflection, it lost much of its theological particularity and became increasingly secularized during the Progressive era. This shift toward a more general meaning was no doubt due in large part to the rise of the Social Gospel movement, which sought to blur the boundary between social and spiritual work and encouraged a certain measure of ecumenical understanding among Protestant denominations and even with other religions. For example, at the 1893 Parliament of World's Religions, which was held concurrently with the World's Columbian Exposition in Chicago, a Brethren minister from Nebraska named John Duke McFadden delivered a brief statement on "The World's Salvation." "In working for the world's salvation," he claimed, "we are to work for the overthrow of creeds.... The pulpits and churches and organizations must be linked for the work of saving from crime and violence."[81]

In this ecumenical and socially conscious understanding of world-salvation, a number of prominent American writers and intellectuals found a means of calling for transformative social change. In an 1889 essay protesting both the practice of segregation in southern Congregational communities and the blind eye northern Congregationalists were turning to this practice in order to preserve the larger unity of their denomination, George Washington Cable wrote, "In the scheme of the world's salvation, not the life, or numerical or financial prosperity of one or another church, but the maintenance and spread of the Divine Master's teachings in their integrity is the supreme necessity and command."[82] For Cable, who was also an important local colorist from New Orleans, the iniquitous social reality of racial segregation, which ran counter to Christian values, demanded resolution regardless of the well-being of any particular denomination. Even more broadly, in "Pragmatism and Religion," the last of the eight lectures that make up *Pragmatism* (1907), William James extolled the "optimism . . . that thinks the world's salvation possible" and then, despite the title of his lecture, secularized it: "Take, for example, any one of us in this room with the ideals which he cherishes and is willing to live and work for. Every such ideal realized will be one moment in the world's salvation [because] these particular ideals are not bare abstract possibilities. They are grounded, they are *live* possibilities, for we are their live champions and pledges" (original emphasis).[83]

Historian Deborah J. Coon reads James's valorization of individual "ideals" over denominational theology as being "deeply pluralistic," and although Coon does not connect James's argument explicitly to the Social Gospel, she characterizes his concept of world-salvation in a way that emphasizes its ties with the Social Gospel: it constitutes a "devotion to righting injustices" and a belief in "actively improving the world."[84] Like Cable, however, James casts world-salvation as mainly the result of addressing domestic issues, not of spreading Christian civilization abroad: "Does our act then *create* the world's salvation? . . . I ask *why not?* Our acts, our turning-places, where we seem to ourselves to make ourselves and grow, are the parts of the world to which we are closest, the parts of which our knowledge is the most intimate and complete" (original emphasis).[85] Both Cable and James adopt the language of world-salvation, therefore, in order to draw their readers' attention to the world around them and the interventions they might make there. Like charity, salvation begins at home.

For all of Cable's and James's references to domestic conditions, a global vision ultimately emerges out of American intellectuals' deployment of the language of world-salvation. As noted in the introduction, Jane Addams contended that a "nascent world consciousness"—what she characterized as a "lively sense of the unexpected and yet inevitable action and reaction between ourselves and all the others who happen to be living upon the planet at the same moment"—had been "the unique contribution of [her] time."[86] Within the context of *The Second Twenty Years at Hull-House* (1930), which positions her efforts at promoting world peace as an outgrowth of her work with immigrants locally in Chicago, what leads Addams to this conclusion is her realization that no effort at reform can exist in isolation, that only those efforts at reform that attend to "the continuity and interdependence of mankind" can succeed.[87] Noting just how short her own generation fell of its goals at improving the world, Addams gives her younger readers the following piece of advice: "The task of youth is not only its own salvation but the salvation of those against whom it rebels."[88] Here, Addams's sense of world-salvation almost returns to its original cosmic connotations, emphasizing both intergenerational "continuity" and transnational "interdependence."

Where the concept of world-salvation achieved its greatest impact, however, are almost certainly the uses to which it was put in two of the best-selling books of the late nineteenth century: Edward Bellamy's *Looking Backward* and Josiah Strong's *Our Country: Its Possible Future and Its Present Crisis* (1885). In the concluding passages of Bellamy's novel, for instance, as the narrator realizes that his return to the horrors of nineteenth-century society was only a dream and that he remains in the utopia of the year 2000, he muses "with unspeakable thankfulness upon the greatness of the world's salvation and [his] privilege in beholding it."[89] Like William James and Jane Addams, however, he recognizes the responsibility of individuals to work for the social transformation that will render this utopia a reality: "There suddenly pierced me like a knife a pang of shame, remorse, and wondering self-reproach. . . . What had I done to help on the deliverance whereat I now presumed to rejoice?"[90] Yet *Looking Backward*'s call to action does not rest upon personal responsibility alone. Like the Progressives, Bellamy envisions a stronger state as the source of utopia. Referring to "the national party," Dr. Leete, the narrator's guide in *Looking Backward*, explains that "it probably took that name because its aim was to nationalize the functions of production and distribution. . . . Its purpose was to realize the idea of the nation with a grandeur and completeness never before conceived."[91] The "idea of the nation" to which Dr. Leete refers may be more explicitly socialist than the form the Progressive state would assume, but the enormous popularity and influence of Bellamy's novel speaks to its original readers' receptiveness to the basic idea of state intervention.[92]

It is this continued role of the nation-state in Bellamy's vision of the future that some critics miss when they suggest that the logic of Bellamy's utopia calls for "a more or less unified world culture."[93] In point of fact, Bellamy locates his solution not in some sort of new world order, but within the kind of international framework that his contemporaries understood: that of sovereign nation-states interacting with one another. "This principle," Dr. Leete explains, "is an international as well as a national guarantee. . . . The sense of community of interest [is] international as well as national"; nevertheless, "complete autonomy within its own limits is enjoyed by every nation."[94] Moreover, many of the numerous responses, imitations, and rip-offs of Bellamy's best-seller pick up on this internationalist logic. Thomas Kirwan's *Reciprocity (Social and Economic) in the Thirtieth Century* (1909), an otherwise fairly derivative example of the utopian fiction that followed in the wake of *Looking Backward*'s success, even selects as its title a word ("reciprocity") that refers to equal trade relations between individual nation-states.[95] Not even in some of their most fantastic fiction, it seems, did fin de siècle Americans seem inclined toward—or capable of—imagining beyond the nation.

Bellamy was not the only—or even the first—writer to invoke international visions and grand designs for the United States through the rhetoric of world-salvation. Perhaps the text that links the concept of world-salvation most directly to the United States is Strong's *Our Country*. In the second paragraph of the book, Strong quotes Austin Phelps, the former president of Andover Theological Seminary: "Five hundred years of time in the process of the world's salvation may depend on the next twenty years of United States history."[96] Strong's most immediate aim in writing *Our Country* was to raise funds for the American Home Missionary Society. To that end, half of the book's fourteen chapters are dedicated to describing seven "perils" to U.S. cultural homogeneity (immigration, Roman Catholicism, Mormonism, alcoholism, socialism, financial inequality, and urbanization) that, presumably, domestic missionary work would defeat. Nevertheless, Strong's larger argument about the central importance of the United States to the world's future struck a chord with late nineteenth-century American readers. *Our Country* became one of the best-selling nonfiction books of its decade, selling over 175,000 copies in the United States alone.[97] Highlighting Strong's influence on late 1890s imperial discourse, Amy Kaplan attributes this popularity to the way Strong played on the "American anxiety . . . of belatedness on the imperial stage."[98] Anxieties of this sort abound in *Our Country*, to be sure, but in many ways, Strong's argument is even more precisely focused on the relationship between foreign and domestic concerns.

In identifying a more homogeneous religious culture in the United States as the solution to the problems posed by such global movements as immigration and socialism, Strong makes a subtle case for state consolidation. According to Strong, a more unified religious culture (an ideological state apparatus) would transform the United States into a more positive— and more powerful—force for good in the world. "Our plea is not America for America's sake; but America for the world's sake," he writes. "If I were a Christian African or Arab, I should look into the immediate future of the United States with intense and thrilling interest; for, as Professor Hoppin of Yale has said: 'America Christianized means the *world* Christianized'" (original emphasis).[99] Without question, Strong envisions a future where Americanization, Christianization, and civilization have all collapsed into a single global process that can reshape the world into the United States' own image, but he also contends that achieving such a future is impossible until America, Christianity, and civilization first merge *within* U.S. borders. In his follow-up book, *The New Era; or, The Coming Kingdom* (1893), Strong spells out the benefits of consolidation more explicitly:

> One of the most marked tendencies of the times is toward organization, combination, co-operation; illustrations of which are afforded in the consolidation of petty states and principalities into empires. . . . Organization and co-operation multiply effectiveness many-fold. . . . The great forces of modern times are those which as *organized* forces have taken advantage of this mighty "tide in the affairs of men," and the church must lay hold of this same power. (original emphasis)[100]

Invoking "empires" as a model his fellow church leaders might follow in order to "multiply [their] effectiveness," Strong unapologetically reveals his belief in the logic of imperialism, but in singling out state consolidation as his primary illustration of effective organization, Strong also anticipates those more liberal Progressives who sought social justice from a strengthened state. Strong's popularity as a writer, therefore, may have been due to his ability to give voice to the Progressive state's underlying logic, which served to link otherwise divergent political ideologies, including both Theodore Roosevelt's expansionism and William Jennings Bryan's anti-imperialism.

It is here, in stressing the empowerment of the state and state institutions as a means of engaging emerging global conditions, that Strong's identification of the United States as "the world's salvation" coincides with Woodrow Wilson's description of the United States as "the mediating Nation." Just as "world-salvation" connotes the idea of a religious charge that the United States has received, Wilson's mediating nation invites a similarly religious reading, though Wilson's phrase may be far more subtly allusive than the more overt religiosity of "world-salvation." Specifically, the phrase "the mediating nation" appears in the German theologian Heinrich Ewald's 1841 *Commentary on the Prophets of the Old Testament*. In his comments on Isaiah 42, Ewald applies the phrase to ancient Israel, characterizing it as the site of "the salvation of the whole earth."[101] Regardless of whether or not he was actually familiar with Ewald's work, Wilson may very well have intended to evoke the idea of religious intercession, which figures prominently in the definitions that the *American*, *Imperial*, and *Century* dictionaries provide for "mediator" (a role often "given [to Jesus Christ] with reference to his agency in reconciling God and men," according to the *Century*).[102] In other words, in addition to the meanings I already suggested that Wilson's use of "mediating" deploys, Wilson also may have expected his reference to the United States as the mediating nation to remind at least part of his audience of the rhetoric of world-salvation, particularly as such writers as Josiah Strong employed it. Either way, both Strong and Wilson represent the United States as a potential savior for the world.

This representation, of course, depends upon an exclusionary racial politics—explicitly in *Our Country*, where Strong racializes American society as Anglo-Saxon (and Protestant); implicitly in Wilson's speech, which fails to account for the expansion of Jim Crow. It is precisely because of these racist undertones, however, that the status of "world-salvation" as a keyword—indeed, that the dynamism of keywords in general—matters so much. Just as "internationalism" lost its socialist connotations and came to serve the global aspirations of a number of American politicians and intellectuals, the language of world-salvation became, in the hands of a particularly astute African American writer, the very means by which he could both subvert and invert Strong's and Wilson's racist logic. In May 1915, the month following Wilson's speech to the Associated Press, W. E. B. Du Bois published an essay in the *Atlantic Monthly* entitled "The African Roots of the War," in which he applies the language of world-salvation not to the United States as a whole, but rather to his fellow African Americans. In this essay, Du Bois identifies economic competition among the European nations exploiting Africa (the so-called scramble for Africa) as the primary cause of the First World War:

The present world war is, then, the result of jealousies engendered by the recent rise of armed national associations of labor and capital whose aim is the exploitation of the wealth of the world mainly outside the European circle of nations. These associations, grown jealous and suspicious at the division of the spoils of trade-empire, are fighting to enlarge their respective shares; they look for expansion, not in Europe but in Asia, and particularly in Africa.[103]

In a move that underscores the racist hypocrisy of Wilsonian internationalism, which would demand the recognition of statehood for Poland and Czechoslovakia after the war while redistributing the spoils of the German and Ottoman empires to France and Britain, Du Bois suggests a logical solution to the dangers of imperial competition: the extension of the principles and privileges of state sovereignty to the territories then under colonial rule. "If we want real peace and lasting culture," he counsels, "we must extend the democratic ideal to the yellow, brown, and black peoples. . . . The principle of home rule must extend to groups, nations, and races. The ruling of one people for another people's whim or gain must stop."[104]

Du Bois immediately acknowledges the counterargument that colonial peoples, especially Africans, may lack the education to run their own affairs. Pragmatically committing himself to the ideals of modernization and, by extension, westernization, Du Bois admits that "we must train native races in modern civilization. . . . Modern methods of educating children, honestly and effectively applied, would make modern, civilized nations out the vast majority of human beings on earth today."[105] Here, however, Du Bois deploys the rhetoric of world-salvation and stakes out an important role for disenfranchised African Americans:

> In this great work who can help us? In the Orient, the awakened Japanese and the awakening leaders of New China; in India and Egypt, the young men trained in Europe and European ideals, who now form the stuff that Revolution is born of. But in Africa? Who better than the twenty-five million grandchildren of the European slave trade, spread through the Americas, and now writhing desperately for freedom and a place in the world? And of these millions first of all the ten million black folk of the United States, now a problem, then a *world-salvation*. (emphasis added)[106]

Drawing attention to how Du Bois's argument in 1915 anticipates the Pan-African perspective of such later works as *Dark Princess* (1928), David

Luis-Brown emphasizes the overt religiosity of Du Bois's use of the term "world-salvation": "Du Bois makes an unmistakable allusion to messianism's defining formulation, Paul's pronouncement that the weak will prevail over the strong."[107] Just as unmistakably, however, Du Bois also alludes to the wider turn-of-the-twentieth-century discourse about world-salvation that I have examined above. Indeed, I read "The African Roots of the War" as a direct response to the racial politics at work in Josiah Strong's and Woodrow Wilson's portraits of the United States. Where Strong's *Our Country* is in large part a paean to the seemingly limitless resources of the American West and to the providence that brought the Anglo-Saxon race to the West, Du Bois opens and closes his essay with the Latin phrase *semper novi quid ex Africa* (everything new always comes out of Africa), which refers both to the continent's exploited wealth that could sustain its people and to the source of empowerment Africa might provide for African Americans. Likewise, echoing Wilson's depiction of the United States as the mediating nation but also correcting its omission of people of color, Du Bois presents African Americans as the "mediating" peoples of Africa. In a sense, Du Bois is extending the logic of his famous "Talented Tenth." Just as the most highly educated African Americans (the top 10 percent of their race in the United States) bear a duty to lead the rest of the African American community in their struggle for civil rights, African Americans in general bear a duty to lead the peoples of Africa in their struggle for independence. In short, Du Bois implies that African Americans make up the "Talented Tenth" of the entire black world.

Perhaps most important of all, "The African Roots of the War" reaffirms the state as the solution to all social problems. Even more transcendently than the other texts examined in this chapter, Du Bois's essay proffers a global account of the multidirectional and transformative power of the state to rectify social ills both within its own borders and beyond them. On a very basic level, Du Bois is simply being pragmatic: statehood carries with it the privilege of self-determination and, consequently, a greater opportunity for social stability. The "national bond is no mere sentimental patriotism, loyalty, or ancestor-worship," he observes. "It is the increased wealth, power, and luxury for all classes on a scale the world never saw before."[108] On another level, however, Du Bois is being unapologetically visionary insofar as he locates in Africa the source of future African American empowerment. Newly formed African states become a site for redressing social injustices in the United States by providing African Americans with a leadership role upon the world stage that simultaneously empowers both their African protégés and themselves. They cease to be "a problem" when they become "a world-salvation." In some ways, Du Bois's reframing of the rhetoric of world-salvation within the context of European imperialism provides a more ethical model of internationalism than the ones that John Culbert Faries and Paul Samuel Reinsch advocated. Nevertheless, it is important to remember that, in imagining new states in Africa, Du Bois still asserts U.S. power and prestige, even if that power and prestige are particularized to African Americans. Thus what ultimately aligns Du Bois with both the Progressive politicians and intellectuals this chapter has largely focused on and the late realists the next four chapters consider is his effort to imagine the world as a site for reimagining the United States.

Local Color, World Literature, and the Transnational Turn in William Dean Howells's Fiction and Criticism

In June 1895, *Harper's Weekly* published what may constitute the first comprehensive historical overview of the rise of local color in literature: a two-part essay on dialect by William Dean Howells. The essay may have been prompted, at least in part, by the relatively recent death of James Russell Lowell, whose collection of poems entitled *The Biglow Papers* (1848) was already widely regarded as the first serious effort at rendering dialect artistically in literature. As Gavin Jones has shown in his study of late nineteenth-century dialect literature, Lowell was often thought of as "a protorealist" by subsequent writers who employed dialect and the other techniques of local color, and several of them were moved to write posthumous tributes to Lowell and his literary innovations, including even Henry James, despite James's apparent lack of interest in representing dialect in his own fiction.[1] In the *Harper's Weekly* essay, Howells himself claims that "Lowell's accurate and exquisite study of the Yankee dialect in the *Biglow Papers* was the first work of the kind that was truly artistic."[2] Howells goes on to trace Lowell's legacy in American literature from Harriet Beecher Stowe's *Old Town Folks* (1869) and Bret Harte's short stories to Hamlin Garland's *Main-Travelled Roads* (1891) and Stephen Crane's *Maggie* (1893). (The inclusion of Crane's urban novel alongside the rural fiction of Stowe and Garland underscores the breadth of Howells's conception of local color and lends credence to the arguments of Richard Brodhead and Gavin Jones that nineteenth-century authors and critics perceived local-color writing as central to realism.[3]) In this respect, Howells's essay echoes the opinions of other critics who viewed the use of dialect as an especially—or even uniquely—American literary tradition.[4]

The second half of Howells's essay takes an unexpected turn, however. It transforms into a comparative history, examining the parallel use of dialect by such European authors as Robert Burns, Thomas Hardy, and Émile Zola. This shift to an international perspective is important to the essay's larger argument because it provides Howells with evidence that American practitioners of local color have "been part of the world movement in fiction toward greater naturalness and lifelikeness."[5] For Howells, Lowell's innovative use of dialect matters not because it emerged in isolation, but rather because it meant that an American author had contributed to an even more important development in world literature: the emergence of realism itself. To be sure, Howells, like other American critics of his time, believed that American authors were the most adept at utilizing dialect in their fiction, but Howells also seems to have believed that this national quality only had value within a wider international context. According to Howells, the expert use of dialect is part of what gives Americans "the right . . . to a standing with the foremost of the peoples whose authors wished them to appear in literature exactly as they appear in life."[6] In this formulation, realism, including the use of such techniques of local-color writing as dialect, is a global literary movement, and it provides American writers with the opportunity to participate in—and ultimately to shape—world literature as never before.

World literature and American literature's relationship to it concerned Howells greatly from the late 1880s onwards, and his *Harper's Weekly* essay on dialect should be viewed as part of a larger effort to internationalize American literature, by which I mean that Howells strove in the latter half of his career to make American literature more relevant and therefore more vital to global literary trends and developments as well as more capable of representing the newly globalized dimensions of U.S. society itself. This transnational turn expressed itself simultaneously in Howells's fiction and criticism, both of which worked to position realism and, more specifically, the techniques of local color as the most adequate means of representing the United States in its new position at the center of the world economy. As Howells put it in a review of the local-color writer Mary E. Wilkins Freeman's collection *A Humble Romance and Other Stories* (1887), "A new method was necessary in dealing with the new conditions, and the new method is world-wide, because the whole world is more or less Americanized."[7] These efforts on Howells's part also aligned him with other American writers at the turn of the twentieth century who wrote from the assumption that, just as the United States was playing an increasingly powerful role in world affairs politically and economically, U.S. literary production could play an increasingly important role in world literature. As the previous chapter indicated, this thinking is evident in the attempts of Brander Matthews and Henry Dwight Sedgwick to revise Goethe's concept of *Weltliteratur* to accommodate expressions of national identity and pride, and it is evident, albeit sometimes more ambivalently, in the writings of the authors I examine in subsequent chapters, including Henry James, Abraham Cahan, and Lafcadio Hearn.

The "new method" to which Howells referred in his 1887 review of Mary E. Wilkins Freeman, I contend, formed a crucial aesthetic strategy of late American realism: positioning local color, especially the use of dialect, as a transnational literary practice that could produce a more comprehensive understanding of world literature by valorizing a set of techniques that were particularly suited for depicting cultural difference. As a result, late American realism diverges from earlier genres that literary historians have also labeled "transnational," such as the sentimental novel, in two critical ways: its practitioners cultivated techniques for representing the interpenetration of cultures that, as I suggested in the introduction, was serving to globalize the United States, and its advocates actively promoted a wider range of foreign authors as a means of giving American readers a fuller picture of the world itself.[8] This chapter explores how these two practices shaped the later fiction and criticism of William Dean Howells, including such major works published after 1885 as *A Hazard of New Fortunes* (1890) and *Criticism and Fiction* (1891).

As one of the most important practitioners of realism and almost certainly the most influential critic and gatekeeper of his generation, Howells sought to develop, articulate, and carry out a transnational aesthetic theory of realism that relied heavily on what he perceived as local color's widespread applicability. In his later fiction, local color serves to highlight the global processes that were already transforming the United States in profound ways, and in his later criticism, local color becomes a crucial factor in the inherently globalizing aim of American literary realism, which Howells himself described as "the impulse to get the whole of American life into our fiction."[9] Since Howells had already declared the "whole world" to be "more or less Americanized," the impulse to "get the whole of American life" into American literature was necessarily a global project. It is for this reason that the comparative approach of his two-part essay on dialect matters. From the late 1880s onwards, Howells consistently promoted foreign authors, including two I examine in more detail below: the Spaniard Armando Palacio Valdés and the Filipino José Rizal. Doing so enabled Howells to present American literary realism as a model that aspiring foreign writers could follow if they wished to gain greater access to world literature. Somewhat surprisingly, however, Howells made this point not so much by promoting American writers abroad, but rather by engaging the realism that foreign authors were themselves producing. Moreover, the foreign authors Howells engaged in order to position American literature within a truly global context sometimes inhabited spaces far outside the major European centers of London and Paris, including even the colonial spaces that the United States was entering at the end of the nineteenth century.

The paradoxical nature of local color, which involved the use of a standardized set of literary conventions (dialect, episodic narrative structure, and so forth) in order to depict region- and ethnic-specific cultural practices, has occupied numerous critics over the years and deserves brief consideration for how it plays out in Howells's transnational aesthetic. Warner Berthoff noted decades ago that "the same stories are told, in more or less detail, on all sides. Indeed it is in the nature of American life, heterogeneous and disorderly and yet oppressively uniform, that any sector of it, honestly examined, is likely to reveal a logic of occurrence (or nonoccurrence) that holds true for the whole national experience."[10] Whereas Berthoff and other earlier critics tended to regard this standardization as evidence of local colorists' secondary status within the canon of American literary realism, recent critics have viewed it as an effective aesthetic strategy. Richard Brodhead has argued that local color's "heavily conventionalized formulas" served as an enabling constraint, which worked to give first-time writers, including women, African Americans, and working-class people, "literary access in America."[11] If these aspiring writers agreed to fulfill the stylistic and generic expectations of local color, then their work was more likely to appear in the national magazines of the day, thereby giving them relatively easy access to the publishing industry. As Amy Kaplan has pointed out, however, "this profusion of literature known as regionalism or local color [also] contributed to the process of centralization or nationalization" by reassuring readers that underlying similarities bound the nation's various regions together into a single unit.[12] Thus the paradoxes of local color operated simultaneously at the level of individual texts, which used established conventions to represent regional or ethnic differences, and at the level of the U.S. publishing industry, which used these texts to produce a more homogenous mass culture.

On one hand, this chapter extends to a global level the logic of incorporation that Brodhead and Kaplan have ascribed to local color. Howells's later fiction, including *A Hazard of New Fortunes*, enacts a shift toward engaging—and sometimes attempting to resolve the problems of—such global processes as immigration and the circulation of radical art and politics, which were altering the social fabric of the United States. Likewise, his later criticism, including *Criticism and Fiction*, implicitly casts Howells himself not only as an arbiter of American literary taste, but as a gatekeeper of world literature. Howells's assumption that the techniques of local color that American authors practiced could be adopted by writers in other countries as a means of accessing the American and, by extension, the world market is entirely consistent with the picture of the U.S. literary industry that Brodhead paints. Howells's further assumption that American local color provided a model that foreign authors could employ to represent their own cultures provides an aesthetic counterpart to Woodrow Wilson's political vision of the United States as the mediating nation.

On the other hand, my approach to local color also reflects the dynamic, multidirectional understanding of transnational literary production recently advocated by Tom Lutz and Brad Evans, whose scholarship has paid significant attention to the wider patterns of local color's circulation and consumption and has sought to move beyond what Lutz calls "the central debate over . . . regionalism's hegemonic or counterhegemonic force."[13] For Lutz, the transnational aspects of local color operate primarily at the level of the text itself, where constellations of allusions and multilayered points of view help "the implied readers and the implied author . . . meet in a cosmopolitan compact of literary vision," while for Evans, "the confluence of the local and the cosmopolitan . . . had less to do with a sense of place than with a dynamic of circulation," particularly local color's circulation and commodification within the international aesthetic arts movement.[14] This chapter pursues the implications of their arguments, not only placing the production and circulation of local color as much outside U.S. borders as inside, but also highlighting the ways Howells used local color in both his fiction and criticism as a means of critiquing the very same logic of incorporation that Brodhead and Kaplan have attributed to local color. Howells's opposition to U.S. overseas expansion and his tendency to use his reviews of foreign writers as a platform for criticizing the racist rhetoric undergirding the U.S. government's willingness to go to war with Spain and to occupy the Philippines reinforce Carrie Tirado Bramen's description of local color as "a locus for a variety of ideological positions."[15] Like Lutz, Bramen praises local colorists for introducing polyvocality into their fiction, and she ties their representation of multiple voices and points of view to the pluralism advocated by William James and the other Pragmatist philosophers. What Bramen calls William James's "theory of narrative . . . based on a notion of partial stories" finds full expression in his brother Henry's famous metaphor about "the house of fiction" in the 1908 preface to *The Portrait of a Lady* (1881), which equates the "number of possible windows not to be reckoned" with the limitless—and limitlessly interesting—number of perspectives that can be brought to bear on a story, as well as in Howells's tendency to praise marginalized writers, such as the black poet Paul Laurence Dunbar, simply for exposing readers to a new point of view.[16]

The passage to which Bramen refers is also explicitly global in scope. In *Pragmatism* (1907), William James indicates that the entire world can serve as a writer's or a critic's object of analysis, if that writer or critic employs a pluralist methodology:

> The point of view of a many is the more natural one to take. The world is full of partial stories that run parallel to one another, beginning and ending at odd times. They mutually interlace and interfere at points, but we can not unify them completely in our minds. . . . It follows that whoever says that the whole world tells one story utters another of those monistic dogmas that a man believes at his risk. It is easy to see the world's history pluralistically, as a rope of which each fibre tells a separate tale; but to conceive of each cross-section of the rope as an absolutely single fact, and to sum the whole longitudinal series into one being living an undivided life, is harder.[17]

Ultimately, then, James's "theory of narrative" is about world literature, which itself emerges as a composite entity through the interweaving of "many" different voices and points of view. It is precisely this interweaving that I suggest Howells had in mind when he called for a "new method" that was "world-wide" in his 1887 review of Mary E. Wilkins Freeman's local color. In fact, Howells's follow-up suggestion in that essay that such a method would need to be "vertical instead of lateral" if it aimed at producing "a microcosm" shares the same geometric orientation as William James's rope metaphor, with its "longitudinal series" of fibers.[18] In the next section of this chapter, I examine how this "new method" plays out in Howells's own use of local color in *A Hazard of New Fortunes* and how it serves to represent the newly global dimensions of American life. Then, I will return to the understanding of world literature—and American literature's place in it—that Howells develops in his later criticism, including *Criticism and Fiction*.

DIALECT, METONYMY, AND THE LITERARY REPRESENTATION OF GLOBAL INTERPENETRATION

A Hazard of New Fortunes is a novel that exhibits a hyperawareness of dialect and, at times, even a meta-awareness of its own characters' use of dialect. Although only a handful of the novel's characters speak with the kind of pronounced dialect that is typical of local-color fiction—most notably Lindau and Miss Woodburn, though also to a lesser extent Colonel Woodburn and Mrs. Dryfoos—most of the other characters comment extensively upon those accents and sometimes even imitate them. After agreeing to board the Woodburns, who have moved to New York from Virginia, Alma Leighton remarks, "She talked as if they were poor; poo' she called it," to which her mother replies, "Yes, how queerly she pronounced."[19] Later, Angus Beaton tells Miss Woodburn directly, "I should like to hear you say *Soath* and *hoase* and *aboat* for the rest of my life" (209). At one point, Fulkerson playfully imitates Mrs. Dryfoos, the rustic wife of his financial backer, in front of the Dryfoos family: "'Well, Mely, child,' Fulkerson went on, with an open travesty of her mother's habitual address, 'and how are *you* getting along?'" (143, original emphasis) Perhaps unsurprisingly, however, it is the German accent of Lindau, the most controversial character in the book, that attracts the most attention. Basil March, who as a boy had studied German with Lindau, tells his wife that "he says himself that his parg is worse than his pidte, you know" and describes Lindau's political views as "what Lindau calls his 'brincibles'" (263–64). Fulkerson follows March's lead in referring to Lindau's "brinciples" and, just as he did with Mrs. Dryfoos, imitates Lindau's accent in Lindau's presence: "'Look out, Lindau,' said Fulkerson. 'You bite yourself mit dat dog some day'" (287, 286). Not unlike a local colorist, Fulkerson even attempts to replicate Lindau's words in Lindau's own dialect when he explains to March how he made up with Lindau after an argument: "He said I was his chenerous yong friendt, and he begged my barton if he had said anything to wound me" (287).

If Fulkerson's and Mela Dryfoos's own use of slang and Beaton's affectation of a "French manner" of talking are taken into account (111), then virtually every major character in the novel either speaks idiomatically or comments upon such idiomatic speech. "In season[s] of strong excitement," we learn that "Fulkerson lapse[s] more and more into the parlance of his early life," employing such colorful expressions as "I'll be dogged if I could!" (161). Likewise, although Howells never really attempts to represent Beaton's affectation in the dialogue itself, Miss Woodburn nonetheless describes him to Alma Leighton as someone who "talks English like it was something else" (114). It is also partly Mela's inappropriate and overly familiar use of slang, which the young writer Kendricks thinks of as "all her slang and brag" (241), that frustrates the Dryfooses' attempts to gain acceptance into polite society. One of the novel's major plot points even hinges upon Dryfoos's own ethnic background: he is "Pennsylvany Dutch" and therefore able to understand Lindau when Lindau speaks German (404).

The convergence of so many different dialects in the novel—Southern, Pennsylvania Dutch, first-generation German immigrant, Western slang, not to mention the dialect of such fleeting minor characters as a black janitor and the Italian American restaurateur Frescobaldi—reflects the centralization that, by the late 1880s, was already transforming New York into the economic, cultural, and media capital of the United States. Fulkerson lures March to the city because their ambitions for the magazine they plan to launch are national in scope and New York is the "one city that belongs to the whole country" (6). The Woodburns and Dryfooses relocate there for similarly pragmatic reasons: Colonel Woodburn hopes to find a publisher for his book on slavery, and Dryfoos can accumulate even more wealth if he lives near Wall Street. As Howells himself observed in the "Bibliographical" note he appended to the novel in 1909, *Hazard* channeled his own mixed feelings about moving from Boston to New York after being lured there by *Harper's*. He calls the novel the "first fruit" of his "transition to the commercial metropolis."[20] Howells's apparent receptivity to the "incredible diversity" of New York, despite whatever misgivings he may have felt about his move, has led some critics, including both Jay Martin and Tony Tanner, to assume that Howells harbored the same aspirations for his novel that Fulkerson and March express for their magazine and that the intermingling of so many different accents, ethnicities, and regional backgrounds in the novel gives it a national scope.[21]

There is a danger in associating Howells's aims too closely with March's because *Hazard* sometimes employs local color in a way that subverts what Tanner and Martin perceive to be the novel's attempt at achieving national scope. In what is perhaps the most self-referential passage of the novel, Kendricks actually frames his interaction with Mela as an opportunity to expropriate her speech and transform it into local color in the novel he is planning to write. During the conversation with Mela in which he mentally takes note of her "slang and brag," Kendricks wonders "if it would do to put her into literature just as she was" and fancies "that if he could get that in skilfully, it would be a valuable colour" (241–42). The contrast between Mela's physical beauty and wealth, on one hand, and her unsophisticated behavior, on the other, lead Kendricks to conclude that "the great American novel, if true, must be incredible" (241). Kendricks's dilettantish interest in local color—it becomes increasingly clear in *Hazard* that he lacks the discipline to complete the novel he envisions writing—serves as a subtle critique of the popular notion of the time that a single novel could stand in for the nation as a whole.

In this respect, Howells's point is not radically different from that of John William De Forest, who introduced the idea in his 1868 essay "The Great American Novel." De Forest claimed that, because the United States was "a nation of provinces," no "single tale . . . paints American life so broadly, truly, and sympathetically that every American of feeling and culture is forced to acknowledge the picture as a likeness of something which he knows."[22] Yet even more than a decade after Howells published *Hazard*, Frank Norris and other writers continued to invoke the idea. In "The Great American Novelist" (1903), a title that invites comparison to De Forest's essay, Norris argued that "the possibility of *A*—note the indefinite article—*A* Great American Novel is not too remote for discussion. But such a novel will be sectional. The United States is a Union, but not a unit, and the life in one part is very, very different from the life in another. It is as yet impossible to construct a novel which will represent all the various characteristics of the different sections. It is only possible to make a picture of a single locality" (original emphasis).[23] In a novel that, in its attention to variegated characters converging in New York, seems to attempt what Norris describes, Kendricks's dilettantism subverts even the notion that the collective use of local color by multiple authors is adequate to produce a composite picture of the nation.[24]

Instead of working synecdochically to stand in for the various regions and ethnicities of the nation, as several critics contend local color does, the multiple dialects that appear in *Hazard* function metonymically to depict a nation caught up in the even broader processes of globalization.[25] When March and Fulkerson talk about Lindau's "brinciples," they are referring simultaneously to the principles themselves and to their foreign inflection, just as the lady who "always thought of [Beaton] as having spoken French" is indicating how successfully Beaton conveys the "effect" of having cultivated a European manner while studying art in Paris (91). In other words,

cnt

the different dialects that Howells deploys in the novel stand in for—and serve to remind both the characters and the readers of—the wider circulation of people, ideas, and cultural objects and practices that was transforming New York not just into the economic, cultural, and media capital of the United States, but into the epicenter of the world economy as well as into a global city where March and other characters can take pleasure in its seemingly limitless cosmopolitan offerings. Although Brad Evans focuses on the transnational tropes that March, Beaton, and Fulkerson consciously exploit when launching their magazine rather than on the novel's intermingling of dialects and voices, it is precisely this attention to the dynamics of local color's circulation that contributes to what he calls Howells's "*dislocation* of . . . the region" in his fiction and criticism (original emphasis).[26]

Thus the point of the "frantic panorama" that March views during his frequent rides on "the Elevated"—a passage that has attracted considerable critical attention over the years and has even inspired the title of one major study of the period's literature—is that it focuses the reader's attention as much on what the immigrant laborers are producing as on the pleasure March derives from consuming their picturesqueness: "The most picturesque admixture . . . were the brilliant eyes and complexions of the American Hebrews, who otherwise contributed to the effect of well-clad comfort and citizen-self-satisfaction of the crowd[, and the] Neapolitans from the constructions far up the line, where he had read how they are worked and fed and housed like beasts" (163, 161–62).[27] The contributions of Neapolitan manual labor and Jewish tailoring to New York's wealth and power prompt "public-spirited reveries in which [March] dealt with the future economy of our heterogeneous commonwealth" (162). These immigrants, March acknowledges, are making America, and it necessarily follows that they are remaking Americans, including the Marches themselves.[28] Following such experiences as a meal at a restaurant with "a French lady" owner, "a Cuban negro" cook, "a cross-eyed Alsatian" waiter, and "a slim young South American" cashier, the Marches feel "almost [a] loss of individuality" (265–66). Yet these sorts of experiences remain "the chief pleasure of their life" because the Marches have accepted the value of living in a "heterogeneous" economy (264).

Howells's effort to find a means of representing these interpenetrating global processes in his fiction—the "new method" that he called for in his 1887 "Editor's Study"—is what distinguishes *Hazard* as an example of late American realism. Nothing like it appears, for instance, in *The Rise of Silas Lapham* (1885). To be sure, a growing sense of the United States' place in the larger global economy frames the earlier novel, which begins with Lapham boasting that "we ship [our paint] to all parts of the world. It goes to South America, lots of it. It goes to Australia, and it goes to India, and it goes to China, and it goes to the Cape of Good Hope. It'll stand any climate," and ends with the newly married Tom and Penelope "pushing [the paint] in Mexico and Central America."[29] That novel's understanding of U.S. industrial growth is unidirectional, though. Tom's role in Mexico and South America involves "watching the new railroad enterprises and the development of mechanical agriculture and whatever other undertakings offered an opening for the introduction of the paint."[30] Lapham's paint merely follows the routes of U.S. economic expansion, and there is never any indication that Boston is receiving anything in exchange. Even references to Boston's immigrant population, which was already substantial by 1875, the year *Silas Lapham* is set, are rare: some "loafing Irish boys" appear in chapter 3, and during the dinner party in chapter 14, Charles Bellingham patronizingly mentions the "indigent Italians."[31] The influence these immigrants might have on the lives of Bellingham, the Coreys, or the Laphams is never made clear, and the global reach of his paint has no obvious effect one way or the other upon Lapham's moral and financial crises.

By contrast, *Hazard* takes pains to establish the transformative influence of the immigrants living in New York. Hence the "statue of Garibaldi," which had "already taken possession of" Washington Square in "the name of Latin progress," overlooks the "picturesque raggedness of southern Europe, . . . which has invaded the southern border [of the square], and broken it up into lodging-houses, shops, beer gardens, and studios" (44). Even the "Chinese dwellers in Mott Street" take part in this transformation of the city, rendering "not them, but what was foreign to them [including March himself], strange there" (165). The key difference between *The Rise of Silas Lapham* and *A Hazard of New Fortunes*, then, is their respective uses of local color. *Silas Lapham* remains a novel about a relatively insular part of Boston and therefore displays little interest in the multiple intermingling forms of local color that *Hazard* deploys. Gavin Jones makes a similar point about *Hazard*, though he does not pursue the novel's global implications, when he cites it along with Stephen Crane's *Maggie* and Abraham Cahan's *Yekl* (1896) as novels that mark a significant shift from the "provincial, rustic spaces" of local-color fiction of the 1880s to the "increasingly urban and shockingly contemporary" use of dialect during the 1890s.[32]

More unsettling than the physical presence of these immigrants is the potential influence of their ideas, such as Lindau's radical politics, and here, too, *Hazard* addresses the potential influence of these ideas metonymically through the words that carry them. To be more precise, the novel examines how dialects intermingle so subtly and yet so pervasively that the intermingling itself produces involuntarily changes in the way characters speak and think. Just as southern Europeans have "invaded" Washington Square, one character's slang or dialect can invade another character's voice. This interpenetration of voices goes beyond the playful and self-conscious mimicry that Fulkerson, March, and Beaton perform. It begins early in the novel, when March discusses the possibility of moving to New York with his wife and finds that Fulkerson's slangy conception of the magazine is already beginning to affect his way of referring to—and thinking about—the project: "If I had my heart set on this thing—Fulkerson always calls it 'this thing'—I would cheerfully accept any sacrifice you could make to it" (21). Four paragraphs later, the invasion of Fulkerson's slang into his own speech begins to trouble March: "If I do this thing—Fulkerson again! I can't get away from 'this thing'; it's ominous—I must do it because I want to do it" (21). March's protestations notwithstanding, he ultimately accepts Fulkerson's influence upon his speech and thoughts, just as he accepts the job and many of the ideas for the magazine Fulkerson offers. Near the end of the novel, while discussing Alma Leighton's rejection of Beaton's romantic overtures, March muses to his wife, "But let's examine this thing. (This thing! I believe Fulkerson is characterising my whole parlance)" (434). March's after-the-fact awareness of what is happening to his vocabulary does not make it any less involuntarily, though it does enable him to recognize when it happens to other characters. When offering March the opportunity to buy the magazine, Dryfoos also adopts Fulkerson's term for it: "'I've been thinkin' whether you wouldn't like to take the thing.' The word, which Dryfoos had now used three times, made March at last think of Fulkerson" (435–36).

Perhaps the most remarkable example of this linguistic invasion occurs in a passage just before Dryfoos's dinner party, when Howells employs free indirect discourse in order to allow Lindau's dialect to invade the narrator's voice. After Fulkerson makes up with Lindau following one of their arguments over Fulkerson's complicity in the capitalist system Lindau despises, Fulkerson spends "the rest of the summer in keeping Lindau smoothed up" (288). Then the narrator assumes Fulkerson's point of view as Fulkerson imagines what Lindau's feelings are: "It is doubtful if Lindau altogether liked this as well. Perhaps he missed the occasions Fulkerson used to give him of bursting out against the millionaires; and he could not well go on denouncing as the slafe of gabidal a man who had behaved to him as Fulkerson had done, though Fulkerson's servile relations to capital had been in nowise changed by his nople gonduct" (288). Since Fulkerson has already imitated Lindau's accent several times by this point in the novel, it is likely that the misspelled words ("slafe," "gabidal," "nople," and "gonduct") represent Fulkerson's attempt to give voice to what he imagines Lindau's point of view to be rather than the narrator's attempt to explain Lindau's own feelings. Howells's decision to convey Fulkerson's attitude toward Lindau through free indirect rather than direct discourse, however, creates ambiguity. It is almost as if the narrator is just as susceptible as March or Dryfoos to the influence of other voices. Several critics have recently reaffirmed the importance of free indirect discourse to American literary realism because of its ability to produce just this sort of ambiguity, and Phillip Barrish emphasizes the power this technique gives a "character's moment-by-moment thoughts temporarily [to] assume partial control of the narrator's voice."[33] In this instance, the added dimension of Lindau's foreign accent produces even more tension, particularly in view of the later implication that the violence that erupts during the streetcar strike can be attributed at least partly to Lindau's ideas. Lindau's presence at the strike only underscores his revolutionary fervor, which is already made obvious to the reader through the dialogue.

Thus it is not so much the *presence* of so many different dialects in *Hazard* that matters as it is their *intermingling*, and this intermingling of dialects matters because it draws attention to the potential intermingling of the ideas that the people who speak with these dialects bring to New York. Some of these ideas are explicitly disavowed by the characters themselves. Since Alma Leighton rejects Beaton partly because she wishes to retain her artistic independence, this rejection is in some ways a rejection of Beaton's Europeanized aesthetic sensibility. Similarly, when imitating Lindau, Fulkerson is careful to distance himself from the words he burlesques: "*I* don't believe in his brincibles" (287, original emphasis). The very act of imitation serves to burlesque both the words and the ideas those words convey. Nevertheless, these disavowals are undercut by the inability of either Fulkerson or March to escape the influence of the ideas they disavow. In the same lengthy monologue in which he tells March that he would "like to see these [Socialists] shut up in jail and left to jaw each other to death," Fulkerson praises the Midwestern city of Moffitt for practicing its own form of socialism: the city has taken "possession of every [gas] well that was put down, and [holds] it for the common good" (71). Later, Fulkerson commends March's selection and arrangement of stories and articles in their magazine—"all of them palpitant, all of 'em on the keen jump with actuality"—and March is amused by "the mixture of American slang with the jargon of European criticism in Fulkerson's talk" (179). For his part, March is caught off guard when his son Tom begins complaining about the unfair advantages rich citizens enjoy. When asked by his father where Tom has gotten such ideas, Tom admits, "It's what Mr. Lindau says" (269), but as Russ Castronovo points out, Tom has effectively translated Lindau's ideas (and words) into "the native idiom of Americanism."[34]

Whereas Castronovo reads this and similar passages in *Hazard* as "ambivalent" because they are presented from the point of view of March, whose "struggle" to reconcile the "art and beauty" of New York with "the grotesqueness of urban squalor" structures much of the novel, I suggest that the passage in which Fulkerson's imagining of Lindau's dialect is rendered through free indirect discourse invites a more optimistic reading of the forms of global interpenetration *Hazard* explores.[35] What is even more remarkable about that passage than the intermingling of three different voices (Lindau's, Fulkerson's, and the narrator's) is the fact that Fulkerson, who is good-natured but fairly superficial, is capable of occupying Lindau's point of view, imagining Lindau's feelings, and attempting to express those feelings in Lindau's voice. As noted earlier, one of the reasons Howells valued the use of dialect in literature, such as the dialect poetry of Paul Laurence Dunbar, was that it granted readers access to another point of view. In *Hazard*, Fulkerson's imitation of Lindau's dialect achieves a similar end, enabling him to imagine what Lindau's point of view might be. However much he mimics other characters, Fulkerson rarely comes across as nasty or judgmental, and he ends up marrying Miss Woodburn, the only character whose dialogue rivals Lindau's in its nonstandard spelling and punctuation. In fact, the only instance of one character in the novel drawing attention to another's nonstandard English in order to correct it occurs when Mrs. Mandel tells Mela to say "allowable" instead of "rulable" (though she does not correct Mela's use of the word "ain't" in the same sentence) (237). Mrs. Mandel has been hired by the status-conscience Dryfoos in order to improve his daughters' social and linguistic behavior. Otherwise, dialect is usually treated respectfully as an expression, however eccentric, of its speaker's personality and point of view.

In addition to standing in metonymically for the variety of people and ideas circulating in New York, therefore, *Hazard*'s intermingling dialects also offer its characters the opportunity to occupy each other's points of view. Indeed, the failures of the various characters in the novel generally result from their inability to see things from another's perspective. When Dryfoos, not knowing that Lindau has already died, futilely attempts to make amends, "March could have laughed to think how far this old man was from even conceiving of Lindau's point of view" (405). In terms of the novel's pattern of intermingling dialects, Dryfoos's failure occurs because he is unwilling—or unable—to engage Lindau in conversation when he has the chance. He may overhear Lindau's German, but he makes no effort to speak it or to let Lindau know that he understands it. Moreover, if occupying another's point of view is the ethical imperative that the novel implies, then March's inability to do so with consistency undercuts his reliability as a mouthpiece for the author. March misreads Conrad's motives during the strike and misrepresents them after Conrad's death. "Perhaps he was of use in dying," he tells Miss Vance. "Who knows? He may have been trying to silence Lindau" (392). The reader, however, knows that March is wrong because the narrator indicated that Conrad's final efforts were on Lindau's behalf: "He was going to say to the policeman, 'Don't strike him! He's an old soldier! You see he has no hand!'" (384) Elsewhere in the novel, March deliberately avoids occupying others' points of view, employing ironic detachment to help him achieve "his character of philosophical observer" (374). His ability to recognize Dryfoos's failure of imagination does not prevent March from experiencing similar failures of his own.

Where March's imagination does not fail him—and where his views align more nearly with those of Howells—is in his ability to conceive of a solution to the social problems that hover around him in New York, and the solution that March conceives and the means for achieving it also align both March and the novel with the emerging Progressive movement. Essentially, what March envisions is a planned economy that, not unlike the one proposed by Edward Bellamy in *Looking Backward* (1888), would resolve "this economic chance-world in which we live" (396). "If we felt sure that honest work shared by all would bring them honest food shared by all," March tells his wife, "some heroic few of us, who did not wish our children to rise above their fellows—though we could not bear to have them fall below—might trust them with the truth. But we have no such assurance" (397). The "assurance" that March seeks is something that only the state can provide, as March realizes when he considers how much more efficient the state is than private enterprise in managing and protecting immigrants. While visiting Castle Garden, which preceded Ellis Island as New York's immigrant processing facility, March is forced to acknowledge that "people owned more things in common than they were apt to think" because "the government seemed to manage [the immigrants'] welcome as well as a private company or corporation could have done" (272).

In contrast to the uncertain economic future awaiting these immigrants, the state's efficiency moves March to imagine giving the government power to intervene in other aspects of the immigrants' lives and, by extension, his own life: "In fact, it was after the simple strangers left the government care that March feared their woes might begin; and he would have liked the government to follow each of them to his home, wherever he meant to fix it within our borders. He made note of the looks of the licensed runners and touters waiting for the immigrants outside the government premises" (272–73). The implication here is that, since the state has proven itself reliable in managing the massive influx of immigrants from around the world, it should be empowered to regulate the economic conditions that cause so much uncertainty not only in the lives of immigrants, but also in the lives of March and, if nothing is done, his children. Otherwise, as Colonel Woodburn asserts, the nation's future will rest "in the hands of monopolies" (303). March's logic anticipates the arguments regarding finance capitalism and immigration made by such later Progressives as Louis D. Brandeis and Randolph Bourne, which the next two chapters explore more fully.

That March begins to formulate this solution only after witnessing what he takes to be the state's fair and efficient treatment of immigrants suggests that migration and other global processes enabled Americans to envision such solutions, and the novel hints at the role immigrants themselves played in contributing to Progressive discourse. After all, the clearest articulation of the solution that March stumbles toward comes from Lindau. During Dryfoos's dinner party, Lindau rejects Colonel Woodburn's suggestion that noblesse oblige will prompt the wealthy to protect the poor: "The *State* shall do that—the whole beople. . . . The State will see that he haf voark, and that he haf foodt. All the roadts and mills and mines and landts shall be the beople's and be ron *by* the beople *for* the beople" (309–10, original emphasis). Lindau's allusion to Lincoln's Gettysburg Address is almost certainly deliberate and reminds readers that, unlike Dryfoos and the other men there, Lindau actually fought for the Union during the Civil War.

Despite disagreeing with Lindau's cynicism, March picks up on and reinforces these subtle assertions of Lindau's authority, declaring to Fulkerson that Lindau is "as good an American as any of us" (287). Even in his final conversation about Lindau's ideas with his son, March makes it clear that what he objects to are the violent *means* Lindau advocates, not the ends. Lindau "died in the cause of disorder," he says to Tom; "he was trying to obstruct the law. No doubt there was a wrong there, an inconsistency and an injustice that he felt keenly; but it could not be reached in his way without greater wrong" (409). Tom's conclusion that "we could vote anything we wanted" meets with his father's quick approval and neatly encapsulates the Progressive faith in democratic processes as the most appropriate means of effecting the kinds of social change that both Lindau and March desire (409). In allowing Tom, who stands in for the reader in this passage, to reach this conclusion, *Hazard* exemplifies the work that literature, as an ideological state apparatus, can perform. The novel effectively becomes a Progressive document.

Notwithstanding March's final judgment that Lindau had "renounce[d] the American means" (409), uncertainty over just how "foreign" Lindau and his ideas really are remains embedded in the novel, and this uncertainty finds its most profound expression in the novel's handling of Lindau's dialect when March visits Lindau's rooms for the first time. For a span of ten paragraphs, Lindau's accent disappears from the dialogue as his German is translated into English during a bilingual conversation with March. (This translation of Lindau's German occurs again, though to a lesser extent, during Dryfoos's dinner party, when Lindau complains about Dryfoos's business ethics to March, not knowing that Dryfoos understands German.) During this conversation, Lindau engages March in a series of questions, not unlike the Socratic method Dr. Leete employs with the narrator of Bellamy's *Looking Backward*. Unlike Dr. Leete, however, Lindau is unable to get March to admit that capitalism is an unfair economic system, though it is possible that the seed for March's later conclusions regarding the intervention of the state is planted here. More importantly, translating Lindau's German into Standard English allows readers to encounter Lindau's ideas without the inflection of his accent. In a sense, just as Tom later translates Lindau's ideas into a "native idiom," as Castronovo puts it, Howells does so on the reader's behalf during this earlier conversation.

The possibility that Lindau's ideas might not be so foreign after all or that U.S. social progress is already embedded in larger global processes is something that March himself acknowledges. When he explains Lindau's background to Fulkerson, he highlights a link that Lindau physically embodies between the U.S. abolitionist movement and the European revolutions of 1848: "Lindau was fighting the anti-slavery battle just as naturally at Indianapolis in 1858 as he fought behind the barricades at Berlin in 1848" (80). Metonymically, this link or, more accurately, the blurry distinction between safe "American" ideas and radical "foreign" ones is represented by the cognates Lindau uses when March visits his rooms: "March obeyed the German-English 'Komm!' that followed his knock. . . . On the right, through a door that stood ajar, came the German-English voice again, saying this time, 'Hier!'" (166). The reference to Lindau's "German-English voice" reinforces his status as a foreign immigrant, but the words that Lindau uses are themselves hybrids—"German-English" in the sense that they are cognates and thus intelligible even to English-speaking listeners who do not understand German. The possibility therefore exists that Lindau's radicalism is not just intelligible but related to American ideas about social progress. Just as *komm* and "come" and *hier* and "here" are cognates, Lindau's abolitionism in the United States might very well have been a logical extension of his revolutionary activities in Berlin. How un-American, then, is his socialism?

Howells's *A Hazard of New Fortunes* provides only one example of late American realism's attempt to transform into aesthetic terms the emerging global conditions of the United States at the turn of the twentieth century. A brief reading of Sarah Orne Jewett's short story "The Foreigner" (1900) confirms that other late American realists picked up on and extended Howells's use of the techniques of local color to represent what he called the newly "world-wide" aspects of American life. In recent years, of course, Jewett's *The Country of the Pointed Firs* (1896) has received considerable critical attention because of how it illustrates what Hsuan Hsu calls "the geographical and economic relations . . . between region and globe" and what Stephanie Foote calls the "traces of the foreign [that] underwrite and constitute local color."[36] Jewett's skill at rendering the plight of Dunnet Landing, formerly the beneficiary of one mode of global commerce (sailing ships) but now the victim of another (steam transport), is both moving and evocative.

In "The Foreigner," one of a handful of follow-up stories to *Pointed Firs*, Jewett makes the need for acknowledging the influence of the global on the local her explicit subject. In this story, Mrs. Todd recounts to the unnamed framing narrator her friendship with the late Mrs. Tolland, a "French born" woman whom one of the sea captains of Dunnet Landing married in Jamaica and brought back home.[37] Mrs. Tolland's status as a "foreigner"—"she come a foreigner and she went a foreigner, and never was anything but a stranger among our folks," Mrs. Todd avers—gives the story its title and emphasizes her inability to achieve full acceptance into the community.[38] As the story unfolds, however, it becomes increasingly clear that Mrs. Tolland has, in fact, left a lasting mark upon the community through her relationship with Mrs. Todd. Mrs. Tolland, who like Mrs. Todd loses her husband to the sea, bequeaths her property to Mrs. Todd, which gives Mrs. Todd the financial independence she enjoys, and passes on to Mrs. Todd the knowledge about herbs that, as we learn in *Pointed Firs*, gives her equal standing with the village doctor. "She taught me a sight o' things about herbs I never knew before nor since. . . . Yes, 't was she that learned me the proper use o' parsley too; she was a beautiful cook," Mrs. Todd explains, answering the narrator's unspoken question of "where Mrs. Todd had got such an unusual knowledge of cookery. . . . She could vary her omelettes like a child of France, which was indeed a surprise in Dunnet Landing."[39] Just like the immigrants whose restaurants provide so much pleasure to the Marches in *Hazard*, Mrs. Tolland has enriched Dunnet Landing by making it more gastronomically cosmopolitan.

Also like *Hazard*, "The Foreigner" employs dialect to depict Mrs. Tolland's influence metonymically, though the use of dialect is even more subtle and complex in "The Foreigner" than in *Hazard*. Since Mrs. Tolland's story is told by Mrs. Todd in Mrs. Todd's own dialect, the presence of Mrs. Tolland's voice and dialect is almost—but not quite—invisible. Unlike Fulkerson, Mrs. Todd makes no attempt at replicating Mrs. Tolland's accent. The few times she quotes Mrs. Tolland directly, Mrs. Tolland's voice sounds just like Mrs. Todd's: "She told me she had n't been in France since she was 'so small,'" and ""T is my mother.'"[40] On the contrary, Mrs. Todd repeatedly disavows having any knowledge of, memory of, or even interest in Mrs. Tolland's specific use of French. "I never knew her maiden name," she claims; "'t would mean nothing to me," and she goes on to tell the narrator that, when Mrs. Tolland was dying, she "could n't understand what she wanted from her French speech."[41]

Nevertheless, Mrs. Todd undercuts these protestations of ignorance when she describes the day she had to tell Mrs. Tolland about her husband's death. Before learning the news, Mrs. Tolland was happy "an' begun to talk French, gay as a bird, an' shook hands and behaved very pretty an' girlish, sayin' 't was her fête day. I did n't know what she meant then."[42] The presence of the word "fête" in Mrs. Todd's account of that day gives the game away. There is no reason to doubt Mrs. Todd's assertion that she doesn't understand French, even though Mrs. Tolland's use of this word *after* she had "begun to talk French" raises the possibility that Mrs. Todd may know more than she lets on. Since Mrs. Tolland is not Catholic, there is also no reason to doubt her assertion that she did not know what a fête day was when Mrs. Tolland mentioned the word. Still, the fact that she is able to repeat and presumably, since the narrator includes the circumflex alongside Mrs. Todd's nonstandard English, to pronounce the word correctly indicates that someone, probably Mrs. Tolland, has taught her what it means. Mrs. Todd's use of the word "fête" therefore stands in for all the other words and ideas Mrs. Tolland has shared with her. As Mrs. Todd puts it, "she made me imagine new things, and I got interested watchin' her an' findin' out what she had to say."[43] What Mrs. Tolland "had to say" continues to show up in Mrs. Todd's speech. Thus Jewett's deployment of dialect in a story that helps to explain the source of Mrs. Todd's cosmopolitan knowledge demonstrates that Howells was not the only author of the period to put into practice the "new method" that he claimed American authors were equipped to give to the world.

ARMANDO PALACIO VALDÉS AND JOSÉ RIZAL: READING WORLD LITERATURE IN AMERICA

The reason that Lindau is brought into contact with Dryfoos in *Hazard* is because Fulkerson and March commission him to scour various foreign periodicals and translate any pieces that might complement the aesthetic design of their magazine. Thus even at its conceptual stage, Fulkerson and March envision their work in conversation with wider world literature. Their first issue contains a "translation of a bit of vivid Russian realism, . . . [a] fragment of Dostoyevski" that Lindau, the translator, pronounces "good of its kind" (174). Howells is probably making an inside joke here, for he had been largely responsible for introducing Fyodor Dostoyevsky to American readers when he reviewed a French translation of *Crime and Punishment* (1866; published in French as *Le crime et le châtiment*, 1884) in his September 1886 "Editor's Study" for *Harper's*.[44] That same year marked the beginning of Howells's involvement in the Haymarket affair, which resulted in his increased politicization, and his connection with *Harper's*, which eventually led to his relocation from Boston to New York. Critics traditionally identify the latter two events as key moments in the transition into late realism; however, Howells's biographer Edwin H. Cady argues that 1886 also marked the beginning of a significant internationalization in Howells's conception of literature. As a result of taking over *Harper's* "Editor's Study," Howells began reading and reviewing far more foreign authors than he ever had before, which in turn led him to rethink the work of American literary realism within a much broader context. *Hazard*'s playful reference to one of Howells's most important "discoveries" as a critic draws attention to the need for understanding the transnational turn of his fiction in light of the equally transnational turn of his criticism. Just as Lindau's translation of Dostoyevsky invites readers of Fulkerson and March's magazine to consider its place in world literature, *Hazard* directs us to Howells's own criticism, where his conception of world literature—and American literature's place therein—reminds us of the important contributions that realists' nonfictional writings made to the much wider debate about the United States' place in the world at the turn of the twentieth century.

The notion of world literature that I invoke here is the one that David Damrosch proposes in *What Is World Literature?*: "not an infinite, ungraspable canon of works but rather a mode of circulation and reading, a mode that is as applicable to individual works as to bodies of material, available for reading established classics and new discoveries alike."[45] Approaching world literature as a "mode of circulation and reading," Damrosch contends, serves to correct critics' tendency to succumb to the gravitational pull of authors with longstanding international reputations. Whereas both Georg Lukács and Pascale Casanova have appealed to the concept of "totality" in their discussions of world literature—with Lukács invoking "the living totality of the mutual interactions" of "all national cultures, literatures and great writers" and Casanova referring to "the totality of texts and literary and aesthetic debates with which a particular work of literature enters into relation and resonance"—their attention invariably settles on predictable figures and even, in Lukács's case, on a handful of regions.[46] Instead of fetishizing either "authors of international significance," as Lukács does, or "the great literary revolutions," as Casanova does, Damrosch calls for "a phenomenology [rather] than an ontology of the work of art."[47] Establishing such a phenomenology, Damrosch implies, would return students of world literature to the field's roots: as a "network" of relations, whether personal relations among writers, as Goethe originally meant, or "newly global trade relations," as Marx and Engels meant when they adopted the term in the *Manifesto of the Communist Party*.[48]

Damrosch's conception of world literature as a network of relations produced through patterns of circulation and reception complements *The Mediating Nation*'s approach to globalization. More to the point, his approach enables a more productive discussion of the vicissitudes of translation and reception, including what is lost and what is added when a particular work of literature from one nation is read in a different nation and thus in a different context. These vicissitudes will dominate my discussion of two of the authors Howells read and reviewed. After all, the foreign writer with whom Howells formed his most productive and most meaningful relationship was not Dostoyevsky but the largely forgotten Spanish novelist Armando Palacio Valdés. Cady calls Palacio Valdés Howells's "most congenial extra-American ally" and claims that their correspondence and exchange of ideas provided Howells "with a fresh sanction of his doctrine" as he began to reshape many of his "Editor's Study" columns into what became *Criticism and Fiction*.[49] Instead of attempting a wholesale rehabilitation of Palacio Valdés's literary reputation, I focus on his importance to Howells. Similarly, although I give some consideration to the question of authentic translation in my analysis of José Rizal's *Noli me tangere* (1887), Howells's appreciation of Rizal's writing—both aesthetically and politically—was structured by his access to a bowdlerized translation entitled *An Eagle Flight* (1900). Thus what might initially appear as problematic (Palacio Valdés's present obscurity and a corrupt translation of Rizal's masterpiece) is actually significant, or as Damrosch might put it, such problematics are what constitute world literature. The act of reading and reviewing Palacio Valdés and Rizal, I contend, provided Howells with a means of positioning the global spread of local color as a literary development that could complement and, if needed, counterbalance U.S. aesthetic and political ambitions.

Palacio Valdés's present literary obscurity notwithstanding, Cady's claims about the degree of his influence on Howells's thinking during this period are, if anything, too modest. Palacio Valdés serves as the lynchpin for Howells's conception of realism in *Criticism and Fiction*, as I discuss below. Moreover, the sense of having found a kindred spirit who could help him understand the nature and scope of literary realism registers as early as in Howells's first encounter with the Spanish author's fiction. Reading Palacio Valdés's *Marta y María* (1883) in the original Spanish in early 1886 prompted Howells to tell Thomas Sergeant Perry that "no one invented realism; it came. It's perfectly astonishing that it seems to have come everywhere at once."[50] A few months later, in the more public forum of the "Editor's Study," Howells commented on "the simultaneity of the literary movement" in men of such widely separated civilizations and conditions."[51] What Howells found in Palacio Valdés's fiction was proof that realism was a truly international movement. The discovery of an author who shared his literary convictions but who had emerged independently in Spain was crucial to an idea that Howells would develop in his subsequent criticism: that national literatures developed by way of isomorphism. This isomorphic conception of literary development plays out in a series of collaborative efforts by Howells and Palacio Valdés to shape the future development of each other's national literature and to demonstrate the transnational possibilities of literary production.

By "isomorphism," I refer specifically to a process that sociologist John W. Meyer identifies at work in the production of what he calls "world society." According to Meyer, nation-states legitimize themselves by following models of statehood that are already in circulation within the international community, and they police one another by presenting themselves as models for future nation-states to follow: "Nation-state forms, in many specific areas, reflect world models, change along with these models, and change in similar directions despite obvious international diversities in local culture and resources."[52] Notably, Meyer contends that it is culture itself, organized around discursive practices and therefore essentially diffuse, that enables both established and emerging nation-states to conform to standardized but decentralized expectations of what nation-states look like:

> Many features of the contemporary nation-state derive from worldwide models constructed and propagated through global cultural and associational processes. . . . Worldwide models define and legitimate agendas for local action. . . . The institutionalization of world models helps explain many puzzling features of contemporary national societies such as structural isomorphism in the face of enormous differences in resources and traditions, ritualized and rather loosely coupled organizational efforts, and elaborate structuration to serve purposes that are largely of exogenous origins. World models have long been in operation as shapers of states and societies.[53]

Meyer's concept of isomorphism clearly owes much to the historical "modular" process of nation-formation that Benedict Anderson proposes in his seminal *Imagined Communities*, wherein "the nation was becoming [by the 1890s] an international norm, and . . . it was possible to 'model' nation-ness in a much more complex way than hitherto."[54] Just as importantly, however, Meyer also positions his work on globalization as an alternative to the world-systems approach advocated by Immanuel Wallerstein. Meyer rejects the notion of "worldwide systems of economic or political power," which are "essentially a by-product of hegemony with no causal significance in its own right."[55] While Meyer often downplays the structural imbalances of power and the political and economic coercion that produce the "models" he studies, his attentiveness to the isomorphic work of culture helps to explain historical developments that do not conform to the narratives of Wallerstein and other world-systems theorists, such as Japan's unexpected emergence as a Great Power by following late nineteenth-century models to the extent of modernizing its own society and acquiring overseas colonies.[56]

The isomorphic processes that, according to Meyer, give shape and legitimacy to state institutions also help to explain the historical development of certain ideological state apparatuses, such as national literatures. For Howells in particular—though other critics of the era made similar arguments—local color served as what Meyer calls a "world model": a set of literary practices that, because of their widespread use throughout the world, simultaneously gave legitimacy to the American realists who employed them and provided a means of policing other national literatures by pressuring them to emulate the successful American model.[57] At the same time, this logic satisfied Howells's belief that neither the United States nor the world could have a single literary center that dictated literary practice everywhere. In his 1895 essay on dialect, he repeats the conventional wisdom that local-color writing was part of "the wider diffusion" of American literature, which is "intensely decentralized."[58] Howells's choice of words ("diffusion" and "decentralized") reinforces the notion that the conventions of local color are not the result of a top-down directive from a centralized publishing industry, but rather that they emerge organically out of the relationship between disparate authors and their reading publics. The even more diffuse use of dialect globally—appearing almost simultaneously in the writings of Italian playwright Carlo Goldoni, Swiss novelist Albert Bitzius, Scottish poet Robert Burns, and Irish novelist Maria Edgeworth— indicates to Howells that world literature operates along the same lines. "The cultivation of the Scottish dialect in poetry by Burns, and in prose by Scott [does] not account for it in other languages and other lands," Howells notes, concluding that "there is no telling how quickly and intimately the different literatures influence one another."[59] In short, Howells seems to have envisioned local color, a literary practice at which American authors excelled, as a "world model" that worked to strengthen the United States' cultural authority without direct coercion.

For all his claims about decentralization and simultaneity, Howells seems to have overlooked the fact that his own criticism acted as a powerful centralizing force for giving shape to his American readers' conception of world literature. Thus the relationship between Howells and Palacio Valdés reveals a major paradox in Howells's notion of how world literature comes into being. As Cady points out, Howells's authority was such that, "if Howells praised a foreign author like Valdés, he would be translated

not necessary: may flow in your arg*

and published in America."[60] Many of the foreign novels Howells mentioned in his columns, such as those of Palacio Valdés and Dostoyevsky, were translated and printed shortly thereafter by the New York publishing firm Thomas Y. Crowell and Company, which would in turn cite Howells's glowing reviews of these authors in their advertisements.[61] It is therefore perhaps not going too far to say that Howells's criticism defined the extent of world literature for many Americans.

Even Howells's relationship with Palacio Valdés could be regarded as uneven. More than one critic has suggested that Palacio Valdés was not as committed to realism as Howells would have liked to believe and that Palacio Valdés probably massaged some of his writings to make them conform to the expectations of the more established American critic, who could give the younger Spanish author the international publicity he craved.[62] In other words, what Howells viewed as isomorphism, Palacio Valdés may have viewed to some degree as coercion. That Howells was about as generous a representative of literary authority as one could imagine only underscores the fact that his alternative model of transnational literary production remains just that: a historical alternative to the ever-increasing globalization of the literary industry. That alternative model did not survive Howells himself: the most innovative literary criticism produced after Howells's death would appear not in the large national publications Howells worked for but in the so-called little magazines associated with the rise of modernism.

As important as it is to acknowledge this paradox in Howells's criticism, what nonetheless matters more is that, regardless of how uneven it may have been, his relationship with Palacio Valdés produced significant changes in Howells's own conception of the work of literature. Indeed, the criticism that both men wrote as a result of their interaction with one another demonstrates not only the multidirectional nature of literary production at its most basic level—even to the extent of complicating our assumptions about the very nature of authorship—but also the multiple forms of work that literature itself performs. In particular, I contend that, although Howells's assumptions constrained his interpretations of Palacio Valdés's fiction, his encounters with Palacio Valdés simultaneously reshaped Howells's understanding of literary realism and enabled him to cultivate a more politically engaged mode of reading, which culminated in his review of José Rizal's *Noli me tangere*.

Howells's early reviews of Palacio Valdés's novels suggest that his approval of those novels was due in large part to how well they conformed to his preconception of literary realism. In his April 1886 review of *Marta y María*, the first of Palacio Valdés's novels that he reviewed, Howells praises the Spanish author for systematically deromanticizing his characters and thereby challenging the stale stereotypes of Spanish culture circulating in other media: "One of the uses of realism is to make us know people; to make us understand that the Spaniards, for example, are not the remote cloak-and-sword gentry of opera which romance has painted them, abounding in guitars, poniards, billets, *autos-da-fe*, and confessionals, but are as 'like folks' as we are."[63] Unsurprisingly, what renders Palacio Valdés's characters "like folks"—and what earns Howells's greatest admiration—is the author's skillful application of local color to "the atmosphere" and "the whole social life of the quiet town."[64]

Throughout his reviews of Palacio Valdés's works Howells regularly casts him and other Spanish realists as local colorists. In his April 1891 "Editor's Study," he reviews Emilia Pardo Bazán's *Morriña* (1889) alongside Palacio Valdés's *La espuma* (1890; published in English as *Scum*, 1890), and he explicitly compares Pardo Bazán's skill at capturing "the Galician dialect" to "Miss Jewett's art."[65] In a letter to Henry James, he likewise refers to Palacio Valdés as "Asturian (species of Spanish New Englander, as from Brattleboro', Vt.)."[66] Although intended as compliments, these comparisons to American local colorists and U.S. regions serve primarily to render the Spanish authors' fiction more easily consumable for American readers. Howells begins a lengthy January 1888 review of Palacio Valdés's *Maximina* (1887) by assuring his readers that they can "appreciate the graphic fidelity of his [Palacio Valdés's] pictures of life so remote as that of modern Spain" because it is "very like our own life."[67] Instead of encouraging American readers to approach these foreign texts as culturally distinct objects, Howells consistently seeks to orient his readers' encounters with Palacio Valdés's novels within the context of U.S. literary production and consumption.

Howells nonetheless had some justification for viewing Palacio Valdés as a local colorist, and other American critics certainly shared his view of Palacio Valdés's fiction. In his 1900 survey of Palacio Valdés's literary career for *Atlantic Monthly*, Sylvester Baxter describes the setting of *Marta y María* as "a town on the north coast [of Spain], and in its essentials the life of the place seems much the same that one might find in a town on the New England coast, with minor differences of local color."[68] It is possible that Baxter and other critics had merely internalized Howells's opinions of Palacio Valdés's work, but it is just as possible that Palacio Valdés had internalized those opinions himself, thanks to his growing correspondence with Howells. In 1889, when their correspondence was at its height, Palacio Valdés affixed the subtitle "costumbres Andaluzas" (Andalusian customs) to his novel *La hermana San Sulpicio* (1889; *Sister Saint Sulpice*, 1890). This subtitle draws attention to the novel's regional specificity, and throughout the text, Palacio Valdés focuses extensively on the unique customs of Andalusia, often in ways that parallel the work of American local colorists. The novel is narrated by an outsider from Galicia named Sanjurjo, an aspiring poet who assiduously describes the exotic features of the local culture, including the Andalusian dialect, the Moorish architecture, and the seguidilla and other folk dances. In short, the novel reads in many ways like a work of local color.

Instead of examining the extent to which *Sister Saint Sulpice* fulfills the conventions of local color, however, I will focus on the long prologue that precedes the novel, for it is there that a more equal crosspollination of ideas between Howells and Palacio Valdés manifests itself. Palacio Valdés undoubtedly intended this prologue, which takes up 54 of the entire English translation's 395 pages, to be viewed as a major artistic statement, and American critics complied. In his November 1889 review of *Sister Saint Sulpice*, which is really an extended consideration of the aesthetic ideas contained in the prologue rather than a traditional review of the novel as such, Howells advises "every one intending to read, or even to write, a novel" to "acquaint himself with" the prologue.[69] Baxter likewise ranked it among "the most valuable essays upon the art of fiction ever written."[70] In the prologue, Palacio Valdés expresses a belief in both the global and the globalizing aspects of realism: it is "the legitimate art of my epoch, the adequate expression of our century, that which is felt by us who are living at this moment of history," and it enables "the man of this epoch . . . to know everything and enjoy everything."[71] In other words, realism is important to Palacio Valdés because it is practiced everywhere and makes everything consumable. Like the American realists, Palacio Valdés also emphasizes realism's ability to render the particular universal:

> The trifle does not exist absolutely; it is always a relative term. What is a trifle for some is a great fact for others. The death of a child, for example, is an insignificant fact, a trifle to every village, however small—to the parents it is a great fact; perhaps the most important and transcendent in their lives. . . . And if we follow the course of our reasoning we shall reach the conclusion that the planet that we inhabit is a trifle, sad and insignificant enough in the depths of the

infinite spaces. Either nothing that is created has importance, or it is all important. The latter is what I believe. . . . In all that is particular, we may be shown the general; in all that is finite, the infinite. (15)

Perhaps most important of all, Palacio Valdés presents local color as the means for representing the connection between the "particular" and the "general." "Local color," according to Palacio Valdés, supplies "the link that binds the human being everywhere with the land where he was born and with the race to which he belongs" and thus makes concrete the novelist's attempt at "penetrating the world of intellect . . . , knowing its secrets and being able to reveal them in a beautiful manner" (42). Although Palacio Valdés cautions that "external customs and the nature of a country constitute for the novelist only the background for his painting," describing these features through the techniques of local color still "serves to reveal the mysterious link of which we have just spoken" (42–43). That is because the details of environment and their effect on fictional characters give readers better access to a novel's meaning than plot alone can. Anticipating the implications of Henry James's "house of fiction" metaphor, which privileges point of view ("window") over plot ("scene"), Palacio Valdés argues, "Content . . . is a matter of indifference, because all reality is equally beautiful" (16).

These passages, or rather Howells's and Baxter's praise and legitimization of them, suggest that Palacio Valdés had successfully adopted the American "model" of literary realism that Howells championed; however, the legacy of *Sister Saint Sulpice*'s prologue may rest upon a single word that inspired one of the most important passages in all of Howells's criticism. In the middle of the prologue, Palacio Valdés takes pains to distance his brand of realism from other literary movements, including French Naturalism. In particular, he condemns the tendency of some writers to surrender to what he calls "effectism," "the itch to arouse at any cost in the reader lively and violent emotions which seem to show the writer's originality and inventive powers" (21).

The concept of effectism, a term that Palacio Valdés may have borrowed from John Ruskin's art criticism, seems to have left an impression on Howells and other American writers of the period. Demonstrating just how quick a study he was, Hamlin Garland eagerly adopted the term when he praised Howells's own *A Hazard of New Fortunes* (1890) for "its freedom from 'effectism.'"[72] For Howells, Palacio Valdés's term apparently supplied an insight he needed in order to articulate the aims of realism and the function of literary criticism. In his November 1889 "Editor's Study," which he incorporated with very little alteration into the central chapters of *Criticism and Fiction* (chapters 13 through 15), Howells refers to Palacio Valdés's prologue in order to explain why, in his opinion, English literature had fallen into such decadence since the days of Jane Austen. Victimized by "the mania of romanticism," as Howells puts it, Walter Scott, Charles Dickens, Charlotte Brontë, and William Makepeace Thackeray had all given in to "the rage of *effectism*" (original emphasis), and their continued glorification by English critics made it all the more likely that aspiring writers would follow the lead of those authors instead of Austen in the hopes of achieving literary success.[73] Within this context—and in conversation with Palacio Valdés—Howells positions his own criticism against "the perpetuation of false ideals" and famously declares, "Realism is nothing more and nothing less than the truthful treatment of material."[74] In other words, Howells's most concise definition of "realism" emerges through his reading of Palacio Valdés.

The shadow that Howells casts over Palacio Valdés's prologue to *Sister Saint Sulpice* and Howells's indebtedness to Palacio Valdés for helping him articulate his call for realism in both his November 1889 "Editor's Study" and *Criticism and Fiction* has led at least one critic to question the authorship of either or both essays.[75] To a certain extent, thinking of the ideas, if not the words, as developing collaboratively and transnationally does complicate our assumptions about authorship. Perhaps the clearest evidence of such collaboration lies in the fact that Palacio Valdés wrote his prologue largely *for the benefit* of Howells—in both senses of the phrase. By 1889, Palacio Valdés knew that Howells was reading his work faithfully, and he clearly had Howells in mind as he wrote *Sister Saint Sulpice*. Toward the end of the prologue, he mentions Howells by name, taking the opportunity to acknowledge the American critic's influence on his aesthetic ideas. "The eminent novelist and critic of Harper's New Monthly Magazine, Mr. Dean Howells," as Palacio Valdés calls him (apparently confusing Dean for Howells's paternal family name, just as Howells usually referred to the Spanish author only as Valdés), "wrote me about his impressions" of one of Palacio Valdés's earlier novels (51–52). While Howells's "impressions" were largely positive, Palacio Valdés continues, the critic's reference to "'a false and romantic note' [was] for me like a jar of cold water emptied over my head. I instantly perceived that he was wholly right, and I resolved to relapse no more into such *effectism*" (52, original emphasis). Only slightly hidden between the lines, then, is Palacio Valdés's promise to Howells that *Sister Saint Sulpice* and his future novels will conform to a Howellsian conception of realism.

At the same time, Palacio Valdés frames the prologue as a whole with references to his own unique status as the Spanish author whose work was most frequently translated into English.[76] In the second paragraph, he notes that, "in other more cultured countries, where my books circulate in translations, the number of my readers is far greater" than in Spain itself (1). The realization that he consequently represents Spanish literature in the United States is what motivates him to write the prologue in the first place: "It is not, therefore, from any desire to defend myself [from Spanish critics] that I have been actuated to write these lines, but a sincere desire to spread abroad some of the aesthetic observations which have come into my mind" (1). Knowing ahead of time that his novel would be translated into English, Palacio Valdés contends that he has written the prologue to *Sister Saint Sulpice* for this secondary, American audience and more especially for American critics because, as he concludes the prologue, "foreign criticism has begun to recognize that old Spain is once more wielding the sceptre of the novel" (54). The implication is that the prologue will prove to other critics that Howells's characterization of Palacio Valdés's and other Spanish novelists' fiction is correct. In a sense, Palacio Valdés writes the prologue to give Howells additional ammunition in his fight for American literary realism.

The word "effectism" thus stands as Palacio Valdés's gift to Howells, and this point was not lost on the American critics Palacio Valdés was addressing. An anonymous reviewer for *Literary World* devoted as much space to discussing the prologue as to reviewing the novel and concluded that "Howells and Valdés are practically agreed in their theories of novel-writing," and in *Crumbling Idols*, Garland attributes the "true sense" of realism to Howells and Palacio Valdés equally.[77] As if to drive home its short-term purpose even further, Palacio Valdés omitted the prologue when he reprinted *La hermana San Sulpicio* in various editions of his *Obras completas* (Complete Works). Moreover, if Palacio Valdés felt that his prologue to *Sister Saint Sulpice* had performed whatever work he had designed for it once Howells found inspiration in the concept of effectism, then the fact that Howells did not review another work by Palacio Valdés for twenty years after publishing *Criticism and Fiction* suggests that Howells also felt that he had fulfilled his obligation to introduce the Spanish author to American readers.

By the time Howells finally reviewed another of Palacio Valdés's books, a collection of short fiction and nonfiction entitled *Papeles del doctor Angélico* (1911), he had reached yet another, more overtly political understanding of the work of literature. Praising the book as "sublimely humane" in his November 1911 "Editor's Easy Chair," Howells once again positions Palacio Valdés's work against American stereotypes of Spanish culture, but this time Howells calls explicit attention to the geopolitical implications of such stereotypes: "And this is from a thinker of that Spanish race which we have always tried to believe so atrocious, and which a few years ago we were trying so hard to destroy and humiliate in a war of inexorable aggression."[78] Howells is referring to the Spanish-American War of 1898, which he had opposed from its beginning as a colonial adventure tenuously justified by racist rhetoric directed against the Spanish and Filipinos. Rather than resignedly accept the war's outcome after more than a decade, Howells cites Palacio Valdés's "humane" writing in order to remind readers of the United States' sins of aggression.

For Howells, therefore, the realism that Palacio Valdés continues to embody no longer operates in concert with U.S. geopolitical ambitions; it stands to accuse those ambitions instead. The isomorphic relationship between Howells and Palacio Valdés that helped to spread the model of American literary realism to other national literatures thus also serves as a basis for critiquing political, economic, and cultural expressions of U.S. imperialism. That Howells finds in Palacio Valdés's writings a means of combating Americanization attests both to the multidirectional work of Howells's notion of world literature and to the importance of Palacio Valdés to Howells's own anti-imperialist position. Despite not having reviewed any of Palacio Valdés's works for twenty years, Howells makes it clear in his November 1911 "Editor's Easy Chair" that he had continued to read Palacio Valdés's work, mentioning such titles as *Le alegría del capitán Ribot* (1899; *The Joys of Captain Ribot*, 1900) and *Tristán o el pesimismo* (1906). It is even possible that their friendship and his interest in Palacio Valdés's career informed or intensified Howells's opposition to the Spanish-American War.

Personal friendship alone, however, does not explain the extent of Howells's anti-imperialism or the degree to which his reviews during the early twentieth century emphasize the political work that realism could perform throughout the world. Illustrating the sheer breadth of his conception of world literature, Howells placed what is perhaps his most forceful repudiation of U.S. colonial aggression not in a review of a work by a friend or an established representative of European literature but in a review of a novel by the recently deceased Filipino writer José Rizal, whose memory was already being appropriated by U.S. colonial administrators in the Philippines. Howells's review of Rizal's *Noli me tangere* (1887; *An Eagle Flight*, 1900) appears in his April 1901 "Editor's Easy Chair," where Howells extols the novel as a more moral and aesthetically satisfying alternative to the popular historical romances that were then dominating the U.S. literary market. Recent critics have largely concurred with Howells that such best-sellers as *When Knighthood Was in Flower* (1898), *Richard Carvel* (1899), and *Alice of Old Vincennes* (1900) tended to romanticize Anglo-Saxon identity, the history of westward expansion, and the masculine values that Theodore Roosevelt and other proponents of U.S. imperialism espoused.[79] Against these historical romances, with their "glorification of the bad passions," Howells commends Rizal's novel for its "unimpeachable veracity," which finds expression in the author's skillful re-creation of Filipino local color: "From the pure Spanish to the pure Filipino . . . the many different types and characters are rendered with unerring delicacy and distinctiveness, and the effect of all those strange conditions [the exotic culture and land-scape of the Philippines] is given so fully by the spare means that while you read you are yourself of them."[80]

Just as important to Howells as local color are the political implications of the novel and its author's biography. For Howells, Rizal's execution at the hands of Spanish colonial administrators in 1896 serves not to justify the United States' recent war with Spain, as it does in some English-language accounts of Rizal's life of the period. Rather, responsibility for his death becomes transposed onto the United States, which has "bought a controlling interest in their [Spain's] crimes against his [Rizal's] country."[81] Howells contends that, since Rizal's "whole generous life accused the alien oppression," the American occupiers who replaced the Spanish would "simply have shot him, as the Spaniards did."[82] In transposing Spain and the United States, Howells's essay produces a neat dovetailing of aesthetics and politics: just as Rizal's lifework now accuses the U.S. occupation of his homeland, his novel accuses the trite historical romances that help to underwrite the cultural politics of U.S. imperialism.

Howells's review of Rizal's novel marks a significant turning point in Howells's criticism. In contrast to his tendency in earlier reviews of foreign texts to compare their use of local color to that of American local colorists, Howells takes pains to distance Rizal's accomplishments from the influence of American literature. Whereas in the 1880s and 1890s he had presented the work of Palacio Valdés and other Spanish writers as similar to—or even extensions of—American literary realism, Howells pointedly disclaims any direct connections between Rizal and American authors. On the contrary, Howells claims, "The author learned his trade apparently from the modern Spanish novelists"—presumably including Palacio Valdés—"who are very

Catch phrases of review.... (our x's stand for aesthetics)

admirable teachers of simplicity and directness. . . . But he has gone beyond them."[83] The example of Rizal proves that the isomorphic processes
of world literature still operate, even giving colonial authors access to the
global literary industry, but it also suggests that this isomorphism can bypass the United States altogether. Rizal learned from the models offered by
Spanish, not American, authors. (There is evidence that Rizal had Harriet
Beecher Stowe's *Uncle Tom's Cabin* [1852] in mind as a model for exposing
abuses of power through fiction, but Howells may not have been aware of
this connection in 1901.[84]) To be sure, if those Spanish novelists had modeled their work on American realism, as Palacio Valdés's relationship with
Howells suggests, then Rizal remains indebted indirectly to American literature, but Howells's attempt in this essay to displace the United States from
the center of the global publishing industry deserves to be taken seriously
as a politically charged variation on his comments about the diffuseness of
literary production in his 1895 essay on dialect.

The only relationship that Howells sees existing between Rizal and the
popular American writers of the period is a comparative one, and such a
comparison merely reveals how inferior American best-sellers are. Howells
marvels that "a little saffron man, somewhere in that unhappy archipelago,
should have been born with a gift so far beyond that of any or all the authors of our roaring literary successes," and he concludes that the greatest value of Rizal's novel is that there is "no imaginable leze-America in
it."[85] Howells's unfortunate and condescending characterization of Rizal as
"little" and "saffron" notwithstanding, his words underscore his claim that
a dead Filipino aesthetically surpasses the American literary proponents
of Anglo-Saxonism and annexation. Unlike their best-sellers, which retroactively recast each stage of westward expansion as precursors to turn-of-
the-century U.S. imperialism, Rizal's use of local color gives readers access
to a more authentic representation of the Philippines—free from "leze-
America." In Howells's review of Rizal's novel, local color continues to give
Americans access to a foreign culture, but it also works to resist attempts
to Americanize that same culture.

In simultaneously emphasizing Rizal's politics, use of local color, and
indebtedness to Spanish novelists, Howells anticipates Gilles Deleuze and
Félix Guattari's concept of minor literature, wherein seemingly marginal
authors carve out a political, often national, identity for themselves and
their perceived community through their appropriation of the very same
linguistic and geographic conditions that tend to marginalize them. As
Deleuze and Guattari put it, "minor literature doesn't come from a minor

yikes!

language [but] is rather that which a minority constructs within a major language," and "everything in them is political."⁸⁶ Based on the novel's publication history, Rizal seems to have intuited these principles. Written mostly in Spanish, the language of the nation occupying the Philippines at the time, *Noli me tangere* was first published at Rizal's expense in Germany in order to avoid having the novel's overtly political content censored. The paradox of using Spanish in order both to condemn the Spanish colonial authorities and to create a sense of Filipino identity extends to the power relations that the novel depicts: protagonist Crisótomo Ibarra seeks to carry out the plan of his father, who died in prison after being accused of heresy, to build a school that would offer progressive education to local Filipino children, but his efforts—as well as his romance with María Clara—are forestalled by the machinations of Catholic friars, who wield enormous political power in the Philippines. All of these relations raise inherently political questions about what it means to be simultaneously local (Filipino) and part of an empire (Spanish). Consistent with Deleuze and Guattari's claim that "there isn't a [singular] subject" in minor literature but rather that it is "the people's concern," Ibarra also disappears from his own story for chapters at a time, as if pushed aside by subplots concerning the seemingly minor figures of his community and their personal difficulties with the colonial and church authorities.⁸⁷

Where *Noli me tangere* may fall short of Deleuze and Guattari's ideal form of minor literature, which they somewhat contentiously claim exists in Franz Kafka's steadfast refusal to localize his fiction, is in its use of local color to resolve its paradoxes—what Deleuze and Guattari call "reterritorialization through dialect or patois."⁸⁸ Thus the features of Rizal's writing that Howells has in mind when praising the author for giving "distinctiveness" to the Philippines' "strange conditions," such as extensively describing local landscape and customs, interspersing Tagalog words with Spanish in order to give a sense of the local "patois," and so forth, appear because *Noli me tangere* seeks to confer national identity and, by implication, statehood upon the Philippines. Through exploiting its own status as a work of minor literature, Rizal's book demands recognition for the local culture it represents, a recognition that would enable future Filipino novels to command even more respect within world literature.

Here, of course, it is worth remembering that *Noli me tangere* serves as the first of four works of fiction that Benedict Anderson cites for the exemplary ways in which they "conjure up the imagined community."⁸⁹ According to Anderson, Rizal's novel consistently interpellates its readers as Filipinos, despite their lack of an officially recognized national identity, through the techniques of realism and local color (the references to local geography and topography, the use of Tagalog, etc.). Anderson claims that these literary techniques create a sense of intimacy among readers, characters, and narrator and thus a nascent sense of national belonging: "With *Noli Me Tangere*, fiction seeps quietly and continuously into reality, creating that remarkable confidence of community in anonymity which is the hallmark of modern nations."[90] Were Anderson to approach realism, like the nation itself, as a "model" that was becoming an "international norm," then he might also acknowledge that Rizal had a secondary audience in mind beyond the readers being interpellated as Filipinos: an international audience that, he hoped, could recognize and thereby legitimize its Filipino readers as Filipinos.

The isomorphism at work in Rizal's novel thus operates at two levels: the political and the literary. On one hand, Rizal follows existing literary models of realism—Spanish or otherwise—in order to receive legitimacy from such critics as Howells. In turn, such critical legitimacy calls attention to the Filipinos' aspirations for self-rule and statehood, which Howells also implicitly legitimizes when he refers to the "crimes" against the Philippines that now belong to the United States. Although Rizal could not have foreseen how these events would play out, his text enables just this sort of isomorphic reading. A brief preface, in which the author dedicates his novel "To My Country," clearly invokes an international, not merely a Filipino or even Spanish, audience:

> How often, in the midst of modern civilizations have I wanted to bring you [the Philippines] into the discussion, sometimes to recall these memories, sometimes to compare you to other countries. . . . Because I seek better stewardship for you, I will do with you what the ancients did with their infirmed: they placed them on the steps of their temples so that each in his own way could invoke a divinity that might offer a cure. With that in mind, I will try to reproduce your current condition faithfully, without prejudice; I will lift the veil hiding your ills, and sacrifice everything to truth.[91]

Rizal's preface not only foregrounds the language of realism ("reproduce . . . faithfully," "lift the veil," "truth") and the language of internationalism ("midst of modern civilization," "compare you to other countries"); it casts literary realism as a means of securing national recognition. In order to compare the Philippines to Europe, where Rizal was living when he wrote *Noli me tangere*, or to make possible future statehood, Rizal turns out of necessity to fiction.

Exposing colonial injustices realistically and humanizing Filipinos through local color, Rizal implies, ensures the legitimization of Filipino aspirations for self-rule by other nations.

That the most powerful literary critic in the nation now occupying the Philippines understood, sanctioned, and amplified Rizal's argument indicates that *Noli me tangere* managed to do some of the work Rizal envisioned. In fact, Howells's review stands in direct and pointed opposition to efforts already underway to co-opt Rizal's memory in order to justify U.S. annexation of the Philippines. Meg Wesling has drawn attention to the "strategic misreading" of Rizal by U.S. colonial administrators, who promoted Rizal as a national hero "as a means of deflecting criticism of American colonialism through Rizal's condemnations of the Spanish colonial regime, and by emphasizing what they saw as Rizal's reformist tendencies, rather than his revolutionary ones."[92] So effective were these efforts that, by 1913, Austin Craig, author of the first English-language biography of Rizal, could expect to be taken seriously when he coupled Rizal's name with McKinley's as "heroes of the free Philippines" whose "work combined to make possible the growing democracy of to-day."[93]

These attempts to downplay Rizal's more radical arguments involved excluding his novels from Filipino libraries and classrooms and selectively abridging the earliest English translations of *Noli me tangere*. It is testament both to Rizal's literary skill and Howells's critical perceptiveness that Howells inferred Rizal's radical politics from the bowdlerized translation he read.[94] Published by McClure, Phillips in 1900, that translation, entitled *An Eagle Flight*, compresses Rizal's story to such an extent—from sixty-three chapters and an epilogue to fifty-five chapters—that it alters the rhythm and often the meaning of the novel in significant ways. For example, most of Rizal's anticlericalism is omitted entirely, including several depictions of the friars' casual cruelty and much of the satire aimed at religious hypocrisy in various forms. Rizal's goal had been to expose the enormous political and social power that Catholic friars wielded in the nineteenth-century Philippines, but the anonymous translator of *An Eagle Flight* downplays their role significantly, accentuating the responsibility of the secular Spanish authorities instead and presumably removing any guilt-by-association from the American missionaries who were then flooding into the Philippines. The change in title underscores this secularization of the novel: *noli me tangere* is Latin for "touch me not," the phrase spoken by Jesus to Mary Magdalene after his resurrection, while *An Eagle Flight* is taken from a passage in Shakespeare's *Timon of Athens* extolling heroism and progress.

Perhaps the most significant change, however, appears in the translation of Rizal's preface, which is buried at the end of the translator's introduction. The translator subtly alters Rizal's reference to "other countries" to the more abstract "life . . . about me," which serves to deemphasize Rizal's interest in the possibility of future statehood for the Philippines.[95] This abstract translation comports with the translator's assertion in the introduction that "not . . . at any time did he [Rizal] think his country ready for self-government. He saw as her best present good her continued union to Spain, 'through a stable policy based upon justice and community of interests.' He asked only for the reforms promised again and again by the ministry, and as often frustrated."[96] The implication is that, if the United States supplies the reforms that Spain did not, then "union" with the United States may fulfill Rizal's hopes. Tellingly, a complete English-language version of Rizal's novel, with its political implications intact, did not appear until 1912, long after U.S. pacification of the Philippines was assured.[97]

Ironically, these efforts to elide Rizal's radicalism extended even to how Howells's review of *An Eagle Flight* was used by other writers. In Fred W. Atkinson's *The Philippine Islands* (1905) and Austin Craig's *The Story of José Rizal* (1909), both authors quote those passages in which Howells praises Rizal's realism but strategically omit those passages in which Howells condemns the United States for simply replacing Spain as the colonial power occupying the Philippines.[98] In other words, the U.S. publishing industry colluded with colonial administrators in the Philippines to silence Rizal's radical politics as much as possible. Although he ends his review of Rizal's novel hopefully—"Let us never despair of the Republic of Letters"— Howells seems to have anticipated this failure on the part of a publishing industry that was increasingly promoting the more commercially viable historical romances that stood in opposition to Rizal's and Howells's anti-imperialism: "The books that sweep the country must be of the cheapness of the average person. . . . The advertiser couldn't hopefully take hold of [this] Filipino novel."[99]

To a certain extent, the failure of the publishing industry and the reading public to "take hold of" Rizal's novel constituted a failure for Howells, too. The isomorphic processes that he identified at work in the production of world literature were ultimately insufficient to stave off the centralization of the publishing industry. Nevertheless, Howells's criticism matters insofar as it consistently draws attention to the power relations that often lie hidden behind literary conventions. In both *A Hazard of New Fortunes* and his reviews of Palacio Valdés and Rizal, Howells may approach foreign voices and cultural practices in terms of how consumable they are for Americans, but in valorizing local color's ability to represent multiple points of view, he also practically identifies a set of literary practices for giving marginalized voices access to the U.S. and world literary industries. Howells's legacy, therefore, lies in his attentiveness to the aesthetic and political possibilities of intermingling voices, which helped transform American literary realism into a more globally engaged mode of representation and thereby enabled other late American realists to produce their own accounts of the often messy processes of globalization. The next three chapters examine some of those accounts and the particular processes that they engage.

CHAPTER THREE

Improper Wealth Getting

Henry James, the Rise of Finance Capitalism,
and the Emerging Global Cultural Economy

I n *A Hazard of New Fortunes*, what prompts Lindau's outburst that the
state is the solution to existing social problems is a discussion about
the dangers of monopolies that Colonel Woodburn starts at Dryfoos's
dinner party. Tellingly, it is the socially conservative Colonel Woodburn,
not the radical immigrant Lindau, who gives voice to the fear that unregu-
lated competition necessarily leads to monopolies: "The infernal impulse
of competition ha[s] embroiled us in a perpetual warfare of interests, developing the worst passions of our nature, and teaching us to trick and be-
tray and destroy one another in the strife for money, till now that impulse
ha[s] exhausted itself, and we [find] competition gone and the whole economic problem in the hands of monopolies—the Standard Oil Company,
the Sugar Trust, the Rubber Trust, and what not."[1] The kind of anxiety that
Colonel Woodburn expresses in this passage has long been regarded as
one of the primary motivations for the Progressive movement itself. In his
classic study entitled *The Age of Reform*, for example, Richard Hofstadter
describes a weak and frequently corrupt political system "of diffused
power and unorganized strength" into which "the great corporations and
investment houses had now thrust themselves, gigantic units commanding vast resources and quite capable of buying up political support on a
wholesale basis, just as they bought their other supplies. The Progressives
were thus haunted by the specter of a private power far greater than the
public power of the state."[2] Hofstadter goes on to claim that, in contrast
to earlier periods of limited government, Progressives initiated a trend of
seeking "in governmental action a counterpoise to the power of private
business . . . , which found its beginnings in the Interstate Commerce Act
of 1887 and the Sherman Act of 1890."[3] Although the U.S. Supreme Court
eventually issued decisions that severely limited both acts, the ratifications

of the Interstate Commerce Act and the Sherman Antitrust Act serve as watershed moments in many histories of Progressivism, and they paved the way for future federal regulation of American business.

The somewhat surprising political alignment that occurs between the conservative Colonel Woodburn and the radical Lindau in *A Hazard of New Fortunes* gives a sense of just how widespread the anxiety that Hofstadter describes already was when William Dean Howells began serializing his novel in 1889. This passage also indicates the degree to which Howells himself may have hoped that his American readers, more of whom probably would have identified with Colonel Woodburn than with Lindau, would be willing to rethink their own assumptions about the free market and state regulation if it meant curtailing the various "trusts" that Colonel Woodburn names. In having Colonel Woodburn characterize free-market competition as a "strife for money" that inevitably "exhausts itself" and results in monopoly, Howells anticipates the logic of a number of Progressives, including most notably Louis D. Brandeis, who sought to convince their fellow Americans that only state regulation of a newer and even more troubling form of monopoly could ensure the continued stability—and thus the global supremacy—of the U.S. national economy. The so-called Money Trust may not appear on Colonel Woodburn's list, but growing concern over the rise of finance capitalism—what, in his influential work *Other People's Money and How the Bankers Use It* (1913–14), Brandeis called "improper wealth getting"—seems to have prompted just the kind of rethinking of American big business that *A Hazard of New Fortunes* calls for.[4]

Perhaps the most recursive example of this rethinking plays out in one of the period's most heavily revised works of American literature: the version of Henry James's *The American* that appeared in 1907. Originally serialized in the *Atlantic Monthly* between June 1876 and May 1877, *The American* was revised extensively by its author when he prepared it for inclusion in the New York Edition.[5] Long regarded as "the most rewritten" of all James's novels, the 1907 version of *The American* has attracted considerable critical attention, primarily for the insights its revisions provide into James's thirty-year evolution as an artist.[6] James seems to have anticipated the interest that his decision to revise *The American* and some of his other early novels would arouse, and he dedicates the final five paragraphs of his preface to *The American* to explaining and justifying that novel's revisions. He begins by observing, "What I have recognised then in 'The American,' much to my surprise and after long years, is that the experience here represented is the disconnected and uncontrolled experience—uncontrolled by our general sense of 'the way things happen'—which romance alone more or less successfully palms off on us."[7] This observation triggers one of James's most important discussions of the differences between romance and realism. For James, "the real" represents "the things we cannot possibly *not* know, sooner or later, in one way or another," while "the romantic" stands for "the things that, with all the facilities in the world, all the wealth and all the courage and all the wit and all the adventure, we never *can* directly know" (10–11, original emphasis). Or as he phrases this distinction somewhat more glibly, romance equates to "the way things don't happen" and realism to "the way things do" (12). As an author committed to realism, James registers surprise at his discovery that, despite his original intentions, the world of *The American* is a world of "romance" instead of "the real": "The way things happen is frankly not the way in which they are represented as having happened, in Paris, to my hero: the situation I had conceived only saddled me with that for want of my invention of something better" (13).

While his initial concentration on the fine line between realism and romance helps explain why critical attention often focuses on the formal or aesthetic implications of the novel's revisions, James makes it clear that the need for revision stems from the novel's failure to portray socioeconomic conditions accurately. The "situation" to which he refers is what he labels "the queer falsity—of the Bellegardes" (13). Their "queer falsity" is, of course, the plot point upon which the novel hinges: although impoverished, the aristocratic French Bellegarde family steadfastly refuses to allow their daughter Claire to marry the wealthy businessman Christopher Newman because he is American and therefore unsuitable. In reality, however, impecunious European aristocrats frequently married into newly affluent American families.[8] Instead of opposing his courtship of Claire so vehemently, a real-life Bellegarde family would have compared the size of Newman's bank account to the shabbiness of their ancestral home and accepted him. Far from "not finding Newman good enough for their alliance," James confesses, the Bellegardes' "preferred course, a thousand times preferred, would have been to haul him and his fortune into their boat under cover of night perhaps, in any case as quietly and with as little bumping and splashing as possible, and there accommodate him with the very safest and most convenient seat" (14).

Significantly, James goes on to place the blame for this inconsistency on his own stubborn commitment to "the theme to which I was from so early pledged" (14). That "theme," as James describes it, was a "situation, in another country and an aristocratic society, of some robust but insidiously beguiled and betrayed, some cruelly wronged, compatriot: the point being in especial that he should suffer at the hands of persons pretending to represent the highest possible civilization and to be of an order in every way superior to his own" (4). In short, the flaws that James perceived in his own novel's narrative resulted from his commitment to what is sometimes referred to as the international theme in American literature: a conflict between individual American and European characters that reflects a larger, more symbolic contrast between two opposing cultures and sets of values.[9] In a sense, James's decision to revise *The American*, in the belief that "the way things don't happen may be artfully made to pass for the way things do" (12), serves as a critique of the genre of the "international novel" as an insufficient means of representing global socioeconomic conditions in the early twentieth century. The 1907 version of *The American* thus seems to constitute an about-face for an author who had established his reputation through such works as *Daisy Miller* (1878) and *The Portrait of a Lady* (1881).

Reading the revised version of *The American* alongside the efforts of Brandeis and his fellow Progressives to draw attention to and regulate "improper wealth getting," I argue, reveals the extent to which James's revisions underscore his attentiveness to wider social, cultural, and economic matters. As a fairly straightforward satire, the 1877 version of *The American* responds to Gilded Age excess in a manner similar to other realist novels of the 1870s and early 1880s: proposing that moral decisions can redress unethical economic behavior. The 1907 version, on the other hand, offers a sophisticated critique of finance capitalism that is deeply engaged with the same problems that Brandeis examines in *Other People's Money*. Viewing the two versions of *The American* as separate works, I further contend, provides a notable example of late realism's intersection with Progressive discourse: the revisions transform Christopher Newman, the protagonist of the novel, from a blustery but ultimately decent self-made millionaire, much like Andrew Carnegie, into a far more ambiguous figure whose enormous wealth is accompanied by a disquieting sense of entitlement.[10]

This chapter examines James's revision of *The American* within the context of other early twentieth-century discourse about finance capitalism that, in the United States, formed part of a larger effort to curb the excessive power of the Money Trust. For James, this effort entailed not so much a rejection of his and other realists' early responses to what Alan Trachtenberg, in his classic study of the period, calls "the incorporation of America," but rather as a necessary revision of the relatively naïve solutions they had offered.[11] In the case of *The American*, James's revision was prompted in part by his return visit to the United States after a twenty-year absence, as recounted in his other 1907 study of growing U.S. power, *The American Scene*. Recognizing, as Vladimir Lenin did, that the emergence of finance capitalism at the turn of the twentieth century marked a transition into a troubling form of "new capitalism," James used the opportunity to revise *The American* as a means of exploring what I, expanding slightly on Arjun Appadurai's term, call the emerging global cultural economy, wherein the interests of Europe and the United States had begun to intersect economically, socially, and culturally.[12] In its revised form, *The American* downplays the earlier version's depiction of a chasm existing between the two cultures, instead implicating Newman—and, by extension, the rising economic and cultural power of the nation he represents—more fully in the larger global cultural economy. Like other writers of the period, including Brandeis, James ultimately turns to the United States' place in the global cultural economy in order to criticize and correct the failures of finance capitalism. First, however, I will explain what I mean by the rise of finance capitalism and the global cultural economy in order to establish the economic context in which James revised *The American*, and I will examine Brandeis's *Other People's Money* as a representative, but also particularly influential, example of the wider socioeconomic discourse in which James's revisions may be said to intervene.

"IMPERIAL POWER" VERSUS MULTINATIONAL COOPERATION

In the United States, the transition from the period of rapid industrialization following the Civil War into the era of finance capitalism during the early twentieth century resulted primarily from the emergence of such powerful investment bankers as J. P. Morgan. In the series of essays that makes up *Other People's Money*, which he originally wrote for *Harper's Weekly* in support of Woodrow Wilson's economic policies, Brandeis unapologetically casts Morgan and his fellow investment bankers as the villains of his narrative. Unlike previous industrialists or even the so-called "robber barons" of the Gilded Age, these investment bankers, Brandeis argues, accumulate their enormous wealth without taking any risks because they use the money entrusted to them by their depositors in order to finance their investments. "Today," Brandeis writes, "when a large issue of bonds is made, the banker, while ostensibly paying his own money to the city, actually pays to the city other people's money which he has borrowed from the banks. Then the banks get back, through the city's deposits, a large part of the money so received. And when the money is returned to the bank, the banker has the opportunity of borrowing it again for other operations."[13]

According to Brandeis, this "dynamic" wealth enables Morgan and other U.S. investment bankers to move beyond the traditional banker's role of middleman and disinterested adviser and to force their way, in various industries, onto multiple corporations' boards of directors, concentrating inordinate power into their own hands in the process.[14] For Brandeis, such concentration of power causes several major problems: interlocking directorates create conflicts of interest that reduce competition and subvert the free market; the flow of money to the corporate centers of New York, Boston, Chicago, and Philadelphia erodes the financial independence of other regions of the United States; and the shift in decision-making from experts who helped establish particular industries to financiers who are interested primarily in a company's performance on the stock market results in inefficiency. Worst of all, investment bankers become "builders of imperial power" and encroach upon the power of the state.[15] Brandeis describes this encroachment explicitly when he suggests that "the banker [rather than the state] has become the universal tax gatherer," but he also gestures toward it more subtly when he decries the continental scope of railroad magnate E. H. Harriman's holdings, which "extended from the Atlantic to the Pacific; from the Great Lakes to the Gulf of Mexico."[16] The United States, Brandeis implies, is at risk of becoming an oligarchy of financiers who operate outside of—and perhaps even against—state legitimacy. That Dryfoos, the character most committed to capitalism in A Hazard of New Fortunes, begins his land-development project partly out of fear that "it wouldn't be five years before the Standard [Oil Company] owned the whole region" indicates that Brandeis was not alone in his concern that monopolies might effectively become states within the state.[17]

Brandeis was no Marxist—his larger argument pivots upon the assumption that breaking the Money Trust would restore competition and innovation—but his analysis of investment banking closely aligns with Karl Marx's critique of "the improvised wealth of the financiers," which "endows barren money with the power of breeding and thus turns it into capital, without the necessity of its exposing itself to the troubles and risks inseparable from its employment in industry or even in usury. The state-creditors actually give nothing away, for the sum lent is transformed into public bonds, easily negotiable, which go on functioning in their hands just as so much hard cash would."[18] Moreover, Brandeis's association of "imperial power" with investment banking anticipates V. I. Lenin's conception of imperialism, the "economic quintessence" of which is "monopoly capitalism" and not simply overseas expansion.[19] *Imperialism, the Highest Stage of Capitalism* (1916) does not cite *Other People's Money*, which was published as a book two years earlier, but it is possible that Lenin encountered Brandeis's name, if not his writings, during his research on U.S. monopolies and banking practices. (Lenin refers to J. P. Morgan and U.S. Steel several times, for example.) Like Brandeis, who identifies the formation of the Money Trust as "a revolutionary change" in the U.S. economy, Lenin views the economic order of the early twentieth century as something entirely new:

> Thus, the beginning of the twentieth century marks the turning point at which the old capitalism [based upon free competition] gave way to the new, at which the domination of capital in general made way for the domination of finance capital. . . . The concentration of production; the monopoly arising therefrom; the merging or coalescence of banking with industry: this is the history of finance capital and what gives the term "finance capital" its content.[20]

For Marx and Lenin, the defining characteristics of finance capitalism are its disconnection from industrial production, which no longer serves as the primary means of accumulating wealth, and its freedom from the presumed laws of the free market, due to the systematic formation of monopolies.

These features of finance capitalism proved deeply troubling to many American reformers. The possibility that investment bankers, who produced no useful commodities themselves, now controlled the industrial future of the United States seemed to portend a lack of innovation and therefore a decline in the technological progress that had catapulted the nation into its position of economic supremacy. Brandeis and other commentators explicitly dissociated industrialists, such as Andrew Carnegie, from the investment bankers who had seemingly replaced them. In *The Theory of Business Enterprise* (1904), his historical account of the emergence of corporate capitalism, Thorstein Veblen anticipates Brandeis by drawing a distinction between the innovative industrialist and the conservative "business man" who "has become a controlling force in industry . . . through the mechanism of investments and markets."[21] Although Veblen does not address investment banking specifically, his condescending description of opportunistic entrepreneurship could stand in for the business practices of J. P. Morgan and the other financiers Brandeis targets:

His furtherance of industry is at the second remove, and is chiefly of a negative character. In his capacity as business man he does not go creatively into the work of perfecting mechanical processes and turning the means at hand to new or larger uses. . . . The men in industry must first create the mechanical possibility of such new and more efficient methods and correlations, before the business man sees the chance [and] makes the necessary business arrangements.[22]

While the theoretical nature of Veblen's highly idiosyncratic writing leaves his views on practical social change opaque, he clearly states that the "solutions" to the problems of "social welfare" require deep engagement with the emerging features of "business enterprise—the phenomena of price, earnings, and capitalization"—rather than the traditional economic "facts of production and consumption."[23] Brandeis, who would later cite Veblen in Supreme Court decisions, took this point to heart. *Other People's Money* is no mere exercise in nostalgia for the era of rags-to-riches industrialists but a carefully researched examination of how investment bankers conjured their vast earnings.

Brandeis's commitment to practical social change—perhaps even more than his general commitment to a capitalist economy—explains a crucial difference between his thinking and that of Marx, Lenin, and Veblen: the anxiety that the emergence of finance capitalism posed a threat to state sovereignty and thus the continued economic strength and social stability of the United States. Veblen had argued, "Legislation, police surveillance, the administration of justice, the military and diplomatic service, all are chiefly concerned with business relations, pecuniary interests."[24] Lenin would conclude that "the supremacy of finance capital over all other forms of capital means . . . the crystallization of a small number of financially 'powerful' states from among all the rest."[25] *Other People's Money*, on the other hand, works from the assumption that the Money Trust functions outside the interests of the state and thus requires state regulation. Among the solutions he outlines, Brandeis suggests that "the Sherman Law should be supplemented both by providing more efficient judicial machinery, and by creating a commission with administrative functions to aid in enforcing the law. . . . We [also] should conserve all rights which the Federal Government and the States have in our natural resources."[26] Such a proposal was not all that different from the ideas voiced by other notable figures of the period, indicating that Brandeis was part of a fairly broad-based effort to expand the state's regulatory powers through democratic means. For instance,

Andrew Carnegie, who had strenuously opposed antitrust legislation in the late-1880s, claimed in a 1909 interview that "monopolies must be controlled in some way or another. A supreme industrial court will have to be created, and eventually will have to pass [judgment] upon prices. . . . There must be control in some form, and that, so far as one sees, must be in the hands of the General Government."[27] The critical point, however, is that, for Brandeis, the rise of finance capitalism did not, in and of itself, ensure the United States' economic or geopolitical supremacy.

Expanding significantly on the Marxist analysis of finance capitalism, Giovanni Arrighi helps to explain why Brandeis and other Americans experienced such anxiety over the emergence of finance capitalism and why they turned to the state as a means of distributing the resulting increase in wealth more productively. In the history of capitalism he outlines in *The Long Twentieth Century*, Arrighi provides an account of the shift of global socioeconomic power from Europe to the United States at the end of the nineteenth century. Building on the work of Fernand Braudel and Immanuel Wallerstein, Arrighi traces the history of the capitalist world-economy from the fifteenth century to the present through four "successive systemic cycles of accumulation": Genoese, Dutch, British, and U.S.[28] Arrighi argues that periods of intense finance capitalism, when "an increasing mass of money capital 'sets itself free' from its commodity form and accumulation proceeds through financial deals" alone, mark transitional moments when the balance of power shifts from one systemic cycle to another.[29] For Arrighi, the end of the nineteenth century was one such transitional moment: "From the 1870s onwards . . . the capacity of the United Kingdom to hold the center of the capitalist world-economy was being undermined by the emergence of a new national economy of greater wealth, size, and resources than its own. This was the United States."[30] At the same time, however, periods of finance capitalism are extremely unstable, and according to Arrighi, it falls to the state to ensure that an emerging national economy is stabilized in such a way that the nation in question can achieve global hegemony: "The state that controlled or came to control the most abundant sources of surplus capital tended also to acquire the organizational capabilities needed to promote, organize, and regulate a new phase of capitalist expansion of greater scale and scope than the preceding one."[31]

Although Arrighi focuses more on the declining power of Britain than on the rising power of the United States, his assertion that less stable periods of finance capitalism give way to more stable periods of material and financial expansion during which an emerging power can consolidate its national economy holds true for the United States during the Progressive era. After the Civil War, despite massive industrial growth, the U.S. economy suffered from a number of financial panics.[32] Speculation and stock-market manipulation led directly to the financial crises of 1866–69 and 1873 and the ensuing depression. Subsequent panics occurred with such frequency that the federal government sponsored O. M. W. Sprague to write a study of the economic conditions that produced these crises. In his *History of Crises under the National Banking System* (1910), Sprague identified four significant crises after 1873: 1884, 1890, 1893, and 1907. Of the 1907 panic, Sprague was quick to note the "powerful influence of Mr. J. P. Morgan" in containing the crisis.[33] Morgan had convinced his fellow investment bankers to channel more money into the economy by providing loans to faltering institutions. Concluding that the only way to avoid future crises was to empower the federal government to respond directly to financial panics without relying on bankers, Sprague argued that the United States should establish a centralized reserve system, like the Bank of England, in order to consolidate its burgeoning economic power. Passing the Federal Reserve Act, which Woodrow Wilson signed into law on December 23, 1913, became one of Brandeis's central aims when, in August of that year, he began publishing the essays that make up *Other People's Money*. In breaking the Money Trust and freeing up capital for reinvestment in industry, Wilson and Brandeis sought to reverse the structural realignment of the U.S. economy that had enabled monopolies to trump competition by controlling the supply of money. Within this context, then, Brandeis's calls for increased federal regulation constitute an effort to expand American production even further, thereby assuring the nation's economic supremacy.

Perhaps what is most striking about Brandeis's and, as I argue below, James's contributions to this engagement with the problems of finance capitalism is the degree to which they invoked the emerging global cultural economy as a means of correcting the cultural practices that had enabled finance capitalism to develop in the United States. In turning to cultural economy, I do not mean to sidestep "hard" economic data. In an extended discussion of Arrighi, who is not particularly helpful in thinking through the cultural implications of his history of globalization, Fredric Jameson suggests that "any comprehensive new theory of finance capitalism will need to reach out into the expanded realm of cultural production to map its effects."[34] Jameson ambitiously goes on to link Arrighi's account of the cyclical patterns of abstracting money with Gilles Deleuze's notion of deterritorialization in order to provide a "global theory" of the historical transitions in the arts, from realism to modernism and postmodernism.[35] By contrast, my aim is to examine how, in the early twentieth century, American writers reached out to an already emerging global culture as a means of responding to pressing economic conditions.

In general terms, "cultural economy" refers to the concept that cultural and economic practices are embedded in one another and that there are cultural facets and implications to economic activity (and vice versa). Paul du Gay and Michael Pryke explain:

> This particular understanding of economics as "culture" focuses attention on the practical ways in which "economically relevant activity" is performed and enacted. It serves to show, in other words, the ways in which the "making up" or "construction" of economic realities is undertaken and achieved; how those activities, objects and persons we categorize as "economic" are built up or assembled from a number of parts, many of them supplied by the disciplines of economics but many drawn from other sources, including, of course, forms of ostensibly non-economic cultural practice.[36]

Throughout *Other People's Money*, Brandeis takes care to identify a number of noneconomic factors at stake in what seems to be an otherwise purely economic problem. "The suppression of industrial liberty," for example, constitutes an attack upon "manhood itself."[37] Brandeis also recognizes that changing a culture in which "investors . . . have been trained to regard the intervention of the banker as necessary" requires extensive "educational work" and "publicity" on the part of the government.[38] His most famous quotation—"sunlight is said to be the best of disinfectants"—appears in a chapter dedicated to "What Publicity Can Do."[39] All of these rhetorical flourishes serve to remind readers that their way of life is inseparably linked with larger economic conditions, which their own everyday practices help to produce. By changing their behavior, Brandeis implies, these readers can effect social change on their own.

More specifically, I borrow the concept of a global cultural economy from Arjun Appadurai, who describes it as "a complex, overlapping, disjunctive order that cannot any longer be understood in terms of existing center-periphery models."[40] For Appadurai, disjuncture is the global cultural economy's defining characteristic, arising as it does from "the tension between cultural homogenization and cultural heterogenization."[41] While economic forces of globalization, such as multinational corporations and the worldwide circulation of goods and products, tend to eliminate cultural difference by giving all societies a relative sameness, they simultaneously provide local forms of cultural expression with new resources and technologies, which are then "indigenized" and reshaped to suit the needs and tastes of the local community.[42] Thus besides assigning culture itself a privileged role in the processes of globalization, operating variously in concert with and in resistance to economic factors, Appadurai underscores the fact that disjuncture occurs because of an underlying tension between similarity and difference. In a global cultural economy, national forms of cultural valuation must coincide with—as well as deviate from—one another, and it is this tension between agreement and variance that, in his preface, for example, James confesses he failed to account for in the marriage plot of *The American* because his "theme" committed him to contrast alone.

Appadurai's identification of modes of national empowerment and local resistance within the very processes of globalization helps to explain what, to twenty-first-century sensibilities, may seem to be two paradoxes at work in Brandeis's response to the Money Trust: first, that a multinational corporation could serve as a model for resisting finance capitalism; second, that the U.S. economy could be strengthened by the state itself encouraging domestic participation in a transnational economic movement. Both of these suggestions find their fullest expression in *Other People's Money*. Brandeis dedicates the last essay of his book to identifying and extolling several functioning alternatives to the United States' economic system that existed in Europe and Canada. All of the models Brandeis points to are cooperatives that still manage to engage in "big business"—the implication being that the introduction of state regulation into the free market does not require the United States to abandon large-scale production.[43] Brandeis's chief model, Britain's Co-operative Wholesale Society (CWS), is a multinational organization that owns "a bacon factory in Denmark, and a tallow and oil factory in Australia. It grows tea in Ceylon."[44] Nevertheless, the structure of this "great business" provides a viable and more just alternative to U.S. corporations: instead of concentrating power into the hands of a few powerful and increasingly wealthy bankers, the CWS functions "democratically," with each of its "2,750,000" members having an equal say in the selection of its modestly salaried directors.[45] The example of the CWS leads Brandeis to conclude *Other People's Money* with a call for Americans to participate in this worldwide "cooperative movement," and he singles out the rise of local credit unions in Germany and Canada as a potential antidote to the United States' undemocratic savings banks, which are "purely commercial enterprises, managed, of course, by the stockholders' representatives" and not "*by* the people, nor, in the full sense, *for* the people" (original emphasis).[46]

Brandeis was by no means the only U.S. Progressive of the early twentieth century to turn to the cooperative movements of Europe and Canada in order to resolve domestic economic problems, nor was he alone in suggesting that fuller engagement with such transnational developments would strengthen the United States' position within the global cultural economy. In a 1913 essay entitled "Consumers' Coöperation," which Brandeis cites in *Other People's Money*, the American journalist Albert Sonnichsen presents the rise of cooperative organizations as a global movement that is truly democratic and thus an alternative to both corporate capitalism and socialism. Sonnichsen quotes Luigi Luzzatti, the former prime minister of Italy, as proclaiming the formation of an international wholesale society "a great idea; that of opposing to the great trusts, the Rockefellers of the world, a world-wide coöperative alliance which shall become so powerful as to crush the trusts."[47] It is unclear whether or not Sonnichsen picks up on the full implication of Luzzatti's decision to name Rockefeller as the representative example of monopolization. In doing so, Luzzatti implies that the global cooperative movement would simultaneously oppose corporate capitalism and the corresponding danger of Americanization.

If Sonnichsen failed to grasp that Luzzatti was staking out an economic system that was designed to curb both economic and cultural incursion from the United States, other commentators did not miss that point. In order to achieve and maintain economic supremacy, many writers maintained, the United States would have to address the wider international systems of economic and cultural valuation that it was entering. One of the recurring arguments of Sprague's 1910 study on banking crises, for instance, is the increased interdependence of U.S. and foreign economies from 1873 onwards, and he identifies the "fictions of speculation" perpetrated by finance capitalists as something that "seriously impairs our credit with foreign nations."[48] In short, in order to replace Great Britain as the world's dominant economic power, Americans would have to learn that their national economy and national forms of valuation did not exist outside the global cultural economy. Rather, they needed to gain a firmer understanding of their place within that global cultural economy. In the remainder of this chapter, I examine how, through his revision of *The American*, Henry James sought to produce just that knowledge.

THE AMERICAN: REVISION AND CRITIQUE

If cultural economy accounts for how and why societies ascribe both monetary and nonmonetary values to cultural objects and practices that do not otherwise appear to possess clear economic functions, then the concepts of cultural economy and the global cultural economy provide an eminently suitable framework for studying James's fiction. Writing of *The American Scene* (1907), which James composed as he revised *The American*, John Carlos Rowe has argued that "James represents . . . the shift in global power from Europe to America, with respect to both political and cultural economies. Even as he criticizes American cultural deficiencies and capitalist excesses, James still takes pride in the growing centrality of the American as the type of the cosmopolitan, as the Italian had been in the Quattrocento and the Englishman in the Victorian era."[49] Indeed, James seems to think about economics primarily in terms of cultural activity. After all, hard economic data are rare in James's writings—and sometimes purposely left vague— but few authors have been more concerned with the valuation of art and historical objects, the hierarchy of status, and the details of conspicuous consumption. In his fiction, economic conditions exist primarily to enable or constrain the cultural practices and ideologies of the social milieus he depicts. James's attentiveness to the increased mobility of American finance capitalists, including Christopher Newman in *The American*, as well as to their aspirations for the sort of status and legitimacy that only their brushes with high culture could bring them illustrate Rowe's assertion that "James consistently implicates culture in the work of imperial expansion and domination."[50]

In *The American*, Newman presents a textbook illustration of Ash Amin and Nigel Thrift's central argument regarding cultural economy: that "the pursuit of prosperity must be seen as the pursuit of many goals at once, from meeting material needs and accumulating riches to seeking symbolic satisfaction and satisfying fleeting pleasures."[51] The desire for the less tangible goals of "symbolic satisfaction" and "fleeting pleasures" is precisely what motivates Newman's journey to Europe in the first place. Early in the novel, Newman informs his friend Tom Tristram that he has "come to see Europe, to *get* the best out of it I can" (original emphasis in both editions).[52] Newman's use of the verb "get" here is significant insofar as it indicates just how much he approaches his sojourn in Europe as a process of acquisition. He relies primarily on his purchasing power to obtain the accoutrements of high status: French lessons, copies of the Old Masters' paintings, and an aristocratic wife. Newman's willingness to pay exorbitant fees for functionless and apparently inferior copies of great artworks is a satirical but still characteristic example of what James's contemporary Thorstein Veblen termed "conspicuous waste" and "conspicuous consumption" in *The Theory of the Leisure Class* (1899), just as Newman's ability to travel extensively in Europe is an example of "conspicuous leisure."[53] Simultaneously acknowledging the limits of money's power yet dismissing any doubts of his ultimate success, Newman tells Tristram, "Didn't I say I wanted the best? I know the best can't be had for mere money, but I rather think money will do a good deal" (*AM1* 35). Newman's pursuit of—and belief that he can obtain—this intangible "best," which for him represents learning, cultivation, status, and eventually a family but which exists somewhere other than the United States, precipitates the novel's plot and speaks to the circulation of forms of cultural and symbolic capital on a global scale.

Newman's use of the language of acquisition also indicates that he is a finance capitalist. In the novel's second chapter, as his recent past is rehearsed for the benefit of both Tristram and the reader, James casts Newman's business dealings as a form of speculation: "Christopher Newman's sole aim in life had been to *make* money; what he had been placed in the world for was, to his own perception, simply to *wrest* a fortune, the bigger the better, from defiant opportunity. . . . Life had been for him an *open game*, and he had *played for high stakes*. He had *won* at last and carried off his *winnings*; and now what was he to do with them?" (*AM1* 32, emphases added). As is typical of James, the exact nature of his protagonist's business remains unclear, but Newman explains that, just before traveling to Europe, "some important business" had involved "getting ahead of another party, in a certain particular way, in the stock-market. . . . There was a matter of some sixty thousand dollars at stake. If I put it out of his way, it was a blow the fellow would feel" (*AM1* 34).

When Newman describes feeling "a mortal disgust for the thing I was going to do," which causes him to become "sick of business" and "throw it all up and break off short" (*AM1* 34–35), it becomes clear that *The American* reflects the same anxieties about the cutthroat business practices of the robber barons that appear in other literary works of the period, such as Charles and Henry Adams's *Chapters of Erie* (1871), Mark Twain and Charles Dudley Warner's *The Gilded Age* (1873), and William Dean Howells's *The*

Rise of Silas Lapham (1885). Like these other works, the 1877 edition of *The American* explicitly rejects the speculation and stock-market manipulation that had caused the financial panics of 1866–69 and 1873 and the resulting depression. James's decision to set the action of the novel in the late 1860s—and to retain that setting in 1907—suggests that Newman may have been involved in the events leading up to Jay Gould's attempt to corner the gold market in 1869. Newman's renunciation of business and growing appreciation for European culture—and the Bellegardes' rejection of him for not being good enough—indicate where the novel's values lie. By making Newman a speculator and by having him embrace the language of gambling so early in the novel, James imbues the ending of the 1877 version with additional irony: Newman burns a note that incriminates the Bellegardes in a murder rather than use it to blackmail or expose them, only to be told by Mrs. Tristram that the Bellegardes had been "bluffing things off" and gambling on Newman's "remarkable good nature" (*AM1* 309). The stock market manipulator has himself been manipulated, and in the novel's final action, he turns "instinctively"—perhaps regretfully—to the fire to see if the note is still there.

In the 1907 edition, however, James's critique of the finance capitalism that Newman represents is more damning but also less conventional. Newman's account of his own history remains much the same, though the amounts of money that he handles swell exponentially. By 1907, Newman is gambling for "half a million" (*AM2* 36), a more realistic sum for a stock market speculator to be pursuing than sixty thousand. His age also increases from "thirty-six" to "forty-two and a half" and he makes his fortune before, instead of after, the Civil War (*AM1* 28; *AM2* 30).[54] If the revised word choice is any indication, James wished to portray Newman's business dealings more negatively in 1907. Whereas the 1877 version depicts "the business of money-getting [as] extremely dry and sterile," the 1907 version objects more judgmentally that "the business of mere money-getting showed only, in its ugliness, as vast and vague and dark, a pirate-ship with lights turned inward" (*AM1* 75; *AM2* 80). Thus Newman's "money-getting," the result of piracy, is not unlike the "improper wealth getting" of Brandeis's investment bankers. At other times, the revised language even becomes violent. Instead of being placed in the world "to wrest a fortune," Newman is placed here "to gouge a fortune" (*AM2* 34). Moreover, instead of renouncing business, the 1907 version of Newman gives it up only temporarily: "I'm not at present transacting any [business]—on any terms. There'll be plenty to be done again if I don't hold out, but I shall hold out as long as possible. I dare say, however, that a twelvemonth hence . . . the pendulum [will] swing back again" (*AM2* 37). The novel's final irony disappears, too. Instead of needling Newman, Mrs. Tristram validates his decision to burn the incriminating note when she remarks, "I like you as you are," and the novel concludes with her lament for "poor, poor Claire!" (*AM2* 363).

That Newman remains a finance capitalist in the 1907 edition without receiving the final stinging irony demonstrates the degree to which James had rejected the "theme" of national contrasts as an insufficient means of examining the United States' place in the world. The revised *American* implies that finance capitalism is not only here to stay in the United States, but also that it is expanding and consolidating instead of being "bluffed off" by the representatives of older cultural values in Europe. If anything, Newman is a more serious threat to the Bellegardes in the revised version of the novel. In both versions, for instance, Valentin, the only male member of the Bellegarde family to befriend Newman, describes him as a man who is both a big "stockholder" and thoroughly "at home in the world," but only in the 1907 edition does Valentin associate Newman's finance-capital cosmopolitanism with his own irrelevance: "You make me feel awfully my want of shares. And yet the world used to be supposed to be ours" (*AM1* 94–95; *AM2* 104). Valentin seems to be speaking both metaphorically and literally here: the world really does belong to Newman and others who can master the new form of accumulating wealth (through manipulating "shares" of stock) rather than to the Bellegardes and their fellow aristocrats, who inherited their ever-diminishing wealth.

As if to emphasize the irresistible rise of finance capitalism and the decline of older economic models, James increases the number of business similes that Newman speaks or thinks in the 1907 edition and directs them at Claire, the woman Newman wants to acquire for his wife. The 1877 Newman's mental characterization of Claire as "frank as flowing water" becomes as "distinct as the big figure on a banknote" in 1907 (*AM1* 98; *AM2* 109). In both versions, Newman "made no violent love" to Claire, but the revised version adds that "he just attended regularly, as he would also have said, in the manner of the 'interested party' present at some great liquidation where he must keep his eye on what concerns him" (*AM1* 150; *AM2* 170). Likewise, instead of characterizing the "secrets" that Newman assumes Claire must be keeping from him as "hateful things," as he does in the earlier edition, the 1907 Newman calls them "things as depressing and detestable as inferior securities" (*AM1* 151; *AM2* 172). All of these similes ("banknote," "liquidation," and "securities") speak to Newman's status as

someone who has earned his wealth through investing rather than producing, and the latter two ("liquidation" and "inferior securities") suggest
that Newman is a speculator all too familiar with the risks and potential
rewards of short selling. Later, when Claire gives Newman up in order to
enter a convent, Newman's reaction is revised from "he didn't see his way
clear to giving her up" to thinking of it as a "case of straight violation of
his right of property" (*AM1* 245; *AM2* 286). This revision, which explicitly
reduces Claire to yet another piece of "property" that Newman is trying to
acquire, aligns the 1907 Newman with *A Hazard of New Fortune*'s Dryfoos,
who similarly thinks of his family and employees as his property and who,
like Newman, travels to Europe in order to find his "apotheosis."[55]

Remarkably, Claire, the primary object of Newman's acquisitiveness, responds to Newman more positively in the revised version of *The American*,
despite his more transparent aggression. In the earlier version, Claire pays
Newman the doubtful compliment that he is "dismally inoffensive," but
1907's Claire more emphatically states: "You're easier than we are, you're
easier than I am, and I quite see that you've reasons, of some sort, that
are as good as ours. . . . It's rather disappointing not to have anything to
show you or to tell you or to teach you, anything that you don't seem quite
capable of knowing and doing and feeling" (*AM1* 184; *AM2* 214). If Claire's
assertion that Newman is just as "capable" as the Bellegardes—and his "reasons" are just as "good" as theirs—is read as sincere rather than ironic, as I
contend it should be, then Claire seems to be hinting at some kind of convergence. Newman and the nation he represents have become equal to the
Bellegardes and, by implication, Europe. Claire's and Newman's interests,
values, and cultural practices may have originated in different parts of the
world, but they no longer stand in opposition to one another.

The key to understanding this suggestion of convergence between Claire
and Newman (and, by extension, the national cultures they represent) lies
in Newman's increased acquisitiveness. Not only Claire but the objects of
her European heritage and her language become objects of Newman's desire, and his more rapid mastery of her heritage in 1907 enables him to in-
filtrate Claire's European milieu with greater ease. James adjusts Newman's
character in the 1907 edition so that he comes to value what the European
aristocrats value, which increases his cultural capital and, consequently, his
aggressiveness as an acquirer. Before the revisions, his attitude toward the
art and architecture he takes in while touring the Continent is dismissive.
In a letter to Mrs. Tristram, he writes, "Belgium, Holland, Switzerland, Germany, Italy—I have been through the whole list, and I don't think I am any

the worse for it. I know more about Madonnas and church-steeples than I supposed any man could" (*AM1* 75). After the revisions, that same passage reads, "Belgium, Holland, Switzerland, Germany, Italy—I've taken the whole list as the bare-backed rider takes the paper hoops at the circus, and I'm not even yet out of breath. I carry about six volumes of Ruskin in my trunk" (*AM2* 82). If the 1907 Newman is actually reading those volumes of Ruskin, then he is a mental heavyweight in comparison to his former self.

The more important implication, however, is that Newman has a voracious appetite for European culture in 1907. When arranging for French lessons with M. Nioche, Newman originally took them up impulsively, as if on a lark: "'Oh yes, I should like to learn French,' Newman went on with democratic confidingness. . . . 'But if you learned my language, why shouldn't I learn yours?'" (*AM1* 25) The later Newman, however, is more conscious of the refinement that learning French would add to his conversation: "'Oh yes, I should like to converse with elegance,' Newman went on. . . . 'If you could catch on at all to our grand language—that of Shakespeare and Milton and Holy Writ—why shouldn't I catch on to yours?'" (*AM2* 26) This particular revision also subtly reveals that Newman is familiar with Shakespeare, Milton, and the King James Version of the Bible and that he is aware that Americans share in the cultural and linguistic traditions of Europe. Newman apparently learns the language much faster in the 1907 edition, too, even engaging in puns. "'Come,' said Newman, 'let us begin'" (*AM1* 54) becomes the more impressive "'*Allons, enfants de la patrie* [Come, children of the fatherland],' said Newman; 'let's begin!'" (*AM2* 59)—proving that Newman knows at least some of the lyrics of his instructor's national anthem.

Newman's desire to acquire representative objects of Old World culture (books, paintings, language, an aristocratic wife) constitutes an example of what historian Kristin L. Hoganson calls "the cosmopolitanism of consumption," by which she means the self-conscious efforts of late nineteenth-century American consumers to model their tastes on European styles.[56] Not unlike John W. Meyer, whose notion of "world models" I discussed in the previous chapter, Hoganson claims that this modeling of taste extended to expressions of imperialism: "Besides linking cosmopolitan household interiors to U.S. political and commercial expansion, . . . copying European styles provided opportunities to experience empire secondhand."[57] Hoganson focuses mainly on the wives, mothers, and daughters whose patterns of consumption played out in the domestic sphere, but Americans at the turn of the twentieth century were also concerned with the influence their speculator husbands, sons, and fathers exerted in the political sphere. In an 1899 speech that was widely circulated, Carl Schurz attributed the United States' entry into "that contest for territorial aggrandizement which distracts other nations and drives them far beyond their original design" to "the greed of speculators working upon our Government."[58] Thus within the context of the novel, Newman is literally acquiring objects from the Second French Empire, but his acquisitiveness represents Americans' willingness to model themselves on Europe to the extent of acquiring an overseas empire.

Some of James's revisions to *The American* suggest that he was aware that anti-imperialists had begun linking the McKinley administration's desire to annex the Philippines to economic speculation. While James does not revise Newman's account of his own career so as to make it explicit that he is involved in overseas trade, he does allow Newman to create several analogies between Asia and Europe that do not exist in the 1877 version. When, in the earlier edition, Newman forgets the names of several aristocrats to whom he has just been introduced, he says, "The people here look very much alike" (*AM1* 188), but in 1907's edition he adds, "Don't all Chinamen—even great Mandarins!—look very much the same to Occidentals?" (*AM2* 220). And a few pages later, he goes on to compare these aristocrats' atmosphere to the "odour of dried spices, something far-away and . . . Mongolian" (*AM2* 224). It is unclear if readers are meant to assume that Newman bases these comparisons on firsthand knowledge, which would make the revised version of *The American* even more global than I am contending it is, but it is clear that these revisions serve to render the European society Newman encounters analogous to Asia in his own mind—and thus just as open to his imperial acquisitiveness.[59]

What the revised version of *The American* emphasizes, then, is the threat of displacement that Newman and everything he represents poses to the Bellegardes, but it is his sense of entitlement rather than his nationality that becomes the most direct threat to their social stability. Instead of 1877 Newman's obliviousness and "tranquil unsuspectingness of the relativity of his own place in the social scale" (*AM1* 152), 1907 Newman's more assertive "air as of not having to account for his own place in the social scale" becomes "irritating" to the Bellegardes (*AM2* 174). The Bellegardes in turn become less explicit in their opposition to him, suggesting that their animosity no longer has anything to do with what his nationality is. Instead, the arrival of businessmen like him in Parisian society signals the inevitable triumph of democracy and capitalism, as well as the Bellegardes' own irrelevance. For a nobleman like Urbain de Bellegarde, who in both versions believes firmly in "the divine right of Henry of Bourbon, Fifth of his name, to the throne of France" (*AM1* 153; *AM2* 176), Newman likely represents what James calls in *The American Scene* "the monstrous form of Democracy, . . . the huge democratic broom that has made the clearance and that one seems to see brandished in the empty sky."[60] When James revised *The American*, he expanded upon this connection, and at least one revision emphasizes Urbain's distaste at the inevitable supremacy of the democracy Newman represents. Simply "holding his breath so as not to inhale the odour of democracy" in 1877 (*AM1* 153), 1907's Urbain "could but hold his breath so as not to inhale the strong smell—since who liked such *very* strong smells?—of a democracy so gregarious as to be unable *not* to engender heat and perspiration" (*AM2* 175, original emphasis). James's decision to retain the novel's original setting of Paris in the closing years of the Second Empire gives this particular revision a sharper edge. As a Bourbonite, Urbain may disapprove of Napoleon III, but the advent of the Third Republic in 1870 and the even more radical Paris Commune of 1871 would dash a real-life Bellegarde's hope for a return to monarchy.

THE AMERICAN SCENE: REVISITING AND REVISION

The connection between James's comments on democracy in *The American Scene* and Urbain's greater revulsion at democracy in the 1907 version of *The American* underscores the way in which that edition of *The American* gains meaning when read alongside *The American Scene*, which recounts James's 1904 return to the United States after a twenty-year absence. James undertook the journey in large part to negotiate the deal with Charles Scribner's Sons that led to the New York Edition, including the revised version of *The American*; however, as depicted in *The American Scene*, this trip also enabled him to see firsthand the evidence that his nation was well on its way to supplanting Britain as the world center of economic, political, and cultural power. Together, *The American Scene* and the revised edition of *The American* constitute both an acknowledgement on James's part of his native land's emergence as a global power during his absence and a two-pronged analysis of the larger global cultural economy that the United States had entered and begun to reshape as a result of its growing power. The complementarities between *The American Scene* and the 1907 edition of *The American* thus simultaneously result from James's renewed impressions of the United States and result in a significant downplaying on James's part of the importance of national identity in providing hard-and-fast rules for understanding either personal or social relationships.

James's revision of the relationship between Newman and Valentin in *The American*, for instance, serves as an aesthetic response to James's encounters with immigrants, which he describes memorably in *The American Scene*. Throughout the four chapters he devotes to New York City in the latter work, James obsesses at length over the presence of the millions of immigrants who had made their home in the United States during his absence and the ethnic diversity they had brought physically into the nation. His anxieties become most acute as he recounts his visit to Ellis Island, already the most famous point of entry for immigrants of the period. James describes the scene as a "visible act of ingurgitation on the part of our body politic and social" and imagines that, like himself, "any sensitive citizen who may have happened to 'look in' . . . comes back from his visit not at all the same person" (*AS* 426). Shaken to its core is his certainty in what makes an American an American. "One's supreme relation, as one had always put it," James writes, "was one's relation to one's country—a conception made up so largely of one's countrymen and one's countrywomen" (*AS* 427). With his visit to Ellis Island, however, "the idea of the country itself underwent something of that profane overhauling through which it appears to suffer the indignity of change" (*AS* 427). These immigrants have literally displaced James. Their influx into the country occurred after his own expatriation, of course, but their presence also overturns James's belief that ethnic, social, and cultural homogeneity forms the foundation of national identity—what he calls "the luxury of some such close and sweet and *whole* national consciousness as that of the Switzer and the Scot" (*AS* 428, original emphasis).

The alteration that James's conception of nationality undergoes mirrors the one that takes place in Ernst Renan's famous 1882 lecture "What Is a Nation?" Renan's essay enacts a shift from thinking about a nation as something tied to race, language, or another essential quality to thinking about it as a convenient construct produced each day by "consent, the desire to live together, . . . a daily plebiscite."[61] For James, the immigrants who arrive at Ellis Island demonstrate the degree to which, as Renan puts it, "desire to live together" rather than some "close . . . and *whole* national consciousness" now defines American identity. These immigrants "desire" to become Americans, too, and native-born Americans must "surrender and accept the [new] orientation" of nationality, which exists as an act of will (*AS* 427). Eventually, James takes comfort in realizing that immigration has always been integral to U.S. history: "Who and what is an alien, when it comes to that, in a country peopled from the first . . . by migrations at once extremely recent, perfectly traceable, and urgently required?" (*AS* 459). Yet James is nagged by a lingering suspicion that these immigrants, poor and crude though they may be, are no less cosmopolitan than he, the son of privilege. "Foreign as they might be, newly inducted as they might be," he notes, "they were *at home*" (*AS* 460, original emphasis). What James seems to recognize is that immigrants comprise a type of global citizenry, capable of being "at home" even in their foreignness, and that immigration is itself a significant force within the larger global cultural economy. I follow up on both these points in the next chapter.

The new notion of national identity that James adopts as a result of his visit to Ellis Island resonates in his revisions of *The American*. As nearly every study of these revisions has observed, Newman's friendship with Claire's younger brother Valentin warms immensely, and Valentin's role as a French foil to the American Newman becomes less pronounced. Reframing their relationship enables James to switch from an essentialist view of national identity to a functionalist one. In 1877, Valentin is "a foreigner to his finger-tips" (*AM1* 89), implying that his foreignness or nationality is a form of identity that is tied to his body. In 1907, however, he is "a foreigner to the last roll of his so frequently rotary *r*" (*AM2* 98), suggesting that foreignness is the result of something one does or says rather than something one is. This functionalist attitude toward the concept of national identity suggests the influence of the Pragmatist philosophy of James's brother William, who tied meaning and identity to experience rather than essence.[62]

Newman's intensified friendship with Valentin also eliminates much of Newman's ethnocentrism and inability to fathom foreign customs. Removed entirely is Newman's condescending opinion that "all Frenchman are of a frothy and imponderable substance" (*AM1* 95). When the two men debate Newman's chances of winning Claire, Newman is also much quicker on the uptake regarding his lack of an aristocratic title:

1877	1907
"Why, you are not noble, for instance," he [Valentin] said.	"Well, for instance you're not, as we call it, if I'm not mistaken, 'born.'"
"The devil I am not!" exclaimed Newman.	"The devil I'm not!" Newman exclaimed.
"Oh," said Bellegarde, a little more seriously, "I did not know you had a title."	"Oh," said his friend a little more seriously, "I didn't

"A title? What do you mean by a title?" asked Newman. "A count, a duke, a marquis? I don't know anything about that, I don't know who is and who is not. But I say I am noble. I don't exactly know what you mean by it, but it's a fine word and a fine idea; I put in a claim to it."
(*AM1* 105)

know you had—well, your quarterings."
"Ah, your quarterings are your little local matter!"
(*AM2* 117)

Newman still dismisses the objection that Claire's nobility will stand in his way in 1907, but he has grown sophisticated enough to know what Valentin means when referring to "quarterings," a term in heraldry. Furthermore, he is confident enough in his own social status not to lay claim to nobility but to dismiss it as a "local matter."

To be sure, in neither the 1907 edition of *The American* nor *The American Scene* does James entirely abandon his "theme" of national contrasts in favor of a vision of global homogeneity. Even in its revised form, *The American* ends without intermarriage, despite Newman's status as a more serious contender for Claire's hand, and as with many travelogues, much of *The American Scene* is dedicated to cataloging and analyzing differences between U.S. and European cities, architecture, customs, and so forth. Moreover, James's decision to retain the definite article in the title of *The American* continues to reify American national identity. James invites his readers to view Newman not just as *a* representative U.S. citizen but as *the* representative U.S. citizen.[63] Even this reification, however, receives qualification as a result of James's revisions. In the novel's second paragraph, during the initial description of Newman, the 1877 edition employs the adjective "national" twice: "An observer, with anything of an eye for national types, would have had no difficulty in determining the local origin of this undeveloped connoisseur, and indeed such an observer might have felt a certain humorous relish of the almost ideal completeness with which he filled out the national mould. The gentleman on the divan was a powerful specimen of an American" (*AM1* 17–18). In 1907, James removes "national" altogether, thereby deemphasizing the role of the nation in determining a person's identity: "An observer with anything of an eye for local types would have had no difficulty in referring this candid connoisseur to the scene of his origin, and indeed such an observer might have made an ironic point of the almost ideal completeness with which he filled out the mould of race. The gentleman on the divan was the superlative American" (*AM2* 17–18). James still draws attention to Newman's Americanness but emphasizes its arbitrariness: it results from the happenstance of birthplace ("scene of his origin") and ancestry ("the mould of race"), not by conforming to some sort of preexisting essence ("national type"). Referring to Newman as "the superlative American" instead of "a powerful specimen of an American" also removes a scientific term for comparing and classifying types ("specimen").[64]

James's 1907 portrait of national character thus makes sense not as an abstract concept but as something that results from the context of traveling across state boundaries. It is in Europe that Newman becomes *the* American rather than *the* businessman or *the* Civil War veteran. Newman's Americanness, in other words, is constituted by his status as the citizen of one state in interaction with the citizens of other states. In drawing attention to James's awareness of an *emerging* global cultural economy, therefore, I wish to emphasize that the convergence of national values was—and continues to remain—gradual and that James's later writings expand upon and problematize, without wholly discarding, his earlier concepts of how cultures contrast at an international level.

James acknowledges the gradual nature of this convergence of national cultures explicitly in *The American Scene*, when he explains his own decision for relocating to Europe. In what is perhaps the most confessional passage of the book, he writes:

> It was "Europe" that had, in very ancient days, held out to the yearning young American some likelihood of impressions more numerous and various and of a higher intensity than those he might gather on the native scene; and it was doubtless in conformity with some such desire more finely and more frequently to vibrate that he had originally begun to consult the European oracle. This had led, in the event, to his settling to live for long years in the very precincts, as it were, of the temple. (*AS* 654)

Echoing his early writings, most notably his criticism of "the coldness, the thinness, the blankness, ... the absent things in American life" in *Hawthorne* (1879), James here suggests that learning how to "vibrate" more intensely, rather than simply collecting bits of knowledge, necessitated abandoning the United States and moving to Europe.[65] The longer James had resided in Europe, however, the more that "higher intensity" had worn off. "The European complexity," he continues, "working clearer to one's vision, had grown usual and calculable. . . . Romance and mystery—in other words the *amusement* of interest—would have therefore at last to provide for themselves elsewhere" (*AS* 654–55, original emphasis). James's use of the word "complexity" is significant, insofar as it implies that whichever "elsewhere" James selects would have to equal or supersede the complexity that he had mastered in Europe.

James, of course, selected the United States: "It was American civilization that had begun to spread itself thick and pile itself high, in short, in proportion as the other, the foreign exhibition had taken to writing itself plain; and to a world so amended and enriched, accordingly, the expatriated observer, with his relaxed curiosity reviving and his limp imagination once more on the stretch, couldn't fail again to address himself" (*AS* 655). Ironically, although James still decries the United States' lack of history and high culture and Americans' lack of discrimination throughout *The American Scene*, returning to the nation he had forsaken so many years before serves as a means of aesthetic rejuvenation ("reviving" his "relaxed curiosity" and "stretching" his "limp imagination"). Tellingly, this renewal is possible because the United States has "amended and enriched" itself. James's choice of words—synonyms for "revised" and "amassed wealth"—could not be more appropriate, indicating that he was as aware as Brandeis of the need to revise the image of American society in light of its altered economic conditions.

That James found his own artistic regeneration in the "spread" of "American civilization" becomes clear when one stops to consider the scope of *The American Scene*: some 150,000 words and presumably only half the length of the project James originally conceived. Unlike his other travel books, such as *English Hours* (1905) and *Italian Hours* (1909), both of which compiled preexisting self-contained essays, *The American Scene* exhibits a sometimes remarkable structural coherency that subtly links, for example, his discussions of immigrants with his discussions of the United States' growing imperial power. (James's decision to use the singular *scene* in the title rather than the plural *hours* underscores both the book's coherency and, through an allusion to the visual and dramatic arts, its overarching concern with describing an entire culture instead of recounting disparate temporal experiences.) Thus when James bemoans the bourgeois tastes of his fellow countrymen, he finds solace in reminding himself that his "vision has a kind of analogy; for what were the Venetians, after all, but the children of a Republic and of trade?" (AS 507) This Venetian analogy seems to have struck James as particularly appropriate because he returns to it in his chapter on the Bowery: "As the Venetian Republic, in the person of the Doge, used to go forth, on occasion, to espouse the Adriatic, so it is quite as if the American, incarnate in its greatest port, were for ever throwing the nuptial ring to the still more richly-endowed Atlantic" (AS 525).

In the above passage, James is referring once again to the immigrants who had transformed the ethnic and cultural character of New York City, but the images of trade and overseas expansion connoted by this passage simultaneously highlight the fact that the United States, like Venice, was a republic that had acquired an empire. Indeed, when James finally arrives in Washington, he remarks on how that city's features "all more or less majestically [play] the administrative, or as we nowadays put it, Imperial part" (AS 633). Here, James employs "imperial" for its political meaning, but in light of the commercial foundations that the U.S. and Venetian empires shared, it is also in keeping with Brandeis's and Lenin's economic usage.

The city of Washington, with its manifestations of newly attained "Imperial" power, presents James with the greatest number of political, economic, and cultural convergences between the United States and the more established imperial powers of Europe. The architecture and landscape of Capitol Hill, for instance, provide evidence of "the *democratic assimilation* of the greater dignities and majesties" of the Roman model (AS 650, original emphasis). Even when James notes that the similarities between America's capital city and the capitals of Europe are as yet merely superficial— "Washington talks about herself, and about almost nothing else; falling superficially indeed, on that ground, but into line with the other capitals" (AS 635)—he never doubts the inevitability of U.S. hegemony. Commenting on the ostensible "historic void" out of which U.S. power has sprung, he worries:

> The danger "in Europe" is of their having too many things to say, and too many others to distinguish these from; the danger in the States is of their not having things enough—with enough tone and resonance furthermore to give them. What therefore will the multitudinous and elaborate forms of the Washington to come have to "say," and what, above all, besides gold and silver, stone and marble and trees and flowers, will they be able to say it *with*? (AS 648, original emphasis)

Driving home the central problem to which he and Brandeis were both responding, James answers his own rhetorical question by pointing out that, in the absence of other qualifications, the ability to have a "say" in the U.S. government is all too often "*directly* made by money" (*AS* 648, original emphasis). Without some sort of intervention, the "Washington to come" may be populated with Christopher Newmans. While he is never as specific in identifying solutions as Brandeis is, James concludes that some agent—presumably the state itself, considering that he is discussing the federal government in this passage—must cultivate other "interests [and] values . . . outside the mere economic" that will provide the United States with the cultural authority to match its economic power (*AS* 648–49). In other words, like Brandeis, James points to cultural economy's alternate mode of valuation as a means of counterbalancing the purely monetary power of those "speculators" that Carl Schurz identified as the driving force behind U.S. imperial expansion.

James ends his chapter on Washington with the haunting image of three Native Americans "dispossessed of forest and prairie" (*AS* 652). Just as clearly as the "immaculate" streets of the city or the buildings on Capitol Hill, they offer physical proof of the United States' emergence as an imperial power; for James, whose mind was "fed betimes on the Leatherstocking Tales," their presence confirms that the United States, like the empires of Europe, has strode "the bloody footsteps of time" (*AS* 652–53). That James himself was haunted by these three Native Americans is evinced by the fact that he returns to them three chapters later, in the penultimate paragraph of *The American Scene* (in a section that was cut by the publisher of the first U.S. edition). In a rather surprising moment of identification with their plight that perhaps grows out of his own sense of having been "dispossessed" by immigrants, James takes his American readers to task for not making that bloody imperial legacy amount to something more than it does:

> If I were one of the painted savages you have dispossessed . . . beauty and charm would be for me in the solitude you have ravaged, and I should owe you my grudge for every disfigurement and every violence, for every wound with which you have caused the face of the land to bleed. No, since I accept your ravage, what strikes me is the long list of the arrears of your undone. . . . You touch the great lonely land—as one feels it still to be—only to plant upon it some ugliness about which, never dreaming of the grace of apology or contrition, you then proceed to brag with a cynicism all your own. (*AS* 734–35)

Perhaps more than any other rhetorical maneuver in *The American Scene*, James's identification of an alternative cultural economy that Americans have "ravaged"—the lost "beauty and charm" that these "painted" Native Americans physically embody—emphasizes the degree to which the United States has taken its place in an aggressive and expanding global cultural economy.

In light of this meditation on the violence that has been suppressed in official and quasi-official accounts of American history, such as the Leatherstocking Tales, some of James's revisions to *The American* take on a slightly sinister tone. I conclude with one such alteration that appears in the first chapter of the novel. In both versions of *The American*, James withholds his protagonist's name for several paragraphs, allowing himself to drive home the symbolism of the name with a joke. While making arrangements with Noémie Nioche for copies of the artworks that surround them in the Louvre, Newman presents her with his card. The changes that James makes to their ensuing exchange reveal the profound shift in his thinking about Euro-American relations that had occurred during the intervening thirty years:

1877	1907
And she took it and read his name: "Christopher Newman." Then she tried to repeat it aloud, and laughed at her bad accent. "Your English names are so droll!"	And she took it and read his name: "Christopher Newman." Then she tried to repeat it aloud and laughed at her bad accent. "Your English names are not *commodes* [easy] to say!"
"Droll?" said Mr. Newman, laughing too. "Did you ever hear of Christopher Columbus?"	"Well, mine's partly celebrated," said Mr. Newman, laughing too. "Did you never hear of Christopher Columbus?"
"*Bien sûr*! [Of course!] He invented America; a very great man. And is he your patron?	"*Bien sûr*! He first showed Americans the way to Europe; a very great man. And is he your patron?
"My patron?"	"My patron?"
"Your patron-saint, in the calendar."	"Your patron saint, such as we all have."
"Oh, exactly; my parents named me for him." (*AM1* 21)	"Oh, exactly; my parents named me after him." (*AM2* 21)

In both versions, James sets up his punch line through slippage. Either Noémie genuinely does not know who Christopher Columbus was, or more likely, she is unable to communicate precisely what it was Columbus accomplished. Either way, her mistaken assumption that Columbus is Newman's patron saint suggests that the novel's Christopher is as much on a voyage of discovery as his more famous namesake.

James's revision of Noémie's muddled description of what Columbus accomplished is even more suggestive. In 1877, James was content to create humor out of her confusion of the verbs "invent" and "discover." The implication of the joke anticipates Renan's views on nationhood: Noémie's confusion invites readers to consider the idea that the United States is a construction, a country that has been "invented" as opposed to one *Anderson* that has come into being organically through ethnic and linguistic homogeneity. In 1907, by contrast, James's humor results from Noémie's confusion of direct and indirect objects. She should have said that Columbus "first showed *Europeans* the way to *America*." Thus the joke remains an outgrowth of the vagaries of grammar, as highlighted by the conversation of two people who do not share the same mother tongue, but the implications of the revised sentence are richer, especially when considered in light of James's comments on the plight of Native Americans in *The American Scene*. In a very real sense, Columbus did show (Native) Americans the way to—and the ways of—Europe. He both transported captive American Indians back to Europe and laid the foundation for the genocidal policies of European and U.S. imperial administrators. Newman's facetious admission that Columbus is his patron saint is therefore an admission that he is the beneficiary of the bloody imperial legacy that Columbus founded and that James denounces in *The American Scene* through his own identification with the three Native Americans he encountered in Washington.

Finally, on an even more basic level, Noémie's new response also evokes an image of transatlantic exchange: that the way from Europe to America is simultaneously the way from America to Europe. Consequently, while her answer may not be technically correct, it is entirely appropriate to the larger issues that concern James. The ramifications of Newman's presence in Europe, including his effect on the lives of Claire and other Europeans, prove that the United States has its role to play on the international stage, too. The United States, James demonstrates, is not simply an extension of Europe, nor does history and culture flow one-directionally westward. At the same time, the fact that Noémie can confuse two *continents*, let alone two individual countries (she does assume at first that Newman is English because of his name), indicates how difficult it is to sustain simple national binary values in James's fiction. Both of these factors—the increased international importance of the United States and the convergence of national values in an emerging global cultural economy—become more prominent in *The American* as a result of James's revisions. In the end, the world of the revised version of the novel is more like the world surrounding Henry James himself in 1907: it is global.

CHAPTER FOUR

Migration Systems and Literary Production

The Global Routes of Abraham Cahan and Knut Hamsun

lfred Stieglitz's *The Steerage*, taken in 1907 and first published in
1911, has become one of the most iconic images from the age of
mass migration to the United States at the turn of the twentieth
century. In recent years, Stieglitz's photograph has graced the cover of the
second volume of the third edition of *The Heath Anthology of American Literature* (1998), thereby underscoring its editors' long-standing commitment
to expanding the canon of American literature by including, among other
neglected texts, immigrant writings. The iconicity of *The Steerage* is somewhat ironic, however, because Stieglitz was traveling eastward from New
York to Germany when he took the photograph and thus captured steerage
passengers returning to Europe rather than arriving in the United States.[1]
Even those commentators who have been aware of this context have sometimes been unable to keep from reading more traditional immigrant experiences, including their own, into Stieglitz's photograph. Alfred Kazin,
who included *The Steerage* as the frontispiece to *A Walker in the City* (1951),
wonders about the people in the image at length in his autobiographical
New York Jew (1978), particularly "the figure of a young woman standing
with her back to me": "I dimly knew that Stieglitz had taken the photograph
going *to* Europe. The figures ... were returning, but no matter. ... She is my
mother—in that picture and for that year" (original emphasis).[2] Other commentators interested in exactly why these travelers were returning to Europe have hypothesized that Stieglitz's subjects were hopeful immigrants
who had been rejected by U.S. immigration authorities at Ellis Island for
financial, health, or political reasons.[3]

What is striking about these responses to *The Steerage* is the degree to
which they reinforce the notion of settling in the United States as the only
possible objective of the figures in the photograph. This sort of logic demands either that Stieglitz's subjects be reincorporated vicariously into

Alfred Stieglitz's *The Steerage*, 1907 (small-format photogravure).
Private collection; courtesy of Christie's Images and the Bridgeman Art Library.

American history through the success stories of Kazin and others or that their forcible exclusion by the state be acknowledged and thereby partially redressed. Such interpretations tend to obscure a third possibility—one that places much more emphasis on the agency of the immigrants themselves but simultaneously destabilizes the accepted narrative of immigration. Although Stieglitz biographer Richard Whelan allows for the possibility that the people captured in the photograph may have been the victims of increasingly strict anti-immigration policies, he suggests that "most were probably 'birds of passage,' skilled artisans who worked in the construction trades and more or less commuted between Europe and America in two-year cycles."[4] In other words, the immigrants who appear in *The Steerage* may have chosen to return to Europe after having accomplished whatever goals had brought them temporarily to the United States in the first place, possibly with the intention of migrating to America again at a later time.

The status of these so-called birds of passage or "sojourners" and the wider networks that enabled the phenomenon of return migration may rank among the most important yet neglected dimensions of U.S. immigration history. If the numbers compiled by the Office [later Bureau] of Immigration are correct, then the rate of return migration was extremely high during the years that mark the peak of European migration to North America. Between 1908, when the government began recording the number of emigrants leaving the United States, through 1913, an estimated 5,490,877 immigrants entered and an estimated 1,760,429 emigrants exited the country, making the rate of return roughly 32 percent.[5] This statistic is corroborated by historians who have studied return migration of specific nationalities. The estimated rate of return migration ranged from about 20 percent for the Scandinavian countries to as much as 50 percent for Italy.[6] On one hand, these numbers suggest that a much broader understanding of turn-of-the-century cosmopolitanism than what we tend to assume is in order. If working-class migrants were capable of traversing oceans on multiple occasions, then they certainly could lay as much of a claim to the title "cosmopolitan" as did travelers from more privileged backgrounds, such as Henry James and Edith Wharton. On the other hand, the high rates of return migration would indicate that these birds of passage probably had considerable impact upon their home cultures once they returned. In the case of the Scandinavian countries, with their relatively small populations, how could some 400,000 returning emigrants *not* affect the local culture and influence their neighbors' perceptions of the United States?[7] In short, the phenomenon of return migration and the networks of travel and communication that enabled such movement provide potentially very rich historical examples of cultural globalization.

Birds of passage and their patterns of circulation, however, do not fit into traditional accounts of immigration to the United States during the late nineteenth and early twentieth centuries. As Philip R. Yannella has noted, their willingness to return to Europe challenges "the official and unofficial core narrative of America as the desired destiny of the world's multitudes."[8] Certainly, the hope—or the impossibility—of returning to one's ethnic homeland often serves as an important motif in the writings of Maxine Hong Kingston, Theresa Hak Kyung Cha, Amy Tan, Sandra Cisneros, and other recent American authors who belong to ethnic minorities, and several literary critics have picked up on this recurring motif in contemporary ethnic fiction.[9] Nevertheless, Kristin L. Hoganson maintains that the dynamic processes at work in the transnational networks that immigrants established before the Second World War remain a significant blind spot among historians and cultural critics: despite "the voluminous literature on immigration, . . . until recently, these histories have focused on the assimilation of immigrants into American ways. . . . Historians have marshaled the history of immigration in behalf of the Americanization-of-the-world argument."[10]

Indeed, those scholars who celebrate the contributions of marginalized immigrant authors to American culture often inadvertently reinscribe the traditional model of assimilation: migration as a one-way journey that involves moving from some other country and settling permanently in the United States. In his groundbreaking 1986 study *Beyond Ethnicity*, for instance, Werner Sollors sought to place ethnic texts at the center of the American literary tradition by examining how they highlight "the conflict between contractual and hereditary, self-made and ancestral, definitions of American identity—between *consent* and *descent*—as the central drama in American culture" (original emphasis).[11] For Sollors, the constructions of ethnicity in such texts, which are predominantly about *becoming* American, serve to critique essentialist notions of American national identity. Further cementing the centrality of immigrants to U.S. history, Matthew Frye Jacobson argues in *Barbarian Virtues* that the nineteenth-century influx of immigrants provided an economic basis for U.S. colonial expansion through their labor and supplied native-born Americans with intellectual and symbolic resources for conceptualizing—and for ranking hierarchically—a variety of non-Anglo-Saxon peoples. "As modern American nationalism took shape within an international crucible of immigration and empire building," Jacobson writes, "American integration into the world economic system in this period of breathtaking industrialization exposed a rather profound dependence upon foreign peoples as imported workers for factories and as overseas consumers of American products."[12] Despite their thoughtful readings of the give-and-take relationship between historical ethnic communities and the larger U.S. culture in which they became embedded, Sollors and Jacobson still privilege the experiences of immigrants who underwent the process of naturalization. Focusing on the problems and debates surrounding the question of Americanization, they tend to overlook the transnational networks that many immigrant communities maintained in order to preserve a means of returning, physically as well as culturally, to their homelands.

While there is perhaps no way of establishing definitively why the anonymous travelers of *The Steerage* were en route to Europe, the possibility that Stieglitz's iconic photograph immortalizes a few of the millions of "birds of passage" provides a dramatic illustration of the existence of global routes of circulation that connected the United States to the rest of the world through the working-class migrants who traveled them. In this chapter, I propose a model for examining the literary work that some of these migrants produced that focuses on immigration itself as a process of circulation rather than absorption. Specifically, I argue that texts about and by immigrants often reveal the vital role immigrants played in the globalization of America and that, by establishing and maintaining transnational networks, immigrant communities in the United States both facilitated and, at times, challenged the worldwide spread of American capitalism and culture. I also contend that the existence of these migration networks helped shape the debate about immigration reform in the United States in significant ways. Rather than supplant the contributions of Sollors, Jacobson, and other scholars who have exposed the multidirectionality of Americanization, however, I seek to extend their multidirectional approach even further by focusing on how migrant communities simultaneously remade American culture at home and helped disseminate particular conceptions of American culture abroad. In order to illustrate the role that these migration systems played in the consolidation of the United States' position at the center of the world economy, I will focus on two authors who participated in the global circulation of American money, products, and culture that resulted directly from the establishment of transnational migratory networks at the turn of the twentieth century: Abraham Cahan, who chose to remain in the United States and whose *The Rise of David Levinsky*

(1917) remains one of the classic novels of immigration, and Knut Hamsun, whose own attempts to settle in the United States met with failure and who later wrote a series of critical studies of the shortcomings of American society and culture, including most notably *On the Cultural Life of Modern America* (1889).[13]

The model of circulation I am advocating here borrows heavily from the work of sociologist Orlando Patterson, who has identified a phenomenon that he calls the "migration system." According to Patterson, a migration system is "any movement of persons between states, the social, economic, and cultural effects of such movements, and the patterned interactions among such effects."[14] By definition, these systems follow specific routes of migration and thus extend beyond national borders, often encompassing multiple countries or regions of countries, and they frequently result in ethnic and cultural enclaves in major cities. Patterson locates such a system—the emerging West Atlantic system—around the present-day Caribbean, with Miami serving as a major hub for immigrants (both legal and illegal), refugees, and migrant workers from Cuba, the Dominican Republic, Columbia, Mexico, and elsewhere—many of whom intend to return eventually to their respective homelands. More recently, historian Nancy Foner has argued that such migration systems represent a continuation of earlier historical processes. Specifically examining Jewish and Italian immigrant communities in New York between 1880 and 1923, Foner reveals how those immigrants "maintained extensive, and intensive, transnational ties and operated in what social scientists now call a transnational social field" through regular communication, business transactions, return visits, and so forth.[15] To a certain extent, Patterson's "migration system" and Foner's "transnational social field" already find their counterpart in existing literary and cultural studies scholarship on diasporic literatures, the most famous and influential of which remains Paul Gilroy's examination of the African diaspora's cultural production in *The Black Atlantic*. Gilroy's focus on "the middle passage, on the various projects for redemptive return to an African homeland, on the circulation of ideas and activists as well as the movement of key cultural and political artifacts," continues to serve as a model of transnational literary analysis, but the *enforced* migration of many diasporas is often their most salient historical feature and distinguishes them from the migratory routes that Cahan and Hamsun followed and that other American writers attempted to make sense of at the turn of the twentieth century.[16]

Likewise, Cahan's and Hamsun's shared interest in representing the global dimensions of their own migration systems distinguishes their work from a much longer tradition with which both, but especially Hamsun, could be associated: the fictional and nonfictional narratives of Europeans encountering American society, including Frances Trollope's *Domestic Manners of the Americans* (1832), Alexis de Tocqueville's *Democracy in America* (1835–40), Charles Dickens's *American Notes* (1842), Ferdinand Kürnberger's *The Man Who Became Weary of America* (1855), Fanny Kemble's *Journal of a Residence on a Georgian Plantation* (1863), and Oscar Wilde's *Impressions of America* (delivered as a lecture in 1883). In contrast with the writings of Cahan, Hamsun, and later immigrant authors, these earlier texts are generally more concerned with interpreting aspects of U.S. society and culture than with exploring the multidirectional implications of Americanization. With the exception of Trollope and Kemble, none of these earlier writers can even be considered immigrants. Tocqueville, Dickens, Wilde, and Kemble were already more or less established figures in their professions when they traveled to the United States, and Kürnberger had not even been to North America when he wrote his novel.[17]

Thus the question of just how authentically the immigrant experience had been represented remained open to realists as late as the 1890s. In his review of Cahan's first novel, *Yekl* (1896), William Dean Howells noted that fiction "is only just beginning to deal with" the reality of urban life and that its absence from American fiction was due largely to the fact that few writers until the 1890s had been capable of reproducing the "composite and strange" patterns of speech that "the mixture of races" had produced in New York.[18] Consistent with his emphasis on dialect as a means of representing intermingling voices and ideas, Howells praises Cahan's handling of dialect and "the picturesque" as even "stronger" than Stephen Crane's in *Maggie* (1893), and Howells attributes this superiority to Cahan's status as "a writer of foreign birth."[19] In other words, Howells recognizes Cahan's unique ground-level perspective of the immigrant experience as something new in American literature, and it is precisely this newness, which Cahan captures through his skillful use of dialect and local color, that helps give his work—and that of other immigrant writers—access to a U.S. literary market increasingly focused on such global processes.[20]

Having already discussed how late American realists employed dialect to capture the "composite" aspects of American society in the second chapter, I concentrate in this chapter on the transnational routes of circulation that both structured immigrant experiences and texts at the turn of the twentieth century and enabled those immigrants to participate in or resist the expansion of the United States' economic and cultural reach throughout the world. As I demonstrate in the final section of this chapter, the United States' expanding global power gives a sense of urgency to Knut Hamsun's depiction of Americanization that does not appear in the writings of Tocqueville, Dickens, or Kürnberger. The efforts of Cahan and Hamsun to represent the individual immigrant's position within larger migration systems thus speak to an increased awareness of the United States' role within the international community.

"WHAT, OH, WHAT AGAIN, WERE HE AND HIS GOING TO MAKE OF US?"

Repeatedly throughout *The American Scene* (1907), as noted in the preceding chapter, Henry James attempts to come to terms with the changes to U.S. society and culture that the vast influx of immigrants had caused during his twenty-year absence. Recounting his reactions to a Yiddish theater company's performance, James comments on the linguistic inventiveness of the boss of the company, and he eventually concedes that immigrant communities are never merely absorbed into the larger American culture but that they instead contribute to its continued formation and circulation. Gavin Jones's reading of this passage emphasizes James's concern over "the effect [foreign] languages would have on the nature of English itself."[21] James thus seems to anticipate, if not entirely to agree with, Michel de Certeau's claim that the immigrant is "the anonymous hero" of modernity because "the immigrant . . . puts our society to the test, for it is by its capacity to tolerate that which does not respect its norms and traditions that the tolerance and open-mindedness of a society, and the real quality of its politics of communication, are judged."[22] Of his encounter with the Yiddish impresario, James writes:

> What remains with me is this expression, and the colour and the quality of it, and the free familiarity and the "damned foreign impudence," with so much taken for granted, and all the hitches and lapses, all the solutions of continuity, in *his* inward assimilation of our heritage and point of view, matched as they were, on our own side, by such signs of large and comparatively witless concession. What, oh, what again, were he and his going to make of us? (original emphasis)[23]

On the surface, this passage seems to acknowledge that the processes of immigration, assimilation, and Americanization work in more than one direction. As immigrants adapt themselves to their new environment, taking on the linguistic and social characteristics of the United States, they simultaneously produce changes within the culture of that environment. By drawing attention to the likelihood that, just as he is trying to make sense of the culture of these immigrants, they will "make" something new "of us," James raises the concern that the Americanization of immigrants also involves the re-Americanization of native-born U.S. citizens.

Read from this perspective, *The American Scene* takes its place in a much wider discourse on the social and cultural ramifications of the nineteenth-century influx of immigrants. From 1880 onwards, Americans began framing immigration as a national problem and empowering the state to regulate it as never before. In 1882, Congress passed the Chinese Exclusion Act, the first of what would become a series of ever more restrictive anti-immigration laws that culminated in the Quota Acts of 1921 and 1924. In 1885, Josiah Strong singled out immigration as the first and most pressing of the seven "perils" he identified as threatening U.S. society in *Our Country*.[24] Although Strong refrained from suggesting that immigration needed to be curtailed, Nathaniel Shaler, a professor of paleontology and geology at Harvard and an adherent of Social Darwinism, felt no qualms about doing so in an 1893 *Atlantic Monthly* essay entitled "European Peasants as Immigrants," perhaps the single most important anti-immigration screed of the period.[25] Unambiguously tying the issue of immigration to assumptions about the nation's need for racial and ethnic purity, Shaler claimed, "We have suffered grievously from the folly of our predecessors in recklessly admitting an essentially alien folk into this land. . . . They [our predecessors] have imperiled the future of their own race in the land best fitted for its nurture. . . . A true democracy cannot be maintained in the presence of a large alien class."[26]

Among the many implications of Shaler's argument was the belief that national identity and a democratic form of government are possible only through racial and ethnic homogeneity. Citing as evidence the recent disenfranchisement of African Americans through Jim Crow legislation in the South, Shaler contended that the introduction of diversity into a community compels the already established members of that community to "maintain their authority in a forcible way": "History makes it plain that a race oligarchy almost inevitably arises wherever a superior and an inferior variety of people are brought together."[27] As far as Shaler was concerned, the "superior" variety of people in the United States were not just white but "the Aryan variety of mankind"—by which he meant those Americans descended from Northern European or Germanic peoples.[28] In identifying the United States as a "land best fitted" for Aryan peoples, Shaler sought to limit American identity to those citizens who descended from English and German settlers, thus racializing the nation and suggesting that some races and ethnicities were simply incapable of becoming part of the body politic. The final implication was, of course, that the body politic ought to begin excluding members of those "inferior" races by preventing them from immigrating into the country in the first place.

The ambivalences, anxieties, and outright hostilities that Shaler and other Americans exhibited toward immigrants were partly due to the fact that they were witnessing one of the greatest mass migrations in human history. Between 1881 and 1924, an explosion of migration took place, with literally millions of Germans, Italians, Scandinavians, and Eastern Europeans making new homes for themselves in the United States. While foreign-born immigrants had always comprised a sizeable portion of the population, especially after hundreds of thousands of Irish and Chinese immigrants had flooded into the country during the 1840s and 1850s, the total number of immigrants rose dramatically during the final two decades of the nineteenth century. For example, between 1845 and 1851, during and immediately after the Irish Potato Famine and shortly after the Taiping Rebellion began in China, the estimated number of immigrants entering the United States was 1,776,752. Thirty-five years later, during the relatively more stable 1880–86 period, the estimated number of immigrants had more than doubled to 3,767,143, despite the fact that immigration from China was almost entirely halted from 1882 onwards. In 1905, while Henry James was revisiting his homeland, the one-year total surpassed one million immigrants for the first time in U.S. history. The demographics of the United States were changing in observable ways, with a greater number of immigrants from a wider range of countries arriving than ever before. Particularly troubling to Shaler and others was the increase in the number of immigrants from Southern and Eastern, as opposed to Northern and Western, Europe. The population of the United States was becoming increasingly more diverse, and immigration was playing its part in globalizing the nation and its culture. Fears within some quarters that these demographic shifts proved that the United States was in the process of becoming foreign to itself were perhaps to be expected.[29]

There is, however, another way of reading James's question, "What, oh, what again, were he and his going to make of us?" To "make," in this context, could also mean to "interpret," which is precisely what James himself tries to do throughout *The American Scene*. Certainly, James frames his encounter with the Yiddish theater impresario no differently from any of the various other "impressions" of the United States that he attempts to interpret retrospectively. James's anxiety, then, may arise from the recognition that he and the American culture he represents are being interpreted, too. Read from this perspective, James's recognition of at least two other agents of interpretation ("he *and his*") takes on a somewhat disquieting ambiguity: who and where are the impresario's "his"? James could simply be referring to the rest of the theatrical troupe, but he also could be gesturing more abstractly to the people this individual immigrant represents. Like James, who early on in *The American Scene* identifies himself as a "returning absentee," the impresario may be capable of disseminating information about the United States elsewhere, including back to the proverbial "old country."[30] If this immigrant is maintaining an open route of communication with his homeland, then he is capable of performing the same sort of cultural work James envisions for *The American Scene*.

Although never explicitly stated, this underlying implication also informs James's descriptions of his encounters with other immigrants, including an unexpected one with a self-assured Armenian immigrant in the New Hampshire countryside. Anticipating Orlando Patterson's identification of ethnic enclaves that result from emerging migration systems, James attributes the Armenian's confidence to the existence of large and apparently self-sufficient immigrant communities already in place in major U.S. cities: "There awaits the disembarked Armenian, for instance, so warm and furnished an Armenian corner that the need of hurrying to get rid of the sense of it," by which James means the immigrant's foreignness, "must become less and less a pressing preliminary. The corner growing warmer and warmer, it is to be supposed, by rich accretions, he may take his time, more and more, for becoming absorbed in the surrounding element, and he may in fact feel more and more that he can do so on his own conditions."[31] James's supposition that immigrants can and do approach assimilation largely on their own terms challenges the assumption that Americanization is—or should be—a fundamental goal of immigrants residing in the United States. Even more significantly, an "Armenian corner" can "await" a newly arrived Armenian immigrant only because some channel of communication connects that corner in the United States with the immigrant's homeland. Each *already* expects to find the other.

That James was conscious of this sort of cultural work is perfectly feasible because, by the early twentieth century, many Americans were keenly aware of the phenomenon of return migration—to such an extent, in fact, that such back-and-forth patterns of movement shaped discussions about revising U.S. immigration policy. Commenting on the complex web of legal and financial connections that had led some Italian politicians to propose giving "expatriated Italians political representation in the home parliament," Gino Speranza, a U.S.-born attorney who helped found the Society for the Protection of Italian Immigrants, could write in 1906 that "many Italians here [in the United States] return to the mother country and that an even greater number hold real property there."[32] Such continued commitment to the "mother country" deeply troubled many federal officials and policy makers. In 1911, the Dillingham Commission issued a report to the Senate that identified the transience of "new" immigrants (i.e., those from Southern and Eastern Europe) as a key reason for passing more restrictive anti-immigration legislation:

> The new immigration is very largely one of individuals[,] a considerable proportion of whom apparently have no intention of permanently changing their residence, their only purpose in coming to America being to temporarily take advantage of the greater wages. . . . From all data that are available it appears that nearly 40 per cent of the new immigration movement returns to Europe and that about two-thirds of those who go remain there.[33]

These more transient immigrants were assumed to be uninterested in contributing to the ongoing stability of U.S. society and thus justified subsequent governmental measures to limit all forms of immigration.

The Progressive response to return migration, however, was more measured and considerably more positive. William B. Bailey, a Yale professor of economics who worked on the 1910 federal census, acknowledged that birds of passage were likely to drive wages down by competing for American jobs and to send their earnings back to their home countries instead of investing locally, but he also noted that their willingness to return home during times of crisis tended "to limit the fall in wages and to free the community from the necessity of supporting a number of unemployed."[34] In addition to arguing that "it is difficult to see how the interests of this country can be injuriously affected" by return migration, Bailey suggested that "temporary" migration is often the norm and that instilling in immigrants a sense of investment in their own labor "may be sufficient to change these temporary into permanent migrants": "Thus thousands of Irish laborers who had temporarily settled in New England and New York were used in building the railroads of this country and when this work was completed a large number of them permanently settled upon the lands which were made available when communication with the rest of the country was possible."[35] Similarly, in his 1915 study of internationalism, John Culbert Faries drew a distinction between the commuter-like birds of passage, whose lack of attachment to any nation-state and consequent lack of stability elicited Faries's condemnation, and what he called the "re-migrant," whose commitment to the old country and transmission of U.S. money there would "raise the standard of living in the home community" and lessen "the differences which make emigration to America desirable" in the first place.[36] Thus far from fearing return migrants, some Americans viewed the circulation of these migrants and of the money they earned as potentially beneficial to conditions in both the United States and Europe.

Perhaps the most celebrated figure to address these issues directly was Randolph Bourne, whose 1916 essay "Trans-National America" unreservedly portrays return migration as a means of empowering the United States. Like Woodrow Wilson's concept of the mediating nation, Bourne's essay famously positions the United States as an exemplary model of peaceful and multiethnic cooperation, a society that offers an alternative to the history of nationalist-driven conflict that, in 1916, was engulfing Europe in war. For Bourne, the diversity of immigrant communities provided the United States with the means of finally achieving a seemingly impossible goal:

> In a world which has dreamed of internationalism, we find that we have all unawares been building up the first international nation. . . . What we have achieved has been rather a cosmopolitan federation of national colonies, of foreign cultures, from whom the sting of devastating competition has been removed. America is already the world-federation in miniature, the continent where for the first time in history has been achieved that miracle of hope, the peaceful living side by side, with character substantially preserved, of the most heterogenous peoples under the sun.[37]

Significantly, Bourne's model does not attempt to subsume immigrants into a larger national entity. On the contrary, Bourne challenges assimilationist assumptions that "mere participation in the political life of the United States must cut the new citizen off from all sympathy with his old allegiance" and that "the immigrant whom we have welcomed escaping from the very exclusive nationalism of his European home shall forthwith adopt a nationalism just as exclusive, just as narrow, and even less legitimate because it is founded on no warm traditions of his own."[38] Instead, Bourne suggests wider acceptance of "dual citizenship," which transforms "masses of aliens, waiting to be 'assimilated,' waiting to be melted down into the indistinguishable dough of Anglo-Saxonism" into "threads of living and potent cultures, blindly striving to weave themselves into a novel international nation, the first the world has seen."[39] Rather than calling for complete assimilation, as Israel Zangwill's contemporaneous play *The Melting Pot* (1908) notoriously seems to do, Bourne identifies ethnic and cultural diversity as the key constitutive characteristic of a globalized nation, wherein citizens may legally—and even necessarily—hold multiple national sympathies and allegiances.[40]

Unsurprisingly for a writer who proposes a policy of "dual citizenship," Bourne views return migration as yet another instance of the sort of internationalism his essay extols, but he goes even further and argues that migration systems themselves form a key part of the United States' rise to a position of international prominence and power. Throughout "Trans-National America," Bourne takes pains to counteract the recommendations of the Dillingham Commission and others who "stigmatize the alien who works in America for a few years and returns to his own land, only perhaps to seek American fortune again"; according to Bourne, to adhere to this point of view is "to think in narrow nationalistic terms" and "to ignore the cosmopolitan significance of this migration."[41] Bourne's argument for allowing and even encouraging transnational circulation hinges upon its global dimensions. He claims that such circulation will help spread American culture, values, and social practices throughout the world and that doing so will make the world a better place:

> The returning immigrant is often a missionary to an inferior civilization. . . . They return with an entirely new critical outlook, and a sense of the superiority of American organization to the primitive living around them. This continued passage to and fro has already raised the material standard of living in many regions of these backward countries. . . . America is thus educating these laggard peoples from the very bottom of society up, awakening vast masses to a new-born hope for the future.[42]

Far from simply helping transform the United States into a truly "transnational" nation by introducing—and weaving together—multiple cultures and national loyalties, immigrants also participate actively in extending American culture abroad by physically carrying it back with them to their homelands. Rather than viewing the multiple migration systems that extended across the United States at the turn of the century as a threat to

I wonder if Cadle realizes it informs his own...?

national unity, as Nathaniel Shaler did, Bourne views them as a means of remaking other nations in the United States' own "trans-national" image.

A utopian impulse clearly informs Bourne's rhetoric, as it does the writings of other Americans who embraced the language of internationalism, but in pinpointing "dual citizenship" as a potential solution, Bourne pragmatically turns to the only entity with the power to carry out his solution: the state. Moreover, while the optimism of "Trans-National America" is no doubt an outgrowth of Bourne's own pacifism, he was hardly alone in suggesting such a solution. Ten years earlier, Gino Speranza concluded his essay on Italian immigrants' voting rights in Italy this way:

> A universal brotherhood may remain a utopian dream, but commercial interests, the "annihilation of time and space" by improved methods of transportation and the ebb and flow of travel, will render the old distinctions of nationalities and the parochial character of present-day patriotism, more and more an anachronism. The conception of citizenship itself is rapidly changing and we may have to recognize a sort of world or international citizenship as more logical than the present peripatetic kind, which makes a man an American while here, and an Italian while in Italy.[43]

— how so

What distinguishes Bourne's essay is the degree to which he frames transnational migration as a means of empowering both the nation (through greater influence in other countries) and the individual immigrant (through greater personal mobility). He concludes that "the attempt to weave a wholly novel international nation out of our chaotic America will liberate and harmonize the creative power of all these peoples."[44] Bourne's vision of a transnational America therefore contains both individual and social components, and it is the interplay between the two that enables immigrants to make his vision possible through their unique but complementary forms of cultural expression, which is what I take Bourne's use of the phrase "creative power" to mean. The remainder of this chapter examines the writings of two of the most notable practitioners of this cultural work.

and where is the state? In chapter on Jews, it still seems peripheral, hypothetical

THE MIGRATION SYSTEMS OF DAVID LEVINSKY AND KNUT HAMSUN

Although different from one another in important respects, both Abraham Cahan's *The Rise of David Levinsky* and Knut Hamsun's early nonfiction demonstrate thoughtful engagement with the specific migration systems that structure their narratives of immigrants encountering the United States. The migratory route that the fictional character David Levinsky follows is easy to establish from even a cursory reading of Cahan's novel. Levinsky is born in 1865 in the Jewish community of Antomir, a town in what is now modern-day Lithuania but was then part of czarist Russia. In 1885, he emigrates from Europe to New York City, where he resides permanently until the end of the novel. To a certain extent, Levinsky's migration system could double for that of his creator: Cahan was a Lithuanian Jew who migrated to New York in 1882, only three years earlier than Levinsky supposedly does. My goal, however, is to illustrate what parallels and differences exist between the immigrant Levinsky and the return migrant Hamsun, not to prove that Levinsky serves as a fictional stand-in for Cahan. By contrast, Hamsun's migratory experiences were much messier, which is reflected in his relatively unsystematic coverage of a variety of topics in his writings about the United States, but several biographies and anthologies of his early nonfiction paint a more or less complete picture of his immigrant years.[45] Hamsun, who was born in 1859 and raised in northern Norway, immigrated to the United States twice: first in 1882, in order to escape rural labor and put his education to better use, and again in 1886, probably with the intention of returning to Norway again after having earned enough money to finance his literary career. Neither sojourn was successful. A serious illness forced Hamsun's first return to Norway in 1884, and despite having earned very little money the second time around, he returned to Europe for good in 1888, living in Oslo and Copenhagen before finally settling in southern Norway. Furthermore, while Levinsky's story centers primarily on New York City, Hamsun, who never quite found a niche for himself in the United States, resided briefly in Chicago and several other communities, including Minneapolis, Minnesota; Madison, Wisconsin; and Fargo in what is now the state of North Dakota.

The migration systems that emerge from the personal routes of Levinsky and Hamsun make a great deal of historical sense. New York City became a major destination for Eastern European Jews, with many of them traveling through the important German port of Bremen. Like Levinsky, many of these Jewish immigrants entered New York's burgeoning garment industry. Meanwhile, like many Norwegian immigrants, Hamsun benefited from a well-established migration system between the Scandinavian countries and the American Midwest. Hamsun's elder brother had already moved to Elroy, Wisconsin, which is where Hamsun headed at the beginning of his first sojourn. Hence the relative unimportance to his writings of New York City, which Hamsun and other Norwegian immigrants more or less passed through en route to the Scandinavian hubs of Chicago and Minneapolis. At a very basic level, then, the experiences of each immigrant appear to be fairly representative.

Despite these historical resonances and despite the fact that, chronologically, Hamsun's journeys back and forth overlap Levinsky's one-way migration, what stands out about their respective migratory routes are the differences, and these differences matter because they structure each author's writings in unique ways. For instance, the personal experiences of Hamsun suggest that life for immigrants to the United States could be extremely restless and unpredictable: living in four different states or territories in the Midwest over what amounted to only four years, suffering financial and health-related setbacks, traversing the Atlantic Ocean multiple times as a working-class immigrant, and so forth. It is therefore unsurprising that Hamsun's vision of immigrant life is consistently pessimistic, rather than simply ambivalent. By contrast, Cahan presents Levinsky's migratory route as much simpler and more logical, with only one transatlantic journey and a state of permanent residence in New York for the majority of the novel. Even when Levinsky travels outside the city, ranging from short trips to upstate New York, Nebraska, and Louisiana to slightly longer stays in the cities of St. Louis and Boston, these other locations serve as mere extensions of his business activities in Manhattan. In the novel, most of these business trips are confined to books 10 and 11. The only extended section that takes place outside the city after Levinsky arrives in the United States is his vacation at a Catskill resort in Tannersville in book 12, and within the context of the novel, its social milieu of wealthy Jews makes it clear that this location is yet another extension of New York. In other words, as the economic and cultural hub of Levinsky's immigrant community, New York City continues to dominate the novel—even in those sections that take place outside the city—in a way that no particular location does for Hamsun's more diffuse immigrant community. More to the point, the limited geography of the novel constrains Levinsky in such a way that it helps shape the novel's meaning: the more Levinsky assimilates, the less he is able to reconnect with his past life in the old country. The unidirectional nature of Americanization that Cahan seeks to critique is underscored by Levinsky's one-way journey. Levinsky's class mobility in the United States both literally and figuratively distances him from Europe.

The novel's pointedly limited depiction of Levinsky's geographical movement once he arrives in New York may offer one explanation for why critics have focused predominantly on Cahan's negative assessment of the practices of assimilation and why this particular critique continues to dominate analyses of classic immigrant literature: the exclusion of any consideration of return migration on Levinsky's (or any other fictional immigrant's) part may have been a necessary convention in order to highlight the problems and paradoxes immigrants faced when they stayed and became American.[46] To indicate that returning to Antomir was always an option for Levinsky, as it was for millions of real-life immigrants, would have complicated the novel's insistence upon the inevitability of Levinsky's change of character as he assimilates to the American capitalist system. This is one reason why examining the writings of an immigrant who exercised the option of returning home, as Hamsun did, serves as an important corrective to existing scholarship. Still, I contend that the larger migration system that enables Levinsky's physical move to the United States in the first quarter of the novel continues to exert a profound influence over the entirety of *The Rise of David Levinsky*.

What an analysis of Levinsky's own *personal* movement fails to account for are the larger patterns of global circulation in which Levinsky keeps becoming entangled throughout the novel, both economically and culturally. These larger patterns manifest themselves most strikingly in Levinsky's complex and continuing relationship with his hometown of Antomir, which is both a specific location in Lithuania and the site of a significant portion of the novel. Four of the novel's fourteen books—a full 15 percent of the novel's length—take place in Antomir. These early sections covering Levinsky's youth in the old country obviously serve as a contrast to the change in course his life takes in the United States, but they also give the novel geographical complexity. Moreover, Antomir continues to exist after Levinsky leaves and, even more importantly, to exert a centripetal pull on him through his encounters and interactions with people from his past. That Levinsky is aware of this pull is emphasized by the fact that the novel opens and closes with his admission that all of his accomplishments have come at the expense of having to conceal his "inner identity," by which he means his status as a Jew and an immigrant.[47] The distinction between Levinsky's "inner" and "superficial" identities, which echoes "all the hitches and lapses" Henry James observed in the Jewish theater impresario's "inward assimilation of our heritage and point of view," reminds readers that Levinsky is capable of returning to his homeland mentally, as he does when he recounts the story of his early years in Antomir. Even more importantly, the economic and cultural practices that remind him of his homeland throughout the novel do so because they are embedded in the larger migration system of which Levinsky remains a part. In the next section, I examine how these transnational practices and the migration system to which Levinsky belongs give additional meaning to Cahan's novel.

ABRAHAM CAHAN: MIGRATION SYSTEMS AND AMERICANIZATION

Insofar as it acknowledges the conflicting loyalties immigrants felt and celebrates the contributions immigrants made to American society and culture, Abraham Cahan's novel *The Rise of David Levinksy* takes as its explicit subject the sort of transnational American identity that Bourne describes; however, Cahan's novel also creates a richly textured mosaic of a particular nineteenth-century migration system as it was experienced on both sides of the Atlantic. For instance, as an orphan, Levinsky clearly has no family connections of any kind in the United States. He starts out only vaguely aware of the existence of Jewish communities there, and he more or less stumbles upon them after he arrives. Nevertheless, it is apparent that some knowledge—or at least some conception—of America is circulating in Antomir before Levinsky decides to emigrate and that he absorbs this knowledge for several months before he makes his decision. (Levinsky does not begin thinking seriously about emigration until book 3.)

If information about recent émigrés is somehow trickling back across the Atlantic to Antomir and influencing decisions made there, then the process of migration has created a connection between the two locations. The twenty-year-old Levinsky already understands that the United States offers an avenue of escape from the increasingly violent anti-Semitic pogroms that were sweeping across Russia following the 1881 assassination of Czar Alexander II. "Over five million people," Levinsky says of the pogroms, "were suddenly made to realize that their birthplace was not their home. . . . Then it was that the cry 'To America!' was raised. It spread like wild-fire, even over those parts of the Pale of Jewish Settlement which lay outside the riot zone. This was the beginning of the great New Exodus that has been in progress for decades" (60–61). For the young Levinsky, America offers more: "The United States lured me not merely as a land of milk and honey, but also, and perhaps chiefly, as one of mystery, of fantastic experiences, of marvelous transformations. To leave my native place and to seek my fortune in that distant, weird world seemed to be just the kind of sensational adventure my heart was hankering for" (61). Thus Levinsky has been acquiring multiple pieces of information about the United States while still remaining in Antomir: it is a place of greater freedom, peace, and stability; a means of achieving social and economic security; and an opportunity for adventure and self-transformation. When Levinsky finally arrives in New York in 1885, he finds a thriving community of Russian Jews who speak his language, take him under their wing, and initiate him into the garment industry and the benefits of rapid Americanization. At the end of the novel, even after Levinsky has ruthlessly cut many of his former friends and associates out of his life, he still maintains social ties with other immigrants from his hometown: "We mostly spoke in Yiddish, and our Antomir enunciation was like a bond of kinship between us" (497).

Perhaps the most beguiling aspect of *David Levinsky* is how Cahan, who was a socialist, manages to make his protagonist, who is a fairly cutthroat capitalist, so sympathetic and introspective. As a result, the novel serves as a highly ambivalent critique of the relationship between the physical and cultural movement of migration systems and the spread of American capitalism. First published in 1917, near the end of the great wave of immigration, Cahan's novel provides a retrospective look back at the entire period through the eyes of its titular protagonist. Levinsky, who narrates his own life story, works his way up the social and economic ladder and eventually achieves spectacular business success by embracing the philosophies of assimilation and free-market capitalism. Echoing Basil March's acknowledgement of the influence of Jewish tailors on American dress in *A Hazard of New Fortunes*, Levinsky proudly points out just how extensively he and his colleagues—and, by extension, the Jewish immigrants they represent—have reshaped U.S. industry and society:

> The sight of the celebrated Avenue swarming with Jewish mechanics out for their lunch hour or going home after a day's work . . . marked the advent of the Russian Jew as head of one of the largest industries in the United States. Also, it had meant that as master of that industry he had made good, for in his hands it had increased a hundredfold, garments that had formerly reached only the few having been placed within the reach of the masses. Foreigners ourselves, and mostly unable to speak English, we had Americanized the system of providing clothes for the American woman of moderate or humble means. . . . We had done away with prohibitive prices and greatly improved the popular taste. Indeed, the Russian Jew had made the average American girl a 'tailor-made' girl. . . . The average

American woman is the best-dressed average woman in the world, and the Russian Jew has had a good deal to do with making her one. (432–33)

While Cahan makes it clear that these accomplishments factor in Levinsky's moral corruption, a point driven home by the title of the novel's final section, "Episodes of a Lonely Life," Cahan allows Levinsky to take delight in the knowledge that he has assimilated so well into his adopted country that he, in turn, has contributed to the efficiency of American business, the growth of the U.S. economy, and the comfort of the American lifestyle. Although a "foreigner" himself, Levinsky has helped maximize the American capitalist system, even to the point of "Americanizing" an entire industry. This seeming paradox is, in fact, an example of how immigrants learned to exploit conditions already in place in the United States.

Throughout the novel, Levinsky draws attention to the multidirectional nature of Americanization and emphasizes how this multidirectionality connects his community, which includes both his fellow Jewish immigrants and New York itself, to the wider world. When observing Passover with the family of a woman he is trying unsuccessfully to court, Levinsky hears her father say, "This is the Fourth of July of our unhappy people" (483). Rather than serving as an acknowledgement of their assimilation into American society, however, this comparison between Jewish Passover and the United States' Independence Day constitutes an assertion of transnational, transhistorical Jewish identity. As they drink "the first of the Four Cups of wine," the father continues: "Scenes like this bind us to the Jews of the whole world, and not only to those living, but to the past generations as well. . . . The wine we are drinking to-night reminds me of the martyr blood of our massacred brethren of all ages" (483). Similarly, when Levinsky comments upon the contributions of Jewish immigrants to the development of New York City, he inverts the notion of assimilation and playfully Judaizes the city, calling its five boroughs "the five Ghettos of Greater New York" (452). "Men like Volodsky," Levinsky says of a former street peddler who had become a real estate developer,

with hosts of carpenters, bricklayers, plumbers—all Russian or Galician Jews—continued to build up the Bronx, Washington Heights, and several sections of Brooklyn. Vast areas of meadowland and rock were turned by them, as by a magic wand, into densely populated avenues and streets of brick and mortar. Under the spell of their activity cities larger than Odessa sprang up within the confines of Greater New York in the course of three or four years. (500)

The use of Odessa as a point of comparison is not arbitrary on Levinsky's part because it underscores the origins of the manual labor that is building the city. Like Certeau, Levinsky seems to believe that acknowledging the existence and source of such immigrant labor expands a society's "capacity to internationalize."[48]

Levinsky's interest in internationalizing New York, even after establishing himself as a successful businessman, expresses itself both financially and culturally in the ties he and his fellow immigrants from Antomir maintain with the old country. Once he becomes wealthy, Levinsky joins and donates to the "new Antomir Synagogue" in New York, which serves immigrants from his hometown (378). This "new" synagogue's connections to the old one exist in more than name. The routes of exchange between New York and Antomir are strong enough to enable the newly formed congregation to bring a "celebrated" cantor from the homeland: "The contract that had induced him to come over to America pledged him nearly five times as much [as he had earned in Antomir]. Thus the New York Sons of Antomir were not only able to parade a famous cantor before the multitude of other New York congregations, but also to prove to the people at home that they were the financial superiors of the whole town of their birth" (380). That Levinsky and the other members of his congregation are able to hire and transport this cantor indicates that they transact business across national borders; that they can boast of luring him away from Antomir indicates that at least some of them remain in communication with friends and family members who have stayed there. Levinsky himself considers fulfilling a promise he had made to his boyhood friend Naphtali "to send him a 'ship ticket'" once Levinsky had earned enough money (389), and although Levinsky never keeps his promise, the fact that Levinsky and Naphtali would think of the idea suggests that it was a fairly common practice for one successful immigrant to pay for another's immigration and that this practice was already known in European Jewish communities like Antomir by the time Levinsky leaves.

The one-upmanship that takes place between the new and old Antomir synagogues over the celebrated cantor reveals the degree to which Levinsky and his fellow immigrants understand that financial wealth and cultural importance go hand in hand. Thus while Levinsky's primary concern remains finding ways "of making my money breed money" (511), which indicates that he has become a finance capitalist, Levinsky also takes great interest in the contributions of Jewish immigrants to the United States' rapidly expanding popular culture. Levinsky admits that "I envy far more than I do a billionaire . . . the Russian Jew who holds the foremost place among American songwriters and whose soulful compositions are sung in almost every English-speaking house in the world" (517). Here, Levinsky is alluding to Irving Berlin, whose influence on popular music from the composition of "Alexander's Ragtime Band" (1911) onwards would be immeasurable. In coming to embody American popular music more than any other composer had done before him, Berlin provides perhaps the most spectacular example of the global dimensions of immigrant culture and of the international platform that the U.S. entertainment industry could give foreign-born artists. By drawing attention to the fact that Berlin's music is "sung in almost every English-speaking house in the world," Cahan simultaneously underscores the extent to which America's immigrant culture was spreading internationally and demonstrates that immigrants were helping to cement the United States' cultural hegemony.

In book II, Cahan counterbalances these ambivalent instances of immigrants' participation in the consolidation of U.S. economic and cultural hegemony with the introduction of other immigrants who support an alternative transnational movement: socialism. In these sections, Cahan makes it clear that immigration and socialism, the two most important global currents in the author's own life, could be linked, even though they do not converge in the capitalist Levinsky. For example, Levinsky recalls how several left-leaning intellectuals within the Jewish immigrant communities of New York took part in or otherwise supported socialist political activities in czarist Russia, including the Russian Revolution of 1905. "The revolutionary movement was then at its height in Russia," Levinsky remarks, "and the Jews were among its foremost and bravest leaders" (372). He goes on to claim that it was just this relationship between Jewish intellectuals and Russian revolutionaries that led to the pogroms of the 1880s, which "the Government inspired and encouraged quite openly" (372). This repressive atmosphere in turn serves to stimulate "the great emigration of Jews to America," to radicalize even more Russian Jews, and to gain sympathy and support for both the Jewish and socialist causes in Russia (372). Thus Cahan exposes the cyclical nature of radical politics as well as the effects of local and national politics upon human migration, but he also indicates that migration systems can elevate local or national crises onto the geopolitical stage when immigrants themselves raise awareness of those crises elsewhere.

More importantly, these episodes enable Cahan, whose political sympathies at the time certainly lay with socialist revolutionaries, to draw attention to the ways in which the global circulation of American money could work to subvert global capitalism. While Levinsky's involvement with these Jewish socialists, both in New York and in Europe, is limited, he is aware that New York serves as an important hub for the socialist movement. At least one "socialist Yiddish daily" advertises meetings for "an organization of Russian revolutionists" in New York, and Levinsky knows that political refugees from Russia frequently speak at those meetings in order to raise funds for further revolutionary activities in the homeland: "From time to time some distinguished revolutionist would be sent to America for subscriptions to the cause. . . . They were here, not as immigrants, but merely to raise funds for the movement at home" (372–73). In this way, Cahan, who founded and edited the "socialist Yiddish daily" *Forward*, demonstrates just how dynamic Levinsky's immigrant community is and how complex the migration system that connects this community with Jewish communities in Russia must be. Levinsky's acknowledgement that some of the Jews with whom he comes into contact in New York are merely travelers who have come to the United States "not as immigrants" but for very specific, short-term goals highlights the fact that the phenomenon of return migration still exerts a powerful influence in his community. The circulation of these persons, who work to overthrow czarist Russia in particular and global capitalism in general, also serves to subvert the model of Americanization to which Levinsky is committed. (One of the activists Levinsky meets, a woman named Matilda, turns out to be a former love-interest who had given him five dollars to help him land on his feet in New York. Their reunion gives both Levinsky and the reader a glimpse of one of the alternative paths his life could have taken.) While the protagonist Levinsky may not choose to return to his homeland after settling in the United States, the presence of other characters who move back and forth between the United States and Eastern Europe strengthens Cahan's critique of assimilation and Americanization and even extends it to the larger economic and cultural processes of globalization.

KNUT HAMSUN: MIGRATION SYSTEMS AND RESISTANCE

If Randolph Bourne envisioned the return migrant as a "missionary" who would spread the gospel of "the superiority of American organization" throughout the world while Abraham Cahan portrayed return migrants as

Jewish ???

politically subversive, then perhaps the most obvious follow-up question becomes: what information about the United States did birds of passage circulate once they returned to their respective homelands? There is some difficulty in answering this question because, as historian Betty Boyd Caroli points out in her study of Italian repatriation, due to widespread illiteracy, very few return migrants published accounts of their experiences in the United States and those who did, while often highly educated, were rarely professional writers.[49] Thus the writings by return migrants that do exist are simultaneously atypical of the experiences of the uneducated laborers who made up the majority of all immigrants and unlikely to have been read by wide audiences in their respective homelands. That is not to say that such texts are uninformative or entirely unrepresentative of most return migrants' impressions of the United States; however, an extensive archival survey of such existing literature falls far beyond the purview of this chapter. Instead, I turn to the writings of perhaps the most prominent professional writer who underwent the process of return migration as a more or less ordinary immigrant and who went on to record his experiences and impressions of the United States for his fellow countrymen: the Norwegian Nobel laureate Knut Hamsun.

While Hamsun's later career as a major European literary figure may distinguish him from the majority of immigrants of the period, I contend that he makes for a particularly salient point of comparison with Abraham Cahan and other classic immigrant authors of American literature because, like them, Hamsun established his literary identity through his writings about his experiences as an immigrant.[50] Quite literally, the writer permanently adopted the name Hamsun in 1885, after a typographical error led to the accidental omission of the letter "d" from an essay on Mark Twain that he had signed "Hamsund."[51] More importantly, however, Hamsun signaled what he considered to be his formal entry into the Norwegian literary community with *On the Cultural Life of Modern America* (1889), the first full-length book that he published under his new name.[52] Even his most famous work, *Hunger* (1890), bears traces of his immigrant years. The inspiration for that heavily autobiographical novel was the time Hamsun spent living hand-to-mouth in Christiania (now Oslo) between his two sojourns in America, and like the author himself, *Hunger*'s protagonist ends his suffering only when he decides to leave the country in the final chapter of the novel. To be clear, I do not mean to suggest that the contrarian Hamsun spoke for *all* return migrants, but a close reading of his nonfictional writings about the United States reveals that the global spread of the

U.S. economy and American culture could serve to empower authors from other nations, even enabling them to establish modes of resistance to that same global hegemony.

Modern America and Hamsun's other early writings reflect deep disillusionment with his experiences as an immigrant in the United States, and they could be read in part as words of warning to future or potential emigrants not to expect too much out of America. Indeed, Hamsun seems almost to be writing *against* the subgenre of emigration literature that was developing among Scandinavian writers at the end of the nineteenth century.[53] In his conclusion to *Modern America*, Hamsun comments sarcastically on a trope that was beginning to emerge: "When really free writers in this country have a hero whom they wish well but who has come to grief in his native land because he is a freethinker and a liberal, they send him to America in the last chapter of their book. There is elbowroom there!"[54] Nothing could be farther from Hamsun's mind than accepting the assumptions of this cliché uncritically. Nor does Hamsun wish to serve as one of Randolph Bourne's missionaries. Hamsun apparently did return to Norway with a "new critical outlook," as Bourne puts it, but that outlook was aimed squarely at U.S. society itself. *Modern America* is a sharp critique of American culture—or, more precisely, what Hamsun perceived as the lack thereof—and a vitriolic condemnation of what he viewed as most Americans' blind commitment to patriotism, capitalism, and religious experience. For Hamsun, the United States is ultimately "a nation of patriots hostile to foreigners, a people without a national literature or art, a corrupt society, a materialistic mode of life, and flourishing inanity!" (139)

There is more to Hamsun's grousing than mere sour grapes over his own disappointed expectations or, as some critics have proposed in light of Hamsun's later collaboration with the Germans during their occupation of Norway in the early 1940s, some sort of anticapitalist, antidemocratic, and protofascist political project.[55] Barbara Gordon Morgridge argues persuasively that *Modern America* should be viewed as a riposte to *The Innocents Abroad* (1869), Mark Twain's equally iconoclastic skewering of European pretensions and American perceptions of high culture. Morgridge claims that Hamsun's "aesthetic appreciation and receptivity [to Twain's] comic style of hyperbole, paradox, and wit . . . helped to shape the tone and treatment of his American experiences in *Cultural Life*."[56] Hamsun's other early essays certainly bear this assertion out. Of all the American writers Hamsun discusses, including Ralph Waldo Emerson and Walt Whitman, Twain earns Hamsun's fullest respect. In his 1885 essay "Mark Twain," Hamsun calls Twain "the greatest and most popular representative of American humor writing" and both "artistically secure" and "*fair* in his judgments" (original emphasis).[57] It is also possible that Hamsun felt a personal connection with Twain, having met Twain after one of Twain's lectures and, as noted above, permanently adopting the name Hamsun after publishing his essay on Twain.

In "Mark Twain," Hamsun claims to draw the line at Twain's travel writing, specifically singling out *The Innocents Abroad* and citing what he considered Twain's lack of experience with European high culture as "poor qualification for rightly judging the conditions and human beings of Europe."[58] Nevertheless, in his other writings, Hamsun is guilty of adopting the very same tone he criticizes in "Mark Twain": being "poised to make fun of everything that was foreign to him," driving "his hosts to despair," confusing historical figures with one another, and relying on "iconoclasm" and "polemic" to make his points.[59] Indeed, what irritates Hamsun about *The Innocents Abroad* is precisely what many readers may find irritating about *Modern America*: it is a highly idiosyncratic, satiric, and impressionistic example of literary reportage, with an almost gleeful disregard for context or factual accuracy. Hamsun regularly misquotes newspaper and magazine articles and even confuses President Zachary Taylor with the journalist Bayard Taylor, even as he takes Twain to task in his essay on that author for confusing "Catherine with Maria de Medici and Raphael with Rubens."[60] To read *Modern America* for an objective description of living conditions in the United States, however, is to miss the point. Instead, Hamsun is cannily inviting his readers to compare his writing with Twain's, while simultaneously defusing potential criticisms of his book's slipshod research. Apparently, contemporary Norwegian reviewers picked up on both points. Many acknowledged the suspect nature of Hamsun's anecdotal evidence but still praised the author's literary gifts, and several expressed admiration for the effectiveness of Hamsun's American-style satire and self-promotion.[61]

Drawing attention to Hamsun's indebtedness both to Twain's literary style and, more generally, to recognizably American forms of self-promotion should not, however, serve to downplay the content of Hamsun's writings about America. In this regard, both Morgridge and Richard Nelson Current go too far in attempting to defang *Modern America* for American readers. Occasionally, of course, some of Hamsun's criticisms are trite and unoriginal, as is his conclusion that the United States lacks a rich culture and unique art because the nation has no "long history behind it—a history that had given the people their characteristic stamp, that, in a word, had endowed the nation with an original intellectual heritage of its own" (15). Here, Hamsun relies on the tired stereotype that "no cultural individuality has yet taken root [and] no distinctive intellectual character has yet taken shape" in America because it is a "pioneer society" (15). Such assertions are not too far removed from the ones Henry James had already made in *Hawthorne* (1879) and are thus relatively benign.

More problematic is that Hamsun's views on immigration are at times worryingly similar to those taken by Nathaniel Shaler. In his first piece of writing about the United States, an 1885 essay entitled "From America," Hamsun predates Shaler's "European Peasants as Immigrants" by eight years in warning of "the danger that arises from the mixing of different kinds of people in a free, uncontrolled, capricious environment."[62] Hamsun's characterization of his fellow immigrants is even more condescending than Shaler's—Hamsun calls them "diseased and degenerate human raw material"—and he is more explicit than Shaler in calling for the state to put "a timely stop to immigration, or at least [to put] some restrictions on it."[63] It is worth noting that, unlike Shaler, Hamsun bases his objections on perceptions of class rather than of race: what concerns him in "From America" is that the majority of immigrants in the United States are made up of "the dregs of the European population," people who were incapable of contributing to the cultural life of their own countries in any meaningful way.[64] His attitude also seems to have changed significantly over time. Four years later, in *Modern America*, Hamsun writes, "The proposals to restrict immigration rest on shaky ground" (13). He rejects the claim that immigrants are overcrowding the United States: "The land is *not* all taken. That is a pretext and a joke" (13, original emphasis). The real cause for anti-immigrant sentiment in the United States, Hamsun avers, is that "foreign labor can neither be acknowledged as necessary nor recognized as superior to the country's own" (13).

At other times, Hamsun makes a number of insightful and sometimes biting observations about American materialism and ethnocentrism. He condemns Americans' preoccupation with business and making money, and in *Modern America*, he attributes the rapidity with which many immigrants Americanize themselves to economic conditions:

The same family that lived on two crowns a day here [in Norway] needs a dollar and a half a day there, and for the great majority it takes considerable doing to get hold of this dollar and a half; it really keeps you whirling to earn that money. . . . Their inner calm is gone, but they have grown active; suddenly they have grown very light-footed. A sojourn in America is very definitely an effective stimulant; people's minds and energy are set in motion. But one grows active and light-footed from the instant one steps ashore and starts to earn money for one's first meal—long before coming into contact with political freedom in the Republic. (6)

According to Hamsun, Americanization is principally about trying to achieve economic stability, not gaining an appreciation for democracy. If the trade-off for becoming American is losing one's "inner calm," then the process is not worth the effort for Hamsun. There is no time for reflection when one is constantly "whirling," and it is partly this constant bustle that prevents Americans from establishing the rich cultural traditions that flourish in the less money-obsessed European societies.

Even worse, in Hamsun's opinion, is the fact that Americans' exaggerated patriotism makes them unwilling to learn a different way of life from Europe or elsewhere. He describes such national arrogance this way: "There is *one* country, America; anything beyond this is no good. Nowhere on earth is there such freedom, such development, such progress, and such intelligent people as in the land of America. A foreigner often feels wounded by this hulking smugness" (8, original emphasis). Again relating the effect of this patriotism on immigrants like himself, Hamsun remarks that Americanization is really a byproduct of needing to accommodate oneself to Americans. The immigrant "tries to become an American as best he can. . . . He learns the formal aspects of Americanism rapidly; he learns to speak English, he learns to wear his hat tilted over his right ear, he learns to surrender himself in every way according to the external patterns of behavior that characterize the Yankee in his own land. Then American national pride has reached fulfillment: there is one more American in America" (8). Americanization is, in effect, loss of individuality.

What is striking about Hamsun's depiction of Americanization is the degree to which it takes on the characteristics of a malignant force that spreads from person to person, threatening to level differences of habit in order to produce social uniformity. In his essay "From America," Hamsun explicitly compares Americanization to a virus, remarking that Americans themselves "suffer from a national mania, an incurable disease, one that keeps spreading."[65] In this passage, however, Hamsun is discussing the threat that Americanization poses not just to Norwegians who relocate to the United States, but also to Norwegians who remain at home. America,

Hamsun notes, already "provides Europe with its best instruments for dentists, midwives, and hospitals. Indeed, when it comes to applied science or technology, the United States is ahead of all other countries."[66] Hamsun specifically links the spreading "national mania" of Americanization with the global reach of U.S. capitalism and culture.

This coupling of the processes of Americanization and globalization is what distinguishes Hamsun's writings about the United States—and his status as a return migrant—from earlier European authors who wrote similarly satiric interpretations of U.S. society and culture for European readers. Not until the 1880s was it clear that North America was displacing Europe as the center of the world economy. As Winfried Fluck says of Ferdinand Kürnberger's *The Man Who Became Weary of America*, an 1855 novel of a German immigrant's disillusionment with life in the United States, "America is an imaginary construct," which serves for Kürnberger, Tocqueville, and other European writers as a *possible* model of democracy that European nations *might* follow, not as the certain future of global capitalism.[67] Although he does not invoke world-systems analysis, Fluck's characterization of Kürnberger's novel as a representation of the "clash between American and German culture in the nineteenth century" points to the historical struggle for hegemony between those two economies that Immanuel Wallerstein and Giovanni Arrighi claim took place from the mid-nineteenth century onward, as Great Britain went into economic decline.[68] Kürnberger's novel thus belongs to a historical moment when the idea of a single German nation-state, the formation of which was already viewed as likely in 1855, contending for global supremacy seemed feasible. One of the characters in Kürnberger's novel actually views German emigration to the United States as an expansion of German, not U.S., power: "All of North-America will become German, because our immigration is based on a powerful motherland, just as Yankee-English profited from Old-England. But why am I saying all of North-America? The whole world will be German, for the rise of Germany will be the fall of England, just as England precipitated Holland's fall."[69] By the time Hamsun was writing in the late 1880s, Kürnberger's vision of the future was not only absurd; the reverse—Germany and the rest of the world becoming Americanized—was increasingly likely.

What registers in the writings of Hamsun is the recognition that the implications of Americanization extend far beyond the transformation of the individual immigrant. Since migration to the United States and the resulting migration systems serve to expand U.S. economic and cultural power, Hamsun seeks a way of using those same migration systems to challenge that power. Thus his writings serve not only as words of warning to future Norwegian emigrants or as American-influenced satire, but also as a calculated attempt to resist the global spread of American capitalism and culture. In a sense, Hamsun utilizes one global network (the migration system that exists between Scandinavia and the American Midwest) to undermine another (the routes of exchange that help spread U.S. products and culture), and Hamsun circulates a particular conception of America in order, paradoxically, to stave off its further spread. That his efforts remain in interactive relation with the processes of globalization demonstrates that globalization is not solely an American phenomenon; some processes of globalization emerge alongside of—and even in contradistinction to—Americanization.

It is because Hamsun understands the global implications of American attitudes and actions that he harps so extensively upon Americans' xenophobia and ignorance of the rest of the world. America, he recognizes in "Mark Twain," is "the world's greatest and richest country," and he acknowledges that the United States now occupies one of the most important positions on the international stage.[70] "There is a greater crossing of cosmopolitan elements" in the United States, he observes in *Modern America*, "than in any other country in the world" (16). Yet Americans themselves remain "systematically aloof," refusing to engage in dialogue with the nations they are coming into contact with (16). More troubling to Hamsun is their seemingly total lack of awareness of the world outside of their own borders. In *Modern America*, he laments:

> Unfamiliarity with foreign peoples and foreign achievements is one of the national vices of the American people. . . . The authorized geography in [their] schools is American geography; the authorized history is American history—all the rest of the world is included in a mere supplement of a couple of pages. . . . American children grow up with no other knowledge of the world than what they have learned about America. (9)

This willful ignorance on the part of the American people frustrates Hamsun precisely because of the United States' importance and power. In his opinion, no sense of international context guides the decisions of U.S. policy makers or businessmen, and Americans are reshaping the world in their own image with little regard for the cultures they are eradicating elsewhere.

Hamsun's criticisms of Mark Twain's *The Innocents Abroad* are likewise the outgrowth of his unwillingness to allow an American author to represent or, more accurately, to rewrite his own European heritage. "To go to Europe and be a critic," Hamsun writes in "Mark Twain," "requires other qualifications than his energy and generally sound instincts."[71] Instead, turning the tables on Twain (as well as on Howells), Hamsun exoticizes the American author and his culture, thereby reframing Twain's writing as local color that is consumable by European readers like himself:

> He is to be fully trusted only when he is dealing with the mining regions, where rich ores lie underfoot, where men shoot each other for sport, and where they fight their way through the impartial air, between outlaws and Indians, over ice fields and deserts. Here he is at home. . . . His powers of invention, boundless imagination, and original style are precisely the qualities that are needed here. They are less useful when it comes to studies of Greek antiques or European theories of government.[72]

Hamsun's objective is to render both Twain and the national culture that Twain represents local rather than universal. What Twain knows about, where he is "at home," is within U.S. borders. He may write perceptively and entertainingly about rough-and-tumble mining towns and frontier life, Hamsun argues, but he has no business forcing other countries and cultures to fit within his limited worldview. When writing about European cultures, Twain carries his typically American ignorance of those cultures with him, and Hamsun is quick to link this ignorance with the narrow-mindedness that European immigrants encounter in America. Twain's contact with Europeans on their own ground is characterized by "exactly the same kind of ignorance that foreigners suffer from when they go to America."[73] For Hamsun, Twain's travel writing represents the extension of Americanization beyond the United States' own borders. Carrying his American attitudes with him as he travels and attempting to reduce European culture into something that his American readers will understand, Twain embodies the encroachment of a U.S. cultural imperialism that Hamsun actively resists in his writings about the United States.

After 1890, explicit references to the United States become rare in Hamsun's writings. Having exploited his experiences there in order to establish his reputation in Norway, he largely dispenses with the United States afterwards. Returning emigrants do appear as characters in several later novels that are set in Norway, including *Vagabonds* (1927), *August* (1930), *The Road*

Leads On (1933), and *The Ring Is Closed* (1936), and although Hamsun pokes fun at them for the Americanisms that they have adopted, these characters are generally sympathetic. For the most part, the social criticisms that appear in these novels are directed at Norway itself, not the United States. By the time he published his last book, a memoir entitled *On Overgrown Paths* (1949), Hamsun's retrospective attitude toward his sojourn in the United States had mellowed to such an extent that the only negative comments he can muster is of the homesickness he felt and of his preference for the company of other, equally homesick immigrants. Hamsun, however, did produce one more notable essay about the United States in his old age: a 1928 newspaper editorial entitled "Festina Lente." More than any other of Hamsun's later writings, this one indicates the degree to which his views on America had softened over the years. He comments without irony on "the Americans' great helpfulness, their sympathy, their generosity" and claims, "To my dying day I will treasure what I learned during my two stays there, and I will always cherish the fine memories of those times."[74]

Nonetheless, in "Festina Lente," Hamsun remains critical of American materialism and nervous of the United States' long-term impact upon European culture and society. Indeed, Hamsun's vision of the future is one of an ever-expanding U.S. economic and cultural hegemony: "God is forgotten, the almighty dollar seems to be taking His place, and machinery provides no relief to the soul. . . . In the face of these conditions, America only increases its speed. America will not be stopped by any obstacle, but will move ahead, will force its way. . . . We in Europe have the word *Americanism*; the ancients had *festina lente* [hasten slowly]."[75] By contrasting the Roman philosophy of approaching social change cautiously with the term "Americanism," Hamsun acknowledges the centrality of the United States to the international community but also the dangers of other countries adopting American social and cultural practices too quickly. The solution, as Hamsun sees it, rests on American shoulders, and he makes a direct appeal to American readers (for, unlike Hamsun's other writings about America, "Festina Lente" was translated into English and appeared in the December 30, 1928, issue of the *St. Louis Post-Dispatch*): "No more than any other country on the planet can America stand alone. America is not the world. America is a part of the world and must live its life together with all the other parts."[76] At once challenging American isolationism *and* American global hegemony (the United States is neither "alone" nor "the world"), Hamsun calls for dialogue and mutual cooperation. Thus Hamsun, the return migrant, completes the route of

is this right?

circulation he entered over forty-five years earlier. Having experienced the United States firsthand and interpreted those experiences for his fellow Norwegians, he now transmits his conception of America back to the United States. Just as the figures in Stieglitz's *The Steerage* look askance at the viewer, Hamsun demands that his American readers acknowledge his position and respond with respect.

CHAPTER FIVE

Freedom amongst Aliens

Jack London, Lafcadio Hearn,

and the Alternative Modernity of Japan

A lthough most Americans tended to fixate on the so-called "new immigrants" from Southern and Eastern Europe when they discussed immigration in the early twentieth century, as the previous chapter demonstrated, immigration from other regions of the world was by no means insignificant. Between December 1, 1905, and November 30, 1906, for example, over seventeen thousand Japanese entered the United States, many of them settling in San Francisco.[1] The presence of these Japanese, as well as immigrants from other parts of Asia, produced their own anxieties, especially among Californians. While the U.S. Congress had passed the Chinese Exclusion Act in 1882 and an 1894 U.S. district court ruling denied citizenship to Japanese immigrants, California's state legislature went even further and, in 1913, enacted the Alien Land Law, which prohibited Japanese from owning land because they were ineligible for citizenship.[2] Perhaps the most notorious literary expression of these anxieties about Asian immigrants appears in Jack London's short story "The Unparalleled Invasion," which was originally published in the July 1910 issue of *McClure's Magazine*. London's story imagines a future rendered dystopian by an overpopulated China, which periodically sends out its excess populace to colonize neighboring regions. By the 1970s, the Chinese outnumber the entire West— "there were two Chinese for every white-skinned human in the world"— and begin to overrun territories in East Asia under European control.[3] In the face of such an overwhelming threat, the Western nations set aside their differences and collectively launch a genocidal war against China, wiping out the Chinese with biological weapons and colonizing their now empty land in a "vast and happy intermingling of nationalities."[4]

Most critical discussions of London's story center on its apparent racial anxieties. A few critics argue that this futuristic fantasy of racial extermination was intended to satirize the West's racist and imperialist assumptions about China, but most contend that its exploitation of American anxieties regarding Asian immigrants indicates that the racism of the story was probably London's own.[5] I suggest, however, that the anxieties that the story exhibits have less to do with race per se than with a particular conception of modernity. Although China serves as the target for London's genocidal fantasy, the specter of Japan hovers over the story's pseudo-historical background. Whereas the Western nations are unable to "awaken" China because *between them and China was no common psychological speech,"* Japan, transformed by "her victory over Russia in 1904 [into] the freak and paradox among Eastern peoples," succeeds at "awakening" China because "the Japanese thought with the same thought-symbols as did the Chinese" (original emphasis).[6] What London seems to mean by the verb "awaken" is modernization. Japan builds railroads and factories in China, which frees the Chinese from an agricultural economy and thus enables their population to explode. At the same time, London does not expect an "awakened" China to adopt Western values because cultural differences continue to obtain: China remains isolationist and self-sufficient and pays no attention to the "comity of nations."[7] For London, in other words, the future may become dystopian precisely because of the rise of alternative forms of modernity in Asia—an alternative modernity that assimilates such Western technologies as railroads and factories but does not entirely conform to the West's notion of international society.

London's reference to Japan's "victory over Russia in 1904" and his decision to set the West's biological attack on China on May 1, 1976, are crucial. For many Americans of London's era, the Battle of the Yalu River denoted a decisive turning point in world history. Fought on April 30 and May 1, 1904, exactly seventy-two years before the climax of London's story, the first major land battle of the Russo-Japanese War resulted in a dramatic victory for the Japanese army and marked the first time in modern warfare that an Eastern nation had defeated a Western power. In the months following the battle, Japan would issue a series of stunning victories against the Russian army and navy, ultimately precipitating the Russian Revolution of 1905 and forcing Czar Nicholas II to sue for peace. The outcome of the Russo-Japanese War transformed Japan into an important imperial power and the first non-Western member of the so-called Great Powers, and it sent shockwaves throughout the Western world, challenging long-held assumptions about the military, intellectual, and cultural supremacy of European civilization and the inability of nonwhite peoples to resist, let alone adopt and exploit, Western imperialism. In *The Rising Tide of Color against White World-Supremacy* (1920), the eugenicist Lothrop Stoddard gives voice to American anxieties about the growing power of Japan when he singles out that nation's defeat of Russia as a dangerous precedent for Western civilization: "It was Russian Pan-Slavism which dealt the first shrewd blow to white solidarity. . . . Pan-Slavists boldly proclaimed the morbid, mystical dogma that Russia was Asiatic, not European. . . . The Russo-Japanese War, that destroyer of white prestige whose ominous results we have already noted, was precipitated mainly by the reckless short-sightedness of white men themselves."[8] Of course, the whiteness of Russians and other Slavic peoples was an open question among advocates of early twentieth-century race-science—it is unclear, for instance, if Stoddard views "Slavism" as an ethnicity that dilutes Russia's whiteness or as a set of cultural values that misleads a white nation—but Russia was unquestionably a member of the Great Powers and, consequently, a representative of Western imperial hegemony.[9] Stoddard's contorted logic bespeaks the conceptual crisis that many Americans were thrown into at the turn of the twentieth century by Japan's rapid modernization and adoption of Western methods of warfare and imperialism.

At the same time, the aftermath of the Russo-Japanese War helped propel the United States into a more central role in the international community. As Gretchen Murphy notes, "the Russo-Japanese War (1904–5) provided a narrative opportunity for locating the United States . . . in the world" because "the United States [had become] one of several 'world powers' with a complicated set of global alliances and responsibilities."[10] One of the key moments in the United States' rise to international prominence was Theodore Roosevelt's negotiation of the Treaty of Portsmouth, which formally ended the Russo-Japanese War and earned Roosevelt the 1906 Nobel Peace Prize. In addition to the prestige that Roosevelt's mediation brought to U.S. diplomacy (and the territory it gave to Japan), the Treaty of Portsmouth also ratified the secret Taft-Katsura Agreement, in which the United States agreed to recognize Korea as belonging within Japan's sphere of influence in exchange for Japan's pledge not to interfere with the U.S. presence in the Philippines.[11] Thus the Russo-Japanese War highlights the closely intertwined histories of the United States and Japan, which at that time already extended back to 1858, when, with the aid of a U.S. naval squadron, Commodore Matthew Perry signed the Kanagawa Treaty and forcibly opened Japan to trade with the West. More importantly, the war and its repercussions also reveal the extent to which the United States depended upon Japanese imperialism for its own rise to global power at the dawn of the twentieth century. The two nations' emergence as Great Powers was simultaneous and reciprocal.

This uneasy relationship between Japan and the United States registers not only in "The Unparalleled Invasion," but also in other writings by London, who witnessed the Battle of the Yalu River firsthand as a war correspondent for William Randolph Hearst's *San Francisco Examiner*. Immediately following the Japanese victory, London penned what is probably the most famous passage of his war correspondence. Describing an encounter with a group of dejected Russian prisoners of war, he writes:

> The sight I saw was as a blow in the face to me. On my mind it had all the stunning effect of the sharp impact of a man's fist. There was a man, a white man, with blue eyes, looking at me. . . . And there were other white men in there with him—many white men. I caught myself gasping. A choking sensation was in my throat. These men were my kind. I found myself suddenly and sharply aware that I was an alien amongst these brown men who peered through the window with me. And I felt myself strangely at one with those other men behind the window—felt that my place was there inside with them in their captivity, rather than outside in freedom amongst aliens.[12]

The shock or "blow" that London records here—he, a "white man," has been rendered "alien" by a situation that leaves him "free" and protected by the very same "brown men" who have imprisoned other "white men"—parallels the "first shrewd blow to white solidarity" that Stoddard discusses. In contrast to other literary scholars who have examined this passage for what it reveals about emerging racial categories in the United States, I suggest that we read London's use of the term "white men" and Stoddard's parallel use of "white solidarity" as avatars for Western modernity. What both London and Stoddard lament is not just the defeat of a particular Western nation or even the defeat of whiteness per se, but rather the defeat of Western modernity by an Eastern nation with its own brand of modernity. In referring ironically to his "freedom amongst aliens" even though he feels that his "place" is with the Russian prisoners "in their captivity" and their defeat, London attempts to distance himself from a relationship with the Japanese that benefits him in practical terms but that deeply troubles him as a representative of Western civilization. In short, he feels threatened by Japan's victory, that nation's newfound modernity, and the potential implications of both for the future of U.S. geopolitical interests.

This chapter explores the confusion and anxiety over the nature of modernity that Japan's status within the international community precipitated for Jack London and Lafcadio Hearn, perhaps the two most famous and widely read authors to visit Japan at the turn of the twentieth century and to write about their experiences there.[13] Positioning themselves as experts on Japan, London and Hearn produced important representations of Japanese society and culture for American readers as tensions between the two nations were increasing. I argue that, in these writings, London and Hearn present us with a nascent recognition of what may be called "alternative modernities." This recognition emerges in both men's writings not only when each one immersed himself fully and sometimes painfully in Asian culture, but also and even more importantly at key moments in Japan's move toward modernization, including that nation's development into a major imperial power in East Asia. The readings I offer in this chapter thus differ from those of Collen Lye, Gretchen Murphy, and other literary scholars who have examined London's war correspondence in terms of how it served to racialize Asian identity. To be sure, both London and Hearn employ the logic of racialism in order to explain what they perceived to be the cultural and psychological differences between themselves and the Japanese they encountered; however, this racialist logic enabled them to reach sometimes surprising conclusions about geopolitics and the nature of modernity itself. In contrast to Murphy, who reads London's understanding of "Asiatic" culture as "a U.S. racial grouping [with] domestic, not international, meanings," and in contrast to Lye, who reads it as an early example of "the discursivity of a neocolonialism that installed the East as a Western proxy," I view both London and Hearn as being deeply engaged by the genuinely international question of what kind of modern state Japan represented.[14] As I demonstrate below, Hearn engaged this internationalism far more productively—and with a much more open mind—than London did, locating in Japan solutions to social problems that continued to plague the United States, but both London and Hearn found in Japan an exemplary counter-modernity in action that forced them to interrogate their assumptions about the modernity that they, as Americans, represented.

Before examining their writings, however, I wish to clarify what the terms "racialism" and "alternative modernities" mean and how they relate to one another. Racialism, it is important to note, is not the same thing as racism. As Anthony Appiah has pointed out, racialism is a "presupposition" of racism, but the discrimination that characterizes racism is not necessarily found in the concept of racialism. Instead, according to Appiah, racialism is the view that "there are heritable characteristics, possessed by members of our species, which allow us to divide them into a small set of races, in such a way that all the members of these races share certain traits and tendencies with each other that they do not share with members of any other race."[15] The ideology of racialism dominated nineteenth-century conceptualizations of nationhood and culture and led to a number of pseudo-scientific attempts to classify the world's peoples into distinct races, each with its own supposed essential characteristics and dispositions. These attempts to categorize individuals racially could—and often did—lead to organizing them into hierarchies, in the mistaken belief that some races possessed inherent traits that rendered them superior to others; however, it was also possible for a person who subscribed to racialism to believe that, again according to Appiah, "provided positive moral qualities are distributed across the races, each can be respected, can have its 'separate but equal' place."[16] Even W. E. B. Du Bois subscribed to certain aspects of racialism for a time. In his 1897 essay "The Conservation of Races," Du Bois writes, "These eight great races of to-day follow the cleavage of physical race distinctions. . . . Yet no mere physical distinctions would really define or explain the deeper significances—the cohesiveness and continuity of these groups. The deeper differences are spiritual, psychical, differences."[17] Clearly, then, racialism was a pervasive but ultimately descriptive worldview that did not necessarily entail a set of prescriptive rules for social behavior—though it did not exclude the possibility of such rules being established, either.

Alternative modernities, on the other hand, is an idea proposed by the philosopher Charles Taylor at the conclusion of his influential essay "Two Theories of Modernity." In this essay, Taylor describes two ways of understanding the rise of modernity: culturally and aculturally. The acultural explanation takes a culture-neutral view of progress, assuming that the road to modernity is universal and that all cultures must eventually follow the same path. Variations among cultures equate to different positions along the same path, with some cultures having reached farther distances than others. Taylor rejects this explanation, claiming that "what this view reads out of the picture is the possibility that Western modernity might be powered by its own positive visions of the good, that is, by one constellation of such views among available others. . . . What gets screened out is the possibility that Western modernity might be sustained by its own spiritual vision."[18] An acultural understanding of modernity thus tends to read the Western experience of modernity as universal, thereby eliding non-Western experiences of modernity and imposing inappropriately uniform standards for evaluating "progress." The cultural theory of modernity, by contrast, is founded upon the recognition that social change is tied to culture-specific values and practices. As Taylor puts it, "a cultural theory supposes the point of view in which we see our own culture [as] one among others" and which in turn leads to a more complete appreciation of "the full gamut of alternative modernities . . . in different parts of the world."[19]

The similarities between Taylor's culture-specific view of modernity and Appiah's description of historic forms of racialism are striking. Both ideologies presuppose that a given social group's values, practices, and ways of understanding itself and its relationship to other social groups are unique and nontransferable because they have evolved within a specific context. In other words, a social group (whether defined as a race or nation in racialist discourse or as a culture by Taylor) is unique because it possesses a unique and continuous history. There are, of course, significant differences, too. For one thing, racialist discourse carries with it all the baggage of the nineteenth century's largely discredited race-science, some of which informed the anti-immigrant writings of Nathaniel Shaler that appeared in the previous chapter. The conception of alternative modernities, by contrast, is an outgrowth of Taylor's own multicultural values and his ties with philosophical communitarianism, which emphasizes the dialectical relationship between an individual's understanding of his or her own identity and that person's membership within a given social group as well as the link between a person's sense of identity and sense of ethics.[20] Likewise, it would be unfair to conflate twentieth-century multiculturalism and nineteenth-century racialism. Multiculturalism and, by extension, the notion of alternative modernities are concerned primarily with political pluralism and empowerment through recognition of—and respect for—cultural differences. What I am suggesting here is that, far from being bad or simply racist, racialism can lead, under certain circumstances, to the recognition of a close cousin of multiculturalism: Taylor's concept of alternative modernities.[21]

The workings of this logic shape the writings of Jack London and Lafcadio Hearn, though the two men reached different conclusions about the place of Japan in the international community. London employed racialism in order to warn Americans of the danger that Japan's alternative modernity posed to U.S. imperial interests in the Pacific, while Hearn embraced that same alternative modernity to criticize what he viewed as the failures and shortcomings of American society and culture. Although it will become quickly apparent that Hearn's view of Japan was more open and comparative than London's, both writers employed the logic of racialism in order to reach their respective conclusions. The modes of transnational circulation that I have examined in preceding chapters—of literary work and of people, including not just London and Hearn but also the Asian immigrants who often caused even greater anxiety than their European counterparts—thus enabled London and Hearn to engage Japanese culture on behalf of an interested reading public, but the simultaneous circulation of competing ideas about imperialism and modernity along those same routes also give their writings unique and geopolitically important inflections. What Japan ultimately represented to both writers was an alternative—and a possible *after*—to the modernity and imperial hegemony that the United States was increasingly coming to embody.

That London and Hearn could respond to these concerns in such markedly different ways also reveals that Americans living in the early twentieth century had access to a much wider range of possible attitudes towards "Oriental" societies than the one Edward Said categorically characterizes as "racist, imperialist, and almost totally ethnocentric."[22] Although subsequent critics have often claimed to reject Said's model as inappropriate to Japan, some simultaneously reinscribe that model through their readings of Hearn and other writers who visited Japan, which in turn underscores the exceptional nature of the two nations' intertwined histories.[23] While the anxieties that London and Stoddard express might suggest a Pacific Rim variation on Said's notion of "Orientalism," which "depends for its strategy on [a] flexible *positional* superiority, which puts the Westerner in a whole series of possible relationships with the Orient without ever losing him the relative upper hand" (original emphasis), Said's argument is ultimately insufficient to account for the complexity of U.S.-Japanese relations or, even more significantly, for Japan's historically unique position within the international community.[24] As Colleen Lye points out, East Asia as a whole has always "signified an exceptional, rather than paradigmatic, Other" for Americans.[25] More specifically, with its long history, seemingly unbroken cultural continuity, and ability to assimilate Western technology without abandoning its own social practices, Japan has been the non-Western nation that most confounds Eurocentric notions of "modernity." Moreover, despite the intensifying imperial rivalry that followed U.S. acquisition of the Hawaiian and Philippine islands, the United States and Japan engaged for a time in mutually agreeable empire-building. The writings of Jack London and Lafcadio Hearn illuminate this unique and sometimes paradoxical relationship between the United States and the Empire of Japan.

JACK LONDON, RACIALISM, AND IMPERIAL COMPETITION

It is perhaps indicative of the American reading public's fascination with Japan, only recently accessible to the West on a large scale, that the most notable English-language writings at the turn of the twentieth century to feature images of life in Japan tended to be nonfiction—as if the foreignness of Japanese culture not only rendered the addition of fictional elements superfluous, but actually demanded the transparency of nonfiction forms in order to make itself appear authentic to Western readers. This attitude is present in William Dean Howells's review of Shiukichi Shigemi's 1889 autobiography *A Japanese Boy*. Evaluating Shigemi's work in the same column in which he reviews Henry James's novel *The Tragic Muse* (1890), Howells praises Shigemi's writing for exhibiting the same qualities that Howells valued in realist fiction. "The excellent simplicity with which he has told [his] story," Howells contends, enables Shigemi to achieve the same sense of authenticity and equal exchange that Howells claimed as the special power of realism: Shigemi's account of "his schools, tasks, plays, punishments; his home life, in kitchen and parlor; the village life outside; the theaters, the manners and customs of the people; his relations and neighbors; the family sports and amusements; the holidays, and the religious rites and feasts" serves as a "contribution to man's knowledge of himself" and teaches "the truth of our solidarity."[26] The details that Howells singles out for praise in Shigemi's writing are clear examples of local color, suggesting that nonfiction about Japan could receive Howells's stamp of approval and participate in the larger project of realism if it exhibited the same attentiveness to local color that fiction did. That Lafcadio Hearn, whose last major work of fiction before his move to Japan, *Youma* (1890), coincidentally was reviewed by Howells in the same column as *A Japanese Boy* and *The Tragic Muse*, could achieve his greatest popularity by publishing sketches of daily life in Japan in the pages of *Atlantic Monthly* only underscores the space the U.S. publishing industry made for nonfictional representations of local color.

Indeed, it is telling that Jack London's "The Unparalleled Invasion" remains controversial precisely because it disregards realism in favor of fantasy, including the imagined destruction of hundreds of millions of Asians. Nevertheless, even this work of fiction points readers back to London's earlier nonfiction writings about Japan, which it occasionally paraphrases. The recycling of passages from London's journalism, including his infamous 1904 essay "The Yellow Peril," reveals the extent to which London's fiction, not unlike that of his peers Frank Norris and Theodore Dreiser, was sometimes shaped by his journalistic experiences. This particular connection between London's fiction and nonfiction also highlights his desire to use his literary skills and reputation to intervene in a particular geopolitical problem: the rise of Japan as a potential imperial rival to the United States in Asia.

The interactions with Japanese culture that led London to make this intervention did not, properly speaking, take place in Japan. In fact, the total duration of his stay in Japan was about two weeks—from January 25 through February 7, 1904. After that, London followed the Japanese army to Korea, where he spent the remainder of his time (about four months) in East Asia covering the Russo-Japanese War. Thus despite positioning himself as an expert on Asian culture in such essays as "The Yellow Peril" and "If Japan Wakens China" (1909), London's firsthand knowledge of Japan in particular and Asia in general was limited, and this limited knowledge is what prompts many critics to read London's conception of Asia as really a response to the Asian Americans he encountered in California. For instance, Japan features prominently in the title of London's first published piece of writing, "Story of a Typhoon off the Coast of Japan" (1893), but its presence matters very little to the actual narrative. Colleen Lye suggests that "'Japan' simply designates the outer horizon of an expansive oceanic world, which is London's stage for adventure" in this and other early texts by the young author.[27] According to Jeanne Campbell Reesman, the San Francisco Bay area, where London grew up and which already possessed a large Asian population, witnessed the "burnings of Asian neighborhoods and even the lynchings of Asian men by armed groups of white hooligans," and it is this racial strife that informs London's depiction of Asian characters is such later works as "Goliah" (1907), The Iron Heel (1908), "The Unparalleled Invasion," and The Valley of the Moon (1913).[28]

Nevertheless, I suggest that it is shortsighted to infer that London was willfully blind to the global implications of Japan's rising economic, military, and political power. On the contrary, London's war correspondence demonstrates how the result of the Russo-Japanese War forced Americans to rethink their assumptions about what constituted international society. The war itself was fought over control of Korea, Manchuria, and the important port city of Port Arthur [Lushun], all of which Russia had begun to occupy in the late 1890s to forestall Japanese expansion.[29] After the Japanese navy attacked the Russian fleet at Port Arthur on February 8 and 9, 1904, the Japanese army launched a quick campaign through the Korean peninsula, across the Yalu River, and into southern Manchuria. It was this campaign that London accompanied during the spring of 1904. The Japanese army's resulting victories established Japan as the dominant power in East Asia and, as noted above, marked the first occasion in modern history in which a European power suffered a decisive military defeat at the hands of an Asian nation. "The ramifications of Japanese victory over Russia in 1905," David Wells and Sandra Wilson remark, "thus ranged from a fundamental change in the balance of power in Asia to a clear challenge to prevailing notions of white, European superiority throughout the world."[30] This "challenge to prevailing notions of white, European superiority" is what registers most keenly in London's correspondence.

As war correspondence, the articles that London produced were widely regarded as failures, even by London himself. They describe surprisingly little action and offer very little insight into the strategy of the Japanese army. London himself ascribed these shortcomings to the amount of censorship he encountered. The Japanese military did indeed restrict foreign journalists' access to information to a degree that many were unused to.[31] In *Notes of a War Correspondent*, Richard Harding Davis, who covered the war for *Collier's Weekly*, evocatively subtitled his lone chapter on the Russo-Japanese War "Battles I Did Not See," and he complained that he "had not been allowed to see anything of the military operations."[32] Nevertheless, it is also clear from his own articles, in which he frequently adopts a sarcastic persona, that London tended to antagonize the Japanese authorities. Taking pride in what he considered his self-reliance, he describes ignoring Japanese directives and traveling on his own initiative, only to fall behind his fellow correspondents. Moreover, London exhibits an almost naïve inability to write *around* the Japanese censors, and he comes nowhere close to the sort of genuinely newsworthy detail, such as troop movements and engagements, that readers typically expect from war correspondence. Despite facing the same restrictions, Davis managed to report on such events as a Japanese military funeral, for example.[33] London's coverage of the Russo-Japanese War remains valuable, then, not because of his skill as a reporter, but because of the uniqueness of his position as a prominent American observer of a war of imperialism fought between two other global powers and the redirection of his literary efforts toward recording local color and commenting on Japan's form of modernity.

A close reading of London's war correspondence reveals that his attitude toward Japan shifted incrementally from a surprisingly positive to an extremely negative one and that this shift was the result of a process of dislocation, as London was plunged by the global reach of the U.S. mass media into a non-Western context for which he had no existing frame of reference. For instance, in his fourth article, dated March 4 from Seoul, London offers almost rapturous admiration for the Japanese army:

> I doubt if there be more peaceable, orderly soldiers in the world than the Japanese. Our own soldiers, long ere this, would have painted Seoul red with their skylarking and good-natured boisterousness, but the Japanese are not boisterous. They are deadly serious. Yet no one of the civilian population is afraid of them. The women are safe; the money is safe; the goods are safe. . . . The Japanese are a race of warriors and their infantry is all the infantry could possibly be. (41–42)

These sentiments are echoed in a letter to his future second wife Charmian Kittredge dated the same day:

> I think as to the quietness, strictness and orderliness of Japanese soldiers it is very hard to find any equals in the world. If it were our boys they would have gone lightheartedly to all the places and we would surely have heard for many a time about them kicking up a row, but such things never happen in Japanese and it is wonderful how they keep so orderly. . . . Japanese is the race who can produce real fighting men, and its infantry is simply superb. (13)

London's admiration for the prowess of these soldiers is clear. Addressing his American audience, he goes so far as to compare them favorably to "our own soldiers," whose "boisterousness" may very well be "good-natured" but still falls far short of the supreme discipline maintained by the Japanese troops.

A significant change in London's attitude emerges within a matter of days. He confides to Kittredge on March 8, "How the letters [I have received] have roused me up! Furthermore, they have proved to me, or, rather, reassured me, that I am a white man. . . . One can scarcely think whiteman's thoughts" (14). Between March 4 and March 8, London composed five more articles, each of which represents Asians in general and the Japanese in particular in increasingly negative ways. On March 5, he writes about witnessing both Koreans and Japanese soldiers mistreating their horses. He saves the bulk of his vitriol for Koreans but also indicts the Japanese by virtue of their shared status as "Asiatic":

> For the Korean is nothing if not a coward, and his fear of bodily hurt is about equal to his inaction. . . . The white man [London himself] knew nothing about horses, and probably the only thing to be said in his favor was that he was not a Korean. . . . The Asiatic is heartless. The suffering of dumb brutes means nothing to him. . . . The Japanese may be the Britisher of the Orient, but he is still Asiatic. The suffering of beasts does not touch him. (44, 46–47)

interest in differentiation

Later the same day but in a different article, London begins to distance himself from his still admiring descriptions of the Japanese army. His use of passive voice dominates the sentences that open the article: "The Japanese soldiery and equipment *seem to command* universal admiration. Not one dissenting voice *is to be heard* among the European and American residents in Korea. On the contrary, favorable comparison *is made* with our own troops and the troops of Europe" (47–48, emphasis added).

Crucially, London's March 7 article casts a breakdown in communication between himself and the Koreans in racialist terms, in which the chasm separating each race's world of experience extends even to horseshoes: "To keep shoes on our horses was the great problem. In the first place, our horseshoes were whiteman's horseshoes, about which the Korean farmers knew nothing. And as their knowledge of their own kind of shoes was the accumulated wisdom of centuries, it was beyond the wildest flights of imagination to dream that they could learn anything about whiteman's shoes inside several centuries more" (56). This passage is certainly condescending, since the basis for his complaint is the expectation that Korean farmers should be willing to accommodate his needs rather than vice versa; however, London's comments are not explicitly racist. He does not suggest that a "whiteman's" horseshoes are inherently superior to a Korean's. Instead, the "problem" London identifies is the fact that the two races possess equally long and rich traditions of horseshoe-making ("the accumulated wisdom of centuries") and that he just happened to bring the wrong horseshoes.

London's racialism extends to his representation of the Japanese army, which he contends has adopted Western methods without altering the essential character of the soldiers themselves. After recounting his horseshoe problem, he observes, "But horses' feet were not the only feet that suffered on the Pekin Road. Sore-footed soldiers were pretty much in the evidence. They trailed along for miles behind every marching company and battalion. . . . Many of them discarded the army shoe of stiff leather, and went back to their native gear, the soft straw sandal" (57). A few days later (March 13), London returns to this topic, suggesting the following reason for the sore feet: "These men, used to the straw sandal all their lives, had been summoned to join their colors and to incase their feet in the harsh leather boot of the West. . . . The whole leg and foot action of a man who has worn sandals is different from that which comes of wearing boots. And even if the boots had fitted the feet, the very action of the feet and the legs alone would have chafed and lacerated" (80). Here, London is applying the logic of racialism to the physical experiences and bodily habits of others, and he ultimately arrives at a Lamarckian conclusion about the ways in which cultural practices can shape the physical body. The Japanese soldiers' feet are sore, he claims, because they have been forced to put on a foreign form of footwear with which they have had no previous experience and to which their manner of walking is indisposed. Just as a society's method of making horseshoes is based upon skills and techniques that have been passed down within that society ("the accumulated wisdom of centuries"), a people's manner of walking is determined by the footwear that has traditionally adorned their feet: the accumulated *walking* of centuries, as it were.

By March 8, the day of the second letter to Kittredge quoted above, London had extended this racialist outlook to language and mental processes: "The Japanese interpreter is Asiatic. He no more understands a white man's mental processes than a white man understands his" (61). What gives London the most anxiety, however, is that he, a "white man," is in fact beginning to understand "Asiatic" mental processes. Also on March 8, he transcribes a press report from the Japanese army written in broken English, and he comments, "I understand every word of it" (62). Elsewhere, London confesses, "I had become used to a people which was not of my kind. My mind had settled down to accepting without question that the men who fought had eyes and cheek bones and skins different from the eyes and cheek bones and skins of my kind" (106). What London's war correspondence ultimately amounts to is an account of the destabilization of his sense of his own identity. Two days later, he revisits these concerns with a lengthy discussion about the unease he feels at being able to function within the Korean economy without knowing "what anything costs me—at least in intelligible terms" (72). By "intelligible terms," London means whatever Korean currency is "equivalent to in terms of American coinage"—something that is "beyond" him (72).

Instead of successfully relating his experiences in Asia to racial categories with which he was already familiar in California, I contend that London recognizes that he has encountered an alternative form of modernity: an Asian form of social organization, complete with its own currency, military, and media restrictions, that exists alongside of—but does not completely correspond to—the American form of social organization he understands. In other words, London's ability to relate his experiences in Korea to terms with which he is already familiar, namely his experiences in the United States, breaks down. His frustrations thus underscore the way of approaching the history of globalization that I discussed in the introduction: as a reformulation of what William James calls "relations"—or the creation of new relations—between already existing entities (what James calls "terms"). In a sense, London's journey to Korea, which had been made possible by Japanese imperialist expansion and the reach of the U.S. news media, juxtaposes Japanese and American ways of understanding the world and thus brings two terms into relation with one another. Likewise, London's anxiety over the influence that these "Asiatic" mental processes might exert on his own thinking echoes the involuntarily intermingling of voices that the characters of *A Hazard of New Fortunes* experience, indicating the extent to which even authors unsympathetic to Howells's anti-imperialism employed techniques similar to the ones Howells advocated for representing their encounters with the world beyond U.S. borders.

Perhaps nothing exemplifies London's inability to reconcile his experiences in Korea with his experiences in the United States so much as his observation of the Japanese army's stunning victory over the Russian army at the Yalu River, an event that shook London's understanding of modernity itself. In his articles, London conceives of modernity as a fall from some sort of superior human condition, as his description of modern combat clearly indicates. "This is modern warfare," he writes somewhat gloomily about the long-range artillery engagements that the Japanese carry out so skillfully, continuing, "But it is long-range fighting which makes modern warfare so different from ancient warfare" (97). Foreseeing a sort of "cold" warfare that primarily involves deterrence, London notes, "Killing decided ancient warfare; the possibility of being killed decides modern warfare. In short, the marvelous and awful machinery of warfare of to-day, defeats its own end. Made pre-eminently to kill, its chief effect is to make killing quite the unusual thing. When the machinery of warfare becomes just about perfect, there won't be any killing at all" (98). Against this view of war as stalemate, London also envisions another, more threatening aspect of modern warfare: industrialized death. "In ancient warfare," he writes in anticipation of the biological warfare he depicts at the end of "The Unparalleled Invasion," "the energy which drove death was generated in a man's body. . . . But to-day the energy which drives home death is generated by the chemists in large factories and must be carted about by the soldiers who are to use it" (78). According to London, these two developments result in a disjunction between a soldier's experiences on the battlefield and his experiences throughout the rest of his life. As opposed to ancient fighters, for whom warfare was part of everyday life, "the conscript of to-day lives a peaceable, industrious life, and has never heard war's alarms until the moment he is jerked from out his little pigeon-hole and hurled onto the field of battle" (79). For London, these developments eliminate the potential for heroism. Modernity has deprived war of its human factor, which was its potential for glory.

The fact that an "Asiatic" race can embrace this aspect of modernity alarms London. When he witnesses Japan defeat Russia at the Battle of the Yalu River, he realizes that Japan has managed not only to modernize its military successfully without abandoning its own racially specific thought processes and customs but also to deploy that modernized military against a Western power with devastating effectiveness. As demonstrated by his May 1 article's depiction of his "freedom amongst aliens," this realization affects London deeply, transforming him into an "alien" who wishes to share in Russia's defeat rather than Japan's victory because Russia is Western and Japan is not. By the time he was preparing to return to the United States, London could promise Kittredge that "in the past I have preached the Economic Yellow Peril; henceforth I shall preach the Militant Yellow Peril" (24). This is exactly what London did in his infamous essay "The Yellow Peril," which although not officially part of his war correspondence was written before he left Asia. In that essay and in some of his subsequent writings for the next few years, London warned of the threat the potential combination of Japanese military and Chinese economic power posed to U.S. hegemony in the Pacific. "A new competitor," London writes in his 1909 essay "If Japan Wakens China," "and a most ominous and formidable one, will enter the arena where the races struggle for the world-market" (361). Yet even while warning Americans of Japan's ability to turn Western imperialism on its head, London simultaneously attempts to dismiss this anxiety by retreating into a position of moral superiority. He writes hopefully in "The Yellow

Peril" that the "two great branches of the Anglo-Saxon race" (the British and Americans) might "despoil [the Japanese] of his spoils" because "we are a right-seeking race" (346, 349). At this point, of course, it is clear that London has moved beyond a relatively neutral racialist outlook and adopted an outright racist attitude, but it is also clear that London's concerns here are geopolitical: Japan's modernity, as well as its empire, represents a threat because it has proven itself a successful—and "ominous"—"competitor."

LAFCADIO HEARN, RACIALISM, AND COSMOPOLITAN CRITIQUE

In defense of the argument he outlines in "The Yellow Peril" and "If Japan Wakens China," London marshals the support of Lafcadio Hearn. At the time, Hearn was a popular journalist and author, though he has been somewhat forgotten in recent years. Characterizing him as an "American" author, however, is problematic. Hearn was born in 1850 on the Greek island of Levkas to an Irish surgeon serving in the British army and a local Greek woman. At the age of nineteen, he moved to the United States, where he lived for the next twenty years. He became a journalist, working first in Cincinnati and then in New Orleans, but he never underwent official naturalization. In 1890, he traveled to Japan on a brief assignment, but he fell in love with the country and its people and decided to stay. He married a Japanese woman and eventually became a Japanese citizen in 1896, taking the name Yakumo Koizumi.[34] He supported himself and his family by teaching English at various Japanese schools and universities, but he made a name for himself between 1894 and his death in 1904 by translating Japanese folk tales and poetry into English and by writing articles and sketches about his experiences for English-speaking readers. Hearn remained popular and respected throughout the 1890s and early 1900s, publishing regularly in such high-profile U.S. magazines as *Harper's* and the *Atlantic Monthly*.

Critical opinion of Hearn's work mostly follows that of his earliest champions, including Elizabeth Bisland and Malcolm Cowley, who considered Hearn's writings about Japan his best work.[35] It is important to note, however, that Hearn emerged out of the same community of New Orleans local colorists that produced George Washington Cable, with whom Hearn occasionally collaborated. Even after beginning to write about foreign societies and their cultures, Hearn's work continued to be regarded as exemplary representations of local color. In his review of Hearn's *Youma* (1890), a short novel set in Martinique, William Dean Howells observed that "the local color is luxuriously given. . . . Here is a man born to do the work he is doing."[36] All the same, Hearn's reputation has always rested upon his books about Japan, and they were certainly what his contemporary readers, including Jack London, knew him best for.

It is because of Hearn's status at the time as one of the Western world's foremost experts on Japanese culture that London calls upon Hearn to support his claim that Asians are ultimately unknowable to Westerners. London's summary of Hearn's conclusions, however, is a mischaracterization. In *Japan: An Attempt at Interpretation* (1904), the final book Hearn sent to his publisher before he died, Hearn admits that "I cannot understand the Japanese at all."[37] Yet what Hearn means by that is something akin to the Socratic position that only the person who claims to know nothing really understands anything. Hearn draws attention to his early use of singular present tense ("I cannot") only to move into plural future tense, arguing that mutual understanding is possible and necessary. "We *can* know something about Japanese character," Hearn concludes, "if we are able to ascertain the nature of the conditions which shaped it" (emphasis added).[38] The potential for mutual intelligibility that London attempts to repress, Hearn wishes to embrace. Indeed, as his biography suggests, Hearn was a consummate cosmopolitan who insisted upon signing his English-language publications with a middle name (Lafcadio) that derived from the name of the island where he was born (Levkas or, sometimes, Lefcada) instead of his given first name (Patricio, or Patrick), thus emphasizing his hybrid identity.[39] As early as 1874, at the age of twenty-four, Hearn could formulate the following statement on the values of pluralism: "The multitude are, therefore, wiser than any man, from the very fact that diverse vocations diversify the gifts and powers of men, and give that variety to character which, securing the world unity in variety, redeems it from the dreariness and desolation of a dead monotony."[40] This appreciation for the richness that diversity brings to society and for the importance of the relations that secure "the world unity" aligns Hearn with other practitioners of local color as well as with such philosophers as Randolph Bourne and William James. It also made him an astute observer of the juxtapositions of various cultures that the processes of globalization were gradually making possible. These views ultimately prepared Hearn for his career as a sympathetic interpreter of a non-Western culture for American readers.

T. J. Jackson Lears has linked the local-colorist approach to Japan that Hearn and other late nineteenth-century American Orientalists took in their writings, which Lears characterizes as "exercise[s] in exoticism" that were "often ignorant of the traditions they claimed to embrace," to the wider "antimodern sentiments" in fin de siècle American culture that he examines in *No Place of Grace.*[41] In suggesting that Hearn mostly "ignored the educated, urban elites in order to create a nation peopled entirely by 'fairy-folk' of childlike grace and simplicity," however, Lears overstates his case.[42] It is true that, in his early writings about Japan, Hearn tended to emphasize Japan's exotic, seemingly innocent appeal. In *Glimpses of Unfamiliar Japan* (1894), his first collection of essays on Japanese culture and society, Hearn writes:

> To find one's self suddenly in a world where everything is upon a smaller and daintier scale than with us,—a world of lesser and seemingly kindlier beings, all smiling at you as if to wish you well,—a world where all movement is slow and soft, and voices are hushed,— a world where all land, life, and sky are unlike all that one has known elsewhere,—this is surely the realization, for imaginations nourished with English folklore, of the old dream of a World of Elves.[43]

Yet from the first, Hearn consistently acknowledged the parallel existence of what he called the "New Japan," often explicitly contrasting the "common people" of the Japanese countryside with the inhabitants of "modernized Japan."[44] In *Kokoro: Hints and Echoes of Japanese Inner Life* (1896), published only two years after *Glimpses of Unfamiliar Japan*, Hearn opens with an essay entitled "At a Railway Station," the first sentence of which refers to a "telegram."[45] Hearn's point is not that modernity has somehow bypassed Japan or that he can escape from modernity by moving there; rather, Hearn seeks to describe a form of modernity that is different from the form he had experienced in the West—a form of modernity that enabled the Japanese to maintain a sense of continuity with their own distinct cultural practices.

Kokoro—and the vision of Japanese modernity that emerges in its pages—offers an instructive comparison to London's war correspondence, in part because it was published just after Japan's previous war of imperialism, the Sino-Japanese War of 1894–95. Although the Russo-Japanese War had a far greater impact upon the West, some historians have argued that the Sino-Japanese War carried more historical significance insofar as it shifted the balance of power in East Asia from China to Japan and gave Japan the island of Formosa [Taiwan], which at least one Japanese historian in the early twentieth century called "Japan's first colony."[46] Like the Russo-Japanese War, the earlier war between Japan and China was fought mainly for dominance over Korea and Manchuria, and just as in the later war against Russia, Japan beat China quickly and decisively. So quickly and decisively, in fact, that Hearn was moved to celebrate—months before he took Japanese citizenship—that it marked "the real birthday of New Japan" (77). In retrospect, Hearn's glorying in Japan's military victory, as well as in its imperial aggression, is somewhat unnerving because he was witnessing and supporting the roots of Japan's militarization and authoritarianism. He writes approvingly that Japan's "educational system, with its twenty-six thousand schools, is an enormous drilling-machine. On her own soil she could face any foreign power" (83). He also offhandedly mentions that "free speech was gagged; the press was severely silenced"; but "the government really acted with faultless wisdom" (84). Even after Hearn registers misgivings when he sees the gaunt, somber faces of a group of returning veterans, he shrugs them off with the remark that "for all of that, the soldiers were better soldiers now" (92). Hearn's celebratory tone stands in stark contrast to London's anxiety. Hearn revels vicariously in his Japanese neighbors' nationalistic pride. For him, as for them, Japan's spectacular victory proves them the equal of any Great Power. Hearn quotes a Japanese seaman as boasting, "The Chinese had European gunners helping them. If we had not had to fight against Western gunners, *our victory would have been too easy*" (88, original emphasis).

The war's outcome also proves to Hearn that Japan has modernized its society successfully without sacrificing any essentially Japanese characteristics. Thus "the glories" of this war can be celebrated by what Hearn calls "the various great industries of the country" (81). But while Hearn identifies Japan as a fully industrialized nation, the industries he mentions are typically Japanese: porcelain, lacquer-ware, silk, and chopsticks. In fact, Hearn's main concern is not that Japan will rival the West imperially or economically, but rather that Japan might become *too* westernized. He warns against "a tendency to hardening,—a danger of changes" (31). These worries were not without warrant in the 1890s. Following the Meiji Restoration (1867–68), which ousted the Tokugawa shogunate and ended Japan's centuries-old feudal system, Japan entered a period of rapid modernization and industrialization.[47] Prompted by concern over Japan's future after the arrival of Perry and the signing of the Kanagawa Treaty, the nobles and politicians who instigated the Meiji Restoration believed that their nation's survival depended upon its ability to compete economically and militarily with the United States and Europe and to assimilate Western political and social practices. As noted in the second chapter, this drive to adopt and exploit preexisting models of statehood reflects the process that John

W. Meyer calls "isomorphism" at work within "world society." During the next forty-five years, known as the Meiji period (literally, the "period of enlightened rule"), Japan's leaders began introducing land reform, compulsory education and military service, representative government, new tax and trade laws, and improved networks of communication and transportation. As historian Thomas Bender points out, many of these reforms were modeled on the efforts and achievements of U.S. Progressivism.[48] Thus the Meiji government made it clear that it rejected Japan's former isolationist policies and encouraged contact and trade with the West. By 1902, Japan had entered into an alliance with Britain, and Japan ratified the Taft-Katsura Agreement with the United States in 1905.

loose connexion at best

The rapidity with which the Meiji government transformed Japan from an isolated agrarian society into a powerful industrial one nonetheless created considerable concern among many Japanese that the country would lose its cultural identity, and despite his celebratory account of Japan's victory over China, Hearn's writings often align him with these skeptics. Thus Hearn's efforts at drawing attention to the need for preserving as much of Japan's landscape and native culture as possible belong as much to a conservative tradition within Japanese society as they do to the American "antimodernism" Lears analyzes. (Indeed, Hearn's continued popularity among many Japanese readers is no doubt due to his vivid descriptions of a countryside still untouched by industrialization and urbanization and the nostalgic glimpses he offers of a Japan that no longer exists.) Hearn goes to great lengths throughout *Kokoro* and elsewhere to emphasize that he is witnessing a distinctly Japanese strand of industrialization and modernization. Far from simply working to exoticize Japan for American readers, then, Hearn's use of local color often coincides with local Japanese politics and social projects.

As engaged with local Japanese politics as his writings may be, Hearn never loses sight of the global implications of the alternative modernity he sees coalescing. In a chapter of *Kokoro* appropriately entitled "The Genius of Japanese Civilization," he makes a point of comparing the modernity he experiences in Japan quite favorably to the modernity he knew in the West, which he calls "hard, grim, dumb" and "sinister" (14–15). Hearn's negative depiction of Western modernity is based on firsthand knowledge, for he was intimately familiar with the seedy underside of industrialization in both Britain and the United States. Following an eye injury at the age of sixteen, Hearn lived for a time in poverty in London's squalid East End. Later, after a relative paid his fare to the United States, he became a newspaper reporter in Cincinnati, where he spent much of his time among black and white working-class communities. Typical of the more sensational American journalism of the 1870s, Hearn's essays from that period often focused on criminals, prostitutes, and other social outcasts. These early experiences in the United States left a deep impression on Hearn as a young man, and according to Simon J. Bronner, "America became for Hearn the epitome of the clamor of modernization."[49] An 1874 article for the *Cincinnati Enquirer* entitled "Les Chiffonniers" recounts a visit to the rag-pickers at the local dump. For Hearn, the living and working conditions of these people resembled an urban hell: "A wilderness of filthy desolation walled in by dismal factories; a Golgotha of foul bones and refuse; a great grave-yard for worn-out pots and kettles and smashed glasses, and rotten vegetables and animal filth, and shattered household utensils and abominations unutterable."[50] Ten years later, when he was living in New Orleans, Hearn's attitude toward U.S. urban life had only intensified. In "The Roar of a Great City" (1884), originally published in the *New Orleans Times-Democrat*, he envisions the modern city as a "monstrous spider web" and the din of industrial machinery as "the last wail of a dying man, or the shriek of the angel of death as he clasps his victim to him."[51]

The horrors of Western modernity continue to inform and, if anything, take on even more urgency in the writings Hearn produced after his relocation to Japan. In "Growth of Population in America," an article he published in the English-language *Kobe Chronicle* in 1894, Hearn foresees the stagnation of the United States and attributes it to the same kinds of economic consolidation that Louis D. Brandeis would attack twenty years later: "Altogether the condition of the working-classes in America has become almost as hard as in any part of Europe, and is going, in all probability to become harder. Unlimited capital and unlimited power to use it, in the hands of a small class, will certainly produce conditions impossible in England or in Germany."[52] Hearn plainly shares London's misgivings about modern life, but in contrast to London, Hearn locates the source for these anxieties in the West itself, not in Japan's efforts at modernization.

On the contrary, according to Hearn, the turn toward modernity in Japan is not accompanied by a fall or by the shortcomings of Western capitalism. Nor, apparently, does it necessarily entail westernization. In *Kokoro*, he claims that

the land remains what it was before; its face has scarcely been modified by all the changes of Meiji. . . . In all the cities, with the exception of the open ports and their little foreign settlements, there exists hardly a street vista suggesting the teaching of Western ideas. You might journey two hundred miles through the interior of the country, looking in vain for large manifestations of the new civilization. . . . A Japanese city is still as it was ten centuries ago. (12)

Like London, Hearn recognizes that Japan has entered modernity without sacrificing its culture-specific values or social practices. Japan remains—for now—fundamentally Asian and thus presents a model alternative modernity.

[handwritten margin note: hence importance of realism]

The primary reason for Japan's ability to avoid the pitfalls of Western modernity, Hearn concludes, is the nation's reliance on small industries rather than "vast integrations of industrial capital" (29). Marveling at the ability of Japan's textile manufacturers to operate out of modest, preexisting buildings, hence significantly reducing overhead and inefficiency, Hearn claims, "Japan is producing without capital, in our large sense of the word. She has become industrial without becoming essentially mechanical and artificial" (27). The resulting efficiency and mobility of Japan's small industries, as opposed to the West's "vast integrations of industrial capital," explains Hearn's optimism regarding Japan's future. In "Growth of Population in America," written around the same time that he published *Kokoro*, Hearn echoes the despair expressed by Henry James about the transformation of the North American landscape at the end of *The American Scene*:

Within a quarter of a century America has been totally changed. The plains, the prairies of romance, can no longer be said to exist; they are covered with farms, villages, towns, cities. The railroads have not only "built up" the West; they have forced the expansion of industrialism to its utmost limit. . . . Social conditions have hardened and stratified. There are no more chances to make a fortune in a day. Becoming more and more ordered, the West has also become more and more in all things like "the effete monarchies of Europe."[53]

But while the United States' economic and social prospects are stagnating, Japan's remain dynamic. In *Kokoro*, Hearn suggests that this dynamism not only gives Japan the capacity "to threaten Western manufacturers," but even to "ruin foreign industries of far vaster capacity" (26, 28). One wonders how London rationalized the views Hearn expresses in *Kokoro* once London made his self-professed turn from preaching Economic Yellow Peril to preaching Militant Yellow Peril.

Hearn's preaching may carry a very different hue, but his understanding of Japan, like London's, is based on racialism. After praising Japan's progress in *Kokoro*, Hearn explains its uniqueness this way: "The explanation is in the race character,—a race character in more ways than one the very opposite of our own" (30). Hearn is able to read Japan's recent modernization as a story of continuity rather than discontinuity. Despite having "changed the whole political face of the east" and having undergone "the so-called 'adoption of Western civilization,'" Japan has experienced "no transformation,—nothing more than the turning of old abilities into new and larger channels" (7–8). This continuity between past and present is simultaneously what creates the gulf between East and West: "The more complex feelings of the Oriental have been composed by combinations of experiences, ancestral and individual, which have had no really precise correspondence in Western life, and which we [Westerners] can therefore not fully know. For converse reasons, the Japanese cannot, even though they would, give Europeans their best sympathy" (10). The Japanese possess their own history and traditions, which a Westerner like Hearn can never fully share.

As Daniel Stempel argued persuasively in his early study of Hearn's Japanese writings, Hearn's theory of racial differences is really grounded upon an understanding of the "acquisition of *cultural* traits through *environmental* influence," which is precisely the link between racialism and Taylor's "alternative modernities" I noted earlier: that the uniqueness of a specific culture is the direct result of its evolution within a stable environment and its emergence into modernity on its own terms (emphasis added).[54] In *Japan: An Attempt at Interpretation*, Hearn's musings upon his own difficulties in mastering spoken Japanese—even after more than a decade of total immersion, his mangling of the pronunciation was notorious—lead him to speculate:

> No adult Occidental can perfectly master the language. East and West, the fundamental parts of human nature—the emotional bases of it—are much the same: the mental difference between a Japanese and a European child is mainly potential. But with growth the difference rapidly develops and widens, till it becomes, in adult life, inexpressible. The whole of the Japanese mental superstructure evolves into forms having nothing in common with Western psychological development: the expression of thought becomes regulated, and the expression of emotion inhibited in ways that bewilder and astound. The ideas of this people are not our ideas; their sentiments are not

our sentiments; their ethical life represents for us regions of thought and emotion yet unexplored, or perhaps long forgotten.[55]

In a sense, then, Hearn rejects Woodrow Wilson's concept of a mediating nation, pointing out that it is an impossible dream for any single nation or race to "comprehend and embody" all others. Hearn, however, simply accepts the gulf that such psychological development causes, even taking refuge in it instead of allowing it to trouble him as it did London. Hearn never faces the sort of anxiety over his identity that London does because he realizes that he can never actually "go native."[56] The "freedom amongst aliens" he discovers is genuine rather than ironic, as it was for London. Hearn is therefore able to embrace Japanese culture and, more importantly, learn from it instead of dismissing it as "Asiatic." Japan enables him to explore those "regions of thought and emotion . . . long forgotten."

One such lesson that Hearn learns and discusses in *Kokoro* serves as a final point of contrast between his views and those of London. Like London, Hearn meditates briefly on the differences between Japanese and Western footwear. Both writers agree that Americans and Japanese behave differently in part because Americans wear leather shoes or boots and Japanese wear sandals. Hearn writes, "The physical results are not limited to the foot. Whatever acts as a check, directly or indirectly, upon the organs of locomotion must extend its effects to the whole physical constitution" (25). The equation is simple for both men: different traditions of footwear result in different manners of walking, which in turn results in different bodily habits and physical experiences. Unsurprisingly, London comes down in favor of leather boots, ultimately dismissing the Japanese soldiers' sore feet as "the breaking-in process" (57), and the Japanese high command apparently sided with him. After imagining how much the Japanese soldiers "must have yearned for the pliant sandals to which they had been accustomed," London simply notes that "it was a vain yearning, for sandals were prohibited under severe penalties" (80). The discomfort of learning to wear leather boots was part of the process of making them soldiers.

Hearn, who favored sandals, manages to turn this masculine logic on its head. He characterizes "the habit of wearing leather shoes" as a sign of the need for "superfluous comforts" (24). He goes on to argue, not entirely tongue-in-cheek:

It [the leather shoe] has distorted the Western foot out of the original shape, and rendered it incapable of the work for which it was evolved. . . . We have too long submitted to the tyranny of

shoemakers. There may be defects in our politics, in our social ethics, in our religious system, more or less related to the habit of wearing leather shoes. Submission to the cramping of the body must certainly aid in developing submission to the cramping of the mind.
(24–25)

This example leads Hearn to conclude that life in Japan reveals "the real
character of some weaknesses in our own civilization" (26–27). Ultimately,
what Japan offers to Hearn is a different perspective, a more comparative
understanding of the world and its nations and cultures.

RACIALISM, THE STATE, AND IMPERIALIST RECIPROCITY

In the years following Hearn's death and London's return from the Russo-
Japanese War, the primary source of tension between Japan and the United
States remained immigration. The U.S. federal government demonstrated
a continued commitment to friendly relations with Japan, allaying the
American public's fears on several occasions, but anti-Japanese sentiment
remained strong. By 1907 anxiety over Japanese immigration was on the
verge of triggering a crisis between the two nations.[57] On October 11, 1906,
the San Francisco school board passed a resolution to segregate the city's
public schools and to send all Asian children to a separate Oriental Public
School. News of this decision quickly traveled to Japan, where it was decried in the press. In order to save face, President Theodore Roosevelt, who
believed that stronger immigration policies would reduce anti-Japanese
feelings along the West Coast, worked to reach an agreement with Japan's
foreign minister Tadasu Hayashi. The resulting settlement, known as the
Gentlemen's Agreement, ensured that the Japanese government itself would
restrict emigration to the United States. Simultaneously, the Immigration
Act of 1907 gave Roosevelt the power to limit the entry of Japanese laborers.
On May 20, 1907, however, a riot broke out, during which a mob attacked
a Japanese restaurant and bath house. The riot was widely perceived to be
the product of racial strife, and in their attempt to sensationalize the event,
Japanese newspapers played up the fact that the police failed to apprehend
a single member of the mob. Then, on June 27, the San Francisco Board of
Police Commissioners refused to license six Japanese to run employment
agencies. This decision was a clear case of discrimination, since four of the
licenses were simply up for renewal. Although official relations between
Japan and the United States remained cordial throughout these events,

journalists in both countries exaggerated the situation's seriousness and suggested that war-clouds were on the horizon. Even before the license fiasco of June 27, Roosevelt was persuaded by members of his cabinet that greater U.S. naval presence in the Pacific would calm these fears, but when plans for the Great White Fleet's transfer to the Pacific were announced, American newspapers assumed the worst, forcing Roosevelt to recast the fleet's purpose as a peaceful circumnavigation of the world.

In responding to the 1907 crisis, Roosevelt based his decisions on the same racialist logic that guided the thinking of Jack London and Lafcadio Hearn, but Roosevelt's interactions with the Japanese government indicate that the desire for reciprocity with another growing imperial power, rather than racial competition or cosmopolitan self-critique, was his primary motivation. According to historian Raymond A. Esthus, Roosevelt "deplored the manifestations of anti-Japanese sentiment [but] was in agreement with the Californians that Japanese immigration should be checked. He felt that the Japanese could not be readily assimilated—not because they were racially *inferior* but because they were racially *different*" (original emphasis).[58] Eventually, Roosevelt sent William Howard Taft, then secretary of war, to Tokyo, where Taft helped defuse the crisis in September and October of 1907. When the Great White Fleet reached Yokohama in October of 1908, it was greeted enthusiastically, and the following month the two nations signed the Root-Takahira Agreement, which reinforced the Taft-Katsura Agreement of 1905 and reaffirmed the two nations' respective spheres of influence in the Pacific. Official U.S. policy, both foreign and domestic, had been shaped by the logic of racialism, but that logic ultimately enabled the United States and Japan to work out a series of policies whereby both states could engage in mutually beneficial international diplomacy.

In the minds of the American public, however, a perceived relationship between Japanese imperialist expansion in the Pacific and inassimilable Japanese immigrants in the United States resulted in expressions of racial anxiety more in tune with Jack London's dystopian vision of racial competition in "The Unparalleled Invasion." For many Americans, the presence of Japanese immigrants in California threatened to make the West Coast foreign to the rest of the nation, thus paving the way for Japan's total dominance of the Pacific Rim. Perhaps the fullest expression of these fears appears in Montaville Flowers's book *The Japanese Conquest of American Opinion* (1917). Flowers, a Californian who ran an unsuccessful bid for Congress in 1918, was one of several writers who predicted war with Japan and, on the basis of race alone, opposed granting equal rights to Japanese immigrants.[59] Flowers unequivocally identified a connection not only between Japan's expanding empire and the United States' burgeoning Japanese population but also between the racial strife local to California in 1917 and the global impact of the Russo-Japanese War over a decade earlier:

> When these Japanese first arrived upon our shores, they were as peaceable and as amicable as any immigrant, and their home government in Japan readily accepted the treatment accorded them. But as they increased in numbers, and especially as their country rose in the rank of nations, their attitude became insistent—almost commanding. . . . [Japan] had gradually assumed control of Korea, and she had just whipped Russia! It was then, when Japan, swollen with pride, and conscious of the power of conquest, announced herself as a World Empire, that the Japanese in the United States, although not citizens, began to demand all the rights and privileges of citizens; and it was then that we discovered we have in the United States an acute Japanese Problem.[60]

These fears reached a head when, in 1913, the California legislature passed the Alien Land Act, which barred Japanese from owning land. Tokyo protested the measure, leaving Woodrow Wilson with no option but to reassure Japan by openly opposing the new act. With the outbreak of World War I the following year, however, Japan shifted its energies to occupying those Pacific islands formerly held by Germany, thereby avoiding a replay of the 1907 crisis. As the United States began closing its borders to the nation it had helped open to the West, Japan was rejecting its isolationist history and embracing its contact with the West. This historical irony was not lost on Seiji Hishida, a U.S.-educated Japanese historian who, as an apologist for Japanese modernization and imperialist expansion, served as a sort of Japanese counterpart to the American Josiah Strong.[61] Even before the Russo-Japanese War had officially ended, Hishida was responding directly to Jack London and other prophets of an impending "yellow peril." "An attempt is made," he writes in *The International Position of Japan as a Great Power* (1905), "to create antagonism to [Japan's] mission in China by invoking the apparition of the 'yellow peril,' which is supposed to endanger western civilization."[62] Then, anticipating and defusing London's own language of "Economic Yellow Peril" and Japan "awakening" China, he continues, "From the economic point of view, the 'yellow peril' is interpreted to signify that all western trade would be excluded from China should the Chinese, awakened by

Japan, develop their industrial resources with 'cheap labor' and thus supply themselves" (261). In response to this concern, Hishida points out that the modernization of Japan has, in actuality, made the Japanese "better customers in European and American markets" and predicts that China will follow suit, under Japan's guidance (262).

Hishida also addresses London's fear of a "Militant Yellow Peril": "From the military point of view, it is suggested that . . . the combination of Japan with an empire of four hundred million people will endanger the western nations just as the Mongol hordes threatened Europe in the thirteenth century" (262). He dismisses this fear, too, calling attention to the fact that Japan sided with the Western nations against China during the Boxer Rebellion of 1900 and arguing that his nation would do likewise in the future in order to protect its interests. He then takes a swipe at the parochialism of this sort of thinking: "Modern nations really struggle against universalism in order to preserve their own consciousness. So long as nations have no world-language or world-literature and no universal consciousness of right and wrong, and so long as national patriotism is not converted into world cosmopolitanism, the world peace of universalism cannot come into existence" (266). Hishida concludes almost sarcastically that "the commercial and colonial jealousies attending the imperial expansion of the great powers would be softened by observing the spirit of cosmopolitanism" (272).

Hishida's goal here is to portray Japan, rather than the Western nations, as the true representative of modernity and internationalism. Indeed, he comes very close to prefiguring Wilson's concept of a mediating nation—except that Hishida casts Japan in that role. Emphasizing Japan's newfound hybridity as a modernized Asian nation that has joined the Western powers, he argues,

> It is the desire of Japan to preserve in the Orient the national status of those of her sister Asiatic nations which are not yet subjugated by foreign powers, and to lead them to that light of western civilization which she is now enjoying, without having abandoned her national individualism. . . . By reason of kindred ideas and a kindred literature, the Japanese, as Dr. Hirth has remarked, are more capable than Europeans and Americans of educating the Chinese as not to destroy the "the old knowledge while familiarizing the students with the advantages of the new." (258–59, 261)

Hishida's vision of Japan as a savior for all of Asia requires a careful balancing act. On one hand, the Japanese must obtain enough of "western civilization" so that they can transmit it to their Asian neighbors; on the other, they must not entirely abandon their "national" culture, which makes them "kin" and, consequently, intelligible to China and Korea. For all his talk of cosmopolitanism, Hishida draws on the same racialist logic that London and Hearn do, though Hishida, like Hearn, uses this logic to challenge the accepted wisdom of the West. Nevertheless, whereas Hearn merely suggested that comparative thinking might enable the West to learn useful lessons from Japan, such as the comfort of wearing sandals, Hishida claims that Japan's status as "Asiatic" makes that nation more adept at spreading modernity throughout East Asia. In other words, Hishida believes that Japan can beat the other Great Powers at their own game and become the dominant imperial force in the region.

In view of the course Japan's empire would follow over the next forty years, Hishida's reasoning is, in its own way, just as troubling as London's. Despite their apparent differences, both Hishida and London seem to think of modernity primarily in terms of imperial competition and the struggle for geopolitical supremacy. In this respect, Hearn's more nuanced, comparative approach serves as a corrective as much for Hishida's arguments as it does for London's. In *Kokoro* Hearn may have gloried in Japan's victory over China as proof of his adopted nation's successful modernization, but by the time he wrote his final book, *Japan: An Attempt at Interpretation*, Hearn had begun to fear that Japanese modernity was beginning to look too much like American modernity. In a chapter entitled "Industrial Danger," Hearn uneasily notes, "Consider the bewildering rapidity of recent changes. . . . Old Japan had never developed a wealthy and powerful middle class: she had not even approached that stage of industrial development which, in the ancient European societies, naturally brought about the first political struggles between rich and poor. Her social organization made industrial oppression impossible."[63] Then, he warns, "But now those commercial classes, set free and highly privileged, are silently and swiftly ousting the aristocratic ruling-class from power,—are becoming supremely important. And under the new order of things, forms of social misery, never before known in the history of the race, are being developed."[64] No doubt, Hearn exaggerates the degree of social equity in "Old Japan," but in identifying the emergence of "money-power" as the source of future danger for twentieth-century Japanese society, Hearn demonstrates the same economic understanding of—and the same desire to expose—imperialism that Louis Brandeis would in *Other People's Money*.[65] Against this increasingly "dark" vision of Japan's future, however, Hearn hopefully positions Japan's

But it wasn't imperialism

continuity with its past: "Yet it were a grievous error to imagine that [Japan] has nothing further to gain from her ancestral faith. All her modern successes have been aided by it; and all her modern failures have been marked by the needless breaking with its ethical custom."[66] The pointed contrast Hearn draws between Japan's "successes" and its "failures," both of which are equally "modern," points to Hearn's continued faith in Japan's ability to model an alternative modernity.

Modernism, Multiculturalism, and the Legacy of the Mediating Nation

I n the years following the First World War, as American literary critics began to assess the career of the recently deceased Henry James, the author's decades-long expatriation surfaced as a major problem—what, in *The Pilgrimage of Henry James* (1925), Van Wyck Brooks called "the problem of his own deracination."[1] Critics as different from one another as Brooks, H. L. Mencken, and Vernon Parrington apparently could not forgive James for officially becoming a British subject at the end of his life, an action they seemed to view as James's final betrayal of his homeland. In the November 1920 issue of *Smart Set*, one of the "little magazines" that had replaced William Dean Howells's *Atlantic Monthly* and *Harper's* as the gatekeepers of U.S. high literary culture, Mencken wryly suggested that James had "made the mistake of going in the wrong direction. . . . Chicago would have developed him. What he needed was intimate contact with the life of his own country. . . . He would have been a great artist in his own country."[2] At the close of the 1920s, Vernon Parrington's opinion was virtually the same as that of Mencken and Brooks. Extending the negative connotations of the word "cosmopolitanism" into the era of modernism, Parrington argued that James "suffered the common fate of the *déraciné*; wandering between worlds, he found a home nowhere. It is not well for the artist to turn cosmopolitan, for the flavor of the fruit comes from the soil and sunshine of its native fields."[3] For Brooks, Mencken, and Parrington, Henry James, the author who had long been cited in the pages of the *Atlantic Monthly* and elsewhere as the most cosmopolitan of his generation, served as a cautionary tale of the dangers of deracination, exemplifying what artists might lose or leave unfulfilled if they uprooted themselves from their national culture.

It is tempting, within the context of this coda, to allow these evaluations of Henry James's career to represent the point of view of all modernists after the First World War. The logic that enabled such dismissals of James simply because of his cosmopolitanism certainly resembles the nativist literary aesthetic that Walter Benn Michaels has identified in the modernist fiction of William Faulkner, F. Scott Fitzgerald, and Ernest Hemingway. Just as Michaels argues of those novelists, Brooks, Mencken, and Parrington seem to engage in a nativist "reassertion of the distinction between American and un-American" as well as the "transformation of identity into an object of desire."[4] Moreover, the suspicion of foreign ideas and influence that registers in the three critics' evaluations of James's time abroad also found expression more overtly in the Red Scare of 1919–20 and in Congress's rejection of the League of Nations and passage of the immigration quota acts of the 1920s, events that figure prominently in many accounts of the end of the Progressive era. Characterizing the debate over the League of Nations as a clash between "unilateralist [and] internationalist" attitudes toward U.S. foreign policy, for example, Thomas Bender suggests that "the spirit of nationalism [that the First World War] enhanced, partly through the repression of dissent, may have reinforced conservative unilateralism."[5] Yet the shortsighted dismissals of James as a "*déraciné*" do not reflect a wholesale disengagement from the global concerns that shaped late realism during the Progressive era. Such modernists as Gertrude Stein, who explicitly called Henry James her "forerunner," and those associated with the Harlem Renaissance, whose early work often appeared in *The Crisis*, the journal edited by W. E. B. Du Bois, complicate the notion of a decisive break between late realism and modernism.[6] Similarly, historian Emily S. Rosenberg's depiction of the 1920s as the era of the "cooperative state," in which successive Republican administrations encouraged private enterprise to carry out U.S. economic and cultural expansion, is more nuanced than simply labeling the politics of the period isolationist.[7]

In order to gesture toward the continuing legacy of the mediating nation, this coda briefly considers a critical tradition that emerged during the modernist era but which differed significantly from the one represented by Brooks, Mencken, and Parrington. Thus having opened this book with a reading of Woodrow Wilson's April 20, 1915, speech, with its celebratory depiction of the United States as a microcosm of the world and its simultaneous dismissal of expressions of racial and ethnic diversity as "racial momentum," I close it by turning to a different Wilson altogether. In the final chapter of *A Prelude* (1967), a memoir of the author's early life, Edmund Wilson offers an account of his experiences during the First World War. Like Woodrow Wilson, Edmund Wilson found in the war proof of the United States' centrality to the international community, and again like Woodrow Wilson, Edmund Wilson associated the United States' importance with the composite identity of its population. In contrast to Woodrow Wilson, however, Edmund Wilson sought to rectify the contradictions within the appealing vision of the mediating nation in order to fulfill that vision's promises. In seeking to recuperate the legacy of that vision and make it relevant for another, more explicitly multicultural era, *A Prelude* retrospectively reimagines the moment of Woodrow Wilson's pronouncement of "the mediating Nation" for the era of Lyndon Johnson's Great Society: the Mediating Nation 2.0. Moreover, as a critic who probably exerted an even more profound influence on the conception of American literature during the twentieth century than Brooks, Mencken, and Parrington did, Wilson embodies a critical tradition that maintained a consistently internationalist perspective and, in so doing, serves as an important link between the late realism of Howells and James and the more recent multicultural and transnational concerns of present-day scholars.

Writing at the extreme chronological margin of American modernism, Wilson chooses to focus the final chapter of *A Prelude* on his personal experiences during the First World War and the ensuing influenza pandemic. The convergence of the war and the pandemic ushers in the concluding passage of *A Prelude* and Wilson's final remarks on his entry into adulthood. Wilson uses this moment from his own past as a means of interrogating and ultimately reaffirming the concept of the mediating nation. Since he was working at an army hospital during the pandemic, it is unsurprising that his description of the event at first focuses primarily on his sense of being overwhelmed by it:

> Before I had left Vittel, the flu epidemic of 1918 had taken, I think, as heavy a toll of our troops as any battle with the Germans had done. The hospitals were crowded with flu patients, many of whom died. I was on night duty and on my feet most of the time.... We would put them [the dead bodies] on a stretcher and carry them down to a basement room, where we sometimes had to pile them up like logs. They were buried in common ditches. This was much the busiest time in our hospitals. We never had a chance to think—though doctors and nurses also died—about catching the disease ourselves.[8]

Wilson is not exaggerating the scale of the pandemic's devastation in this passage. On the contrary, historians and epidemiologists estimate that nearly as many U.S. soldiers died from influenza as from wounds received in battle, and the number of U.S. soldiers who died during the war (117,000) pales in comparison to estimates for the pandemic's death toll, which range between 550,000 and 675,000 out of a national population of 105,000,000.[9] The pandemic almost certainly affected more American lives than the war did.

Although Wilson did not contract the disease himself, the stress of caring for so many ill and dying men took its toll on him. "When the worst of it was over," he continues, "I did collapse, although I had not caught the flu. I was allowed to go to bed for a day or so in a hospital room by myself."[10] As he rested, Wilson found the time and quietude to contemplate his recent experiences in the army, and in his memoir, he describes reaching a deep understanding of what his involvement in the war and the pandemic had signified: "I also had the leisure to think, and it suddenly became very clear to me that I could never go back to my former life—that is, that I could never go back to the habits and standards of even the most cultivated elements of the world in which I had lived. I felt now that I had never quite belonged in that world, that I had never, in fact, quite belonged to it. . . . My experience of the army had had on me a liberating effect."[11] For Wilson, this "liberating effect" results in a newfound ability to connect with others and a willingness to accept and even seek out variety. "I could now get on with all kinds of people," he claims, "and could satisfy my curiosity about aspects of life that otherwise I should not perhaps so soon have known."[12]

What this passage from *A Prelude* is meant to evoke is much the same as the argument Woodrow Wilson made in his 1915 speech. In effect, Edmund Wilson claims that his experiences in the army had enlarged the scope of his imagination by bringing him into contact with a more diverse array of Americans than he had ever known in his insular world of East Coast prep schools and Princeton. He contends that "many of my friends in the American army had been born in other countries than America: they had been Irishmen, Swedes, Danes, Swiss, Belgians and cockneys. . . . My association with all these had given me a strong contempt for the complaints about the 'foreign' immigrants on the part of old-line Americans and for the talk about the necessity for getting them 'Americanized.'"[13] He goes on to individuate his friends in a way that Woodrow Wilson never bothers to do in his speech: an Italian American he spent Christmas with, a Danish immigrant named John Andersen, and the son of a poor English farmer named Roy Gamble who had found a social mobility and independence in the United States that was impossible for him in his native Britain. Whereas Woodrow Wilson speaks of understanding immigrants "in the compound, not separately, as partisans, but unitedly as knowing and comprehending and embodying them all" and thereby erases whatever cultural, ethnic, or personal idiosyncrasies they might exhibit individually, Edmund Wilson attempts to name the immigrants he met in the army, relate their individual histories, and explain how these encounters affected his own outlook. Likewise, Edmund Wilson's efforts to allow these immigrants to speak for themselves by incorporating their stories into his own memoir stand in stark contrast to Woodrow Wilson's insistent use of the first-person plural pronoun *we*, which paradoxically reveals the failure of his vision: in attempting to give voice to a common American identity, he merely ventriloquizes. Far from giving him an excuse for blaming immigrants and excluding them from the body politic, the war and the pandemic helped convince Edmund Wilson of the centrality of immigrants to U.S. society.

In giving voice to those immigrants through his writing, Edmund Wilson is not simply correcting Woodrow Wilson's omissions; he is identifying a source of creative empowerment. In the final paragraph of *A Prelude*, he writes, "When I was back in New York at first, my habits did not change very much, but my life began soon to take a different direction in a way that, I think, otherwise it would hardly have ever done. . . . I was by that time as a much a product of the world of the war as of that of my earlier years, and I had to live now in the world in which I found myself after the war."[14] That "different direction" would ultimately lead Wilson to a distinguished career as one of the most influential literary critics of the twentieth century. By specifying that the shift in his life's course occurred during a few moments of reflection in the aftermath of the First World War and the influenza pandemic, Wilson ascribes extraordinary importance to those two events. (Wilson even incorporates one of his earliest works of fiction, a short story entitled "The Death of a Soldier," into the final chapter of *A Prelude*. The wholesale inclusion of a story written forty-five years earlier signals the seriousness with which Wilson wishes his readers to consider his early career.[15]) Looking back at the beginning of his career from near its very end—he would die within five years of *A Prelude*'s publication—Wilson casts the war and the pandemic not so much as a rupture with the past, which he still acknowledges he is partially a "product" of, but rather as a moment of transition. The "world of the war" prepares Wilson for the "world . . . after the war."

It is easy perhaps to dismiss Wilson's utopian view of the postwar United States in his 1967 memoir as willfully blind and anachronistic, the wishful thinking of an aging critic eager to attach his legacy to the successes of the Civil Rights movement. Certainly, the Red Scare, the Immigration Acts of the 1920s, and the continuation of Jim Crow demonstrate how few other Americans shared Wilson's feelings. Even more troublingly, despite Wilson's claims of having been awakened to the richness of the United States' own ethnic and cultural diversity, little of this appreciation makes its way into his early criticism. Nowhere in *The Shores of Light*, a 1952 collection of his literary criticism from the 1920s and 1930s, does he refer to the figures of the Harlem Renaissance, and that collection notably omits his 1927 essay "A Nation of Foreigners," in which he used the Sacco and Vanzetti executions as a springboard for condemning ethnically narrow definitions of "Americanism" and American literature.[16]

Instead of dismissing Wilson's claims in *A Prelude* out of hand, however, I suggest that the alternative history that Wilson imagines produces its own meaningful legacy. In positioning himself as a living link between the internationalism of early twentieth-century America and the self-aware multiculturalism of the late 1960s, Wilson anticipates the transnational perspectives of many current literary scholars and historians. Indeed, Donald Pease has recently argued that transnational American studies grew partly out of the academic multiculturalism with which Wilson sought to align himself in *A Prelude*. In its early scholarly forms, Pease observes, "the transnational resembled the multicultural . . . in its capacity to disturb the idea that national, cultural, and social formations were unitary and self-contained."[17] Not unlike Winfried Fluck, whose criticisms of the celebratory tone of some transnational scholarship I examined in the introduction, Pease goes on to highlight what he identifies as the chief shortcoming of both the multicultural and transnational approaches to American studies: "But transnational Americanists who encouraged the reformulation of multicultural conflicts that took place *within* nations in terms of the cross-cultural processes carried out *in between* national and transnational imaginaries often ignored the structures of economic and cultural injustice that persisted within the domestic sphere" (original emphasis).[18] A number of Americanists, including Pease himself, have begun to respond to this oversight by focusing greater attention on the role of the state in maintaining those "structures of economic and cultural injustice" despite the increased cultural power of the transnational imaginary.[19]

Just as I indicated in the introduction that the tendency to invoke transnationalism uncritically can itself be historicized, as *The Mediating Nation* has argued through its exploration of the wide appeal of Woodrow Wilson's polysemantic phrase, so too can the responses of Fluck and Pease. Thus by closing with Edmund Wilson's account of his own intellectual maturation in *A Prelude*, I mean to suggest not only that Wilson's memoir serves as an important bridge between the literature that this book has examined and the recent scholarly project to which *The Mediating Nation* contributes, but also that Wilson's concerns as a critic prefigure those of Americanists who now turn, as Pease puts it, to "the role transnational and diaspora formations [have] played in challenging the state as the core governance apparatus."[20] Despite the celebratory tone in those passages of *A Prelude* that depict Wilson's interactions with immigrants, Wilson makes it clear that the new perspective he gained through these interactions provided him with a basis for critiquing power relations. In the concluding paragraphs of *A Prelude*, Wilson acknowledges that the "world . . . after the war"—where immigrants have destabilized his understanding of American identity; where world war has introduced him to new places, people, and ways of life; and where pandemic has prodded him into taking stock of his life, his future, and his relationship to the United States itself—has resulted in both regeneration (his own expanded imaginative powers) and condemnation (his willingness to criticize overly restrictive definitions of American culture).

Ironically, even as *A Prelude* was going to press, the United States' increasingly fraught involvement in the Vietnam War was curtailing many of Lyndon Johnson's hopes for the Great Society, just as U.S. entry into the First World War had slowed the Progressive movement fifty years before. Nevertheless, Edmund Wilson's effort to connect the moment of his intellectual maturation with the political realities of 1960s America resonates with his best literary and cultural criticism and goes a long way toward justifying his attempt at recuperating the legacy of "the mediating Nation." To return to the posthumous evaluations of Henry James, for example, Wilson played a crucial role in rehabilitating James's reputation. In contrast to the condemnations of James as a "*déraciné*" by Brooks, Mencken, and Parrington, Wilson found James's oscillation "between the European and the American points of view" entirely consistent with James's aesthetics of "ambiguity."[21] It is therefore likely that Wilson appreciated the significance that James's transference of citizenship held personally for the author—something that Brooks, Mencken, and Parrington ignore altogether. As Leon Edel has suggested, James invested his July 1915 naturalization with multiple meanings, which ranged from eliminating the inconvenience of living as an alien in a country at war and showing solidarity with the British while the United States remained neutral to commenting subtly on the rapidity with which Americans expected the naturalization of immigrants to their shores.[22] Thus James's decision to become British can be read as a criticism of the United States that implicitly challenges the logic under-pinning Woodrow Wilson's speech, which Wilson had delivered only three months earlier: that U.S. neutrality is desirable and that the United States' treatment of immigrants is exemplary. In a sense, James performed his own international act in order to critique the state to which he had formerly be-longed. Directly repudiating Brooks in his review of *The Pilgrimage of Henry James*, Edmund Wilson indicates that he discerned James's criticism of the state when he concludes that "Henry James was not an intimidated and sidetracked artist, but a writer who . . . was able to say just what he meant about nations and human beings."[23] In so doing, Wilson also indicates the way in which the late realists' engagement with the state continued—and continue—to inform some of their successors' understanding of the global processes that give shape to American literature and history.

Notes

INTRODUCTION

1. "'America First,' Wilson's Slogan," 1.

2. W. Wilson, *The Papers of Woodrow Wilson*, 38.

3. Ibid., 39.

4. See Patler, *Jim Crow and the Wilson Administration*.

5. Significant studies of how forms of racial, ethnic, and sexual exclusion shaped U.S. ideology and culture during the period I am examining include Warren, *Black and White Strangers*; Wald, *Constituting Americans*; and Kaplan, *The Anarchy of Empire*.

6. Addams, *The Second Twenty Years at Hull-House*, 7, 8. Dawley examines the same passage in *Changing the World*, 15–16.

7. Fisher, introduction, vii.

8. Ibid., xxi.

9. G. Murphy, *Shadowing the White Man's Burden*, 5, 17.

10. Some of the historians whose work I engage self-identify as cultural historians. In their introduction, Cook and Glickman argue that American studies should "be understood as part of the larger genealogy of U.S. cultural history," and they go on to describe cultural history as committed to the idea of "culture as a historical motor" and to such methods as "thick description, discourse analysis, close readings of visual imagery, . . . and so forth" (10, 16, 24). Literary scholars, of course, share these assumptions and methods.

11. Althusser explicitly lists literature among "the cultural ISA" in "Ideology and the Ideological State Apparatuses," 143.

12. "America First," 12.

13. "French Look to Us," 2; "Dernburg Asserts Press Is Partial," 3.

14. See *The New York Times Current History*; Robinson and West, *The Foreign Policy of Woodrow Wilson*; and Hart, *Selected Addresses*.

15. Tucker, "The Crux of the Peace Problem," 453.

16. Ibid., 454.

17. See Wallerstein "The Three Instances of Hegemony." See also Arrighi, *The Long Twentieth Century*, 60–63.

18. Arrighi, *The Long Twentieth Century*, 62.

19. Harvey, *Justice, Nature and the Geography of Difference*, 429.

20. Here, I am thinking of the Asian multiple-passport holders in Ong, *Flexible Citizenships*; or the Taliban fighters who carry both Kalashnikovs and Nike sports bags in Legrain, "Cultural Globalization Is Not Americanization," B7.

21. Giddens, *The Consequences of Modernity*, 64.

22. Robertson, *Globalization*, 8.

23. Cazdyn and Szeman, *After Globalization*, 17.

24. Ibid., 20.

25. Ibid., 58–59, 10.

26. Ibid., 50.

27. See R. Williams, *Keywords*.

28. The launching of the *Journal of Global History*, an important forum devoted to the exploration of the historical dimensions of globalization, in March 2006, suggests that these concerns are diminishing and that such research only continues to grow.

29. Bourne's essay predates by five years the first instance of the word's usage given in the first edition of the *Oxford English Dictionary*. See *OED* (1933), s.v. "transnational." An even earlier appearance occurs in Coit, *The Soul of America* (1914), 88. Philosophers whose ideas were aligned with Bourne's, such as John Dewey and Horace Kallen, quickly picked up on Bourne's term; see Kallen, *The Structure of Lasting Peace*, 94; and Dewey, *Reconstruction in Philosophy*, 25.

30. See *OED* (1933), s.v. "imperialism"; and Koebner and Schmidt, *Imperialism*. For a significant challenge to the *OED*'s commentary, see Streeby, "Empire," 98.

31. For a history of the term "globalization," see Waters, *Globalization*, 1–3. Giddens traces the roots of global theory to "the literature of international relations" and the "'world-system theory'" of Wallerstein; see *The Consequences of Modernity*, 65. (It is worth noting that the concept of core, periphery, and semi-periphery nations, so crucial to Wallerstein's world-systems analysis, does indeed derive from the language of dependency theory, which emerged out of international relations.) Robertson goes back even further, identifying "early social theorists and sociologists, such as Comte, Saint-Simon and Marx," as well as "Emile Durkheim, Max Weber, Georg Simmel and their contemporaries," as the major thinkers who anticipated global theory; see *Globalization*, 15.

32. The classic account of these historical developments during the "long sixteenth century" is Wallerstein, *The Modern World-System*. Some scholars, in an attempt to challenge what they view as a Eurocentric model of world development, have traced the roots of globalization as far back as the trade practices of several ancient civilizations; see A. G. Frank, *Reorient*; and Frank and Gills, *The World System*.

33. See Hobsbawm, *The Age of Revolution*; *The Age of Capital*; and *The Age of Empire*.

34. Wallerstein, "World-System Analysis," 140. In *Justice, Nature and the Geography of Difference*, Harvey reaches a similar conclusion: "The economic collapse and political revolutions that swept across the capitals of Europe [in 1848] indicated that the capitalist world was interlinked in ways that had hitherto seemed unimaginable. The speed and simultaneity of it all was deeply troubling and called for some new mode of representation through which this interlinked world could be represented" (244).

35. Robertson, *Globalization*, 52, 59.

36. O'Rourke and Williamson, *Globalization and History*, 286.

37. In their introduction, O'Loughlin, Staeheli, and Greenberg note that "earlier trends toward global openness and diminution of trade controls at the beginning of the 20th century were soon reversed during the global slowdown of the 1920s and 1930s. Many governments reintroduced tariffs and quotas in an attempt to protect their domestic manufacturers and farmers" (4).

38. In *World on Fire*, Chua explores the flaws and unexpected paradoxes of the dominant neoliberal argument, while in *After Globalization*, Cazdyn and Szeman claim that the financial meltdown of 2008 and the emergence of an undemocratic China as a major economic power demonstrate the untenability of this argument.

39. W. James, *Essays in Radical Empiricism*, 42.

40. Ibid., 86–88.

41. For James's discussion of "continuous transition" and "discontinuity-experience," see ibid., 47–52. In "Literature as Equipment for Living," McGowan recognizes the potential impact of a reformulation of relations in James's philosophy: "And the very being of those individuals [i.e., terms] will be altered . . . if those relations are changed" (121). McGowan goes on to examine the applications of James's philosophy to literary studies.

42. Ninkovich, *Global Dawn*, 20. For a reading of the International Meridian Conference and its impact upon British literature, see Barrows, *The Cosmic Time of Empire*. The classic account of how technologies of travel and timekeeping "disembed" subjects from their sense of local time and space and "reembed" them in the national and global frameworks of modernity is Giddens, *The Consequences of Modernity*. For an important challenge to this linear model of temporal progression, see Pratt, *Archives of American Time*, 125–56.

43. Twain, *Tom Sawyer Abroad*, 20–21.

44. In *The Beginnings of Critical Realism in America*, Parrington suggests that the "new realism" embraced the "sociological school" in order to develop a "more critical attitude towards the social revolution at work in the land" (238, 179). In *On Native Grounds*, Kazin claims that "realism . . . passed silently into naturalism" as a result of "alienation from the new postbellum order" of a "corporation economy" (10, 19–20). In *The American 1890s*, Ziff identifies the post–Civil War generation of writers who came of age in the 1890s and expressed less concern with aesthetic and political "reunification" than with social disunity as the "true precursors" to twentieth-century modernism (22–23). In *The Social Construction of American Realism*, Kaplan argues that the "realism that develop[ed] in American fiction in the 1880s and 1890s" resulted from intensified "class conflicts" and the rise of a homogeneous and homogenizing "mass culture" (9). All four discuss the significance of the Haymarket affair and the move to New York on Howells's career.

45. In *Cosmopolitan Vistas*, Lutz identifies an important tension between regional authors' "local commitments" and their "commitment to Literature as a universal, cosmopolitan, honorific category" that produced fiction "not opposed to, but completely enmeshed in, literary aesthetics" (12, 15). In *Beautiful Democracy*, Castronovo identifies a similar tension between "aesthetic discourse [that] repositions American literature on an international axis" and the "German radicalism [that] lay dormant in a discourse concerned with common tastes, human solidarity, and universalism" (71).

46. H. James, "Art of Fiction," 509.

47. Ibid., 509–10.

48. In *The Age of Reform*, Hofstadter insists that the Progressives' efforts at initiating "governmental action [as] a counterpoise to the power of private business" found expression almost entirely in the domestic arena (233). Responding to the exigencies of Cold War politics, Hofstadter was reluctant to associate the American liberal tradition with European (i.e., Marxist) thought, preferring instead to emphasize Progressivism's

continuity with Populism and the New Deal. In the concluding paragraph of his book, he describes Franklin Roosevelt as "trying to *continue* to repudiate the European world of ideology" (327, emphasis added).

49. In *The Tragedy of American Diplomacy*, W. A. Williams suggests that, "just as [Roosevelt's] Square Deal program centered on the idea of responsible leaders using the national government to regulate and moderate industrial society at home, so did his international outlook revolve around the idea of American supremacy being used to define and promote the interests of 'collective civilization.' . . . The inherent requirements of economic expansion coincided with such religious, racist, and reformist drives to remake the world" (63). Williams's recognition of a connection existing between the desire to remake American society at home and the vision of remaking the world in America's own image is astute, but his argument risks dismissing the Progressives themselves as easy dupes whose odd mixture of sincerity and racism was exploited by calculating imperialists. It also elides the work of W. E. B. Du Bois and others, who sometimes invoked the rhetoric of the expansionists in order to subvert their logic, as I demonstrate in chapter 1. Notable historians who have followed Williams's lead in arguing for the centrality of empire to American historiography include LaFeber, *The New Empire*; Rosenberg, *Spreading the American Dream*; and Hunt, *Ideology and U.S. Foreign Policy*. For a historiographical overview of this literature, see Fry, "From Open Door to World Systems," 277–303.

50. I discuss the significance of Kloppenberg's *Uncertain Victory* and Rodgers's *Atlantic Crossings*, as well as important works by several other historians, in the next chapter.

51. Wells, *Recent Economic Changes*, 1.

52. Ibid., vi–vii.

53. See B. Anderson, *Imagined Communities*; Bhabha, *Nation and Narration*; and Gilroy, *The Black Atlantic*. A telling contrast can be drawn between Robert Weisbuch's frequent use of the phrase "ontological insecurity" in *Atlantic Double-Cross*, which implies that transatlantic exchange works to reaffirm some sort of essential national identity, and Gilroy's assumption that "cultural historians could take the Atlantic as one single, complex unit of analysis in their discussions of the modern world and use it to produce an explicitly transnational and intercultural perspective" (15).

54. A Boolean keyword search of the *MLA International Bibliography* indicates that, while "globalization" appeared in only 167 journal articles published between January 1990 and December 1999, the number of journal articles dealing with globalization between January 2000 and December 2009 soared to 1,584

55. Pease, introduction, 1.

56. See Lowe, "Globalization," 120–23.

57. Fluck, "A New Beginning?," 375.

58. Ibid., 369–70.

59. Ibid., 366.

60. *Utopia and Cosmopolis* was one of the first attempts to historicize globalization through an examination of American literature, but Peyser identified as important precursors to his own work several studies that drew attention to "the consolidation of a market economy presided over by corporate capitalism" (x), including Trachtenberg, *The Incorporation of America*; Michaels, *The Gold Standard and the Logic of Naturalism*; and Kaplan, *The Social Construction of American Realism*.

61. Peyser, *Utopia and Cosmopolis*, 7, 17.

62. Castronovo, *Beautiful Democracy*, 183.

63. For Peyser, the notion of cosmopolitanism that emerged during this period marked a "shift by which the nation is replaced with the globe as the fundamental unit of human association" (x). Castronovo claims that, "when taken not as a pathway to a theoretical universal but as a sure route to global markets, formalist aesthetics allow economic and imperial interests to condense dispersed geographies into a single unified form as the beauty of empire" (184). By contrast, my first chapter identifies a more complicated notion of cosmopolitanism circulating in late nineteenth-century America, and subsequent chapters highlight writers who opposed both imperialism and finance capitalism.

64. Lloyd and Thomas, *Culture and the State*, 1.

65. Ibid., 4.

66. For "indigenization," see Appadurai, *Modernity at Large*. For the possibilities of multicultural cosmopolitanism, see Appiah, "Cosmopolitan Patriots," 617–39. See also Robbins's discussion of cosmopolitanism's "local applications" in "Comparative Cosmopolitanisms," 260.

CHAPTER I

1. In *My Mark Twain*, Howells, the former editor of the *Atlantic Monthly*, called it "the most scrupulously cultivated of our periodicals" and "the leading periodical of the country" (19–20). In *Reading for Realism*, Glazener claims that the *Atlantic Monthly* "epitomized the influence that these [late nineteenth-century] magazines were designed to exert" (5). Glazener discusses the *Atlantic Monthly*'s status among its peer magazines most fully in her appendix (257–66).

2. Perry, "Number 4 Park Street," 3.

3. Brownell, "Henry James," 516.

4. Boynton, "Books New and Old," 560.

5. Perry, "Number 4 Park Street," 2.

6. Trent, "Cosmopolitanism and Partisanship," 48.

7. Ibid., 48–49.

8. Ibid., 49.

9. Ninkovich, *Global Dawn*, 16–17.

10. Lloyd and Thomas, *Culture and the State*, 1, 4. I discuss Lloyd and Thomas's work in the introduction.

11. Hannerz, "Cosmopolitans and Locals in World Culture," 237, 250.

12. Appiah, "Cosmopolitan Patriots," 618.

13. Ibid.

14. Since the mid-1990s, there has been a widespread revival of interest in the possibilities and limitations of cosmopolitanism. Perhaps the most notable contribution to this debate remains Nussbaum et al., *For Love of Country*. For an overview of this debate, see A. Anderson, "Cosmopolitanism, Universalism, and the Divided Legacies of Modernity," 265–89. For an overview of its implications for literary studies, see Lutz, *Cosmopolitan Vistas*, 49–58.

15. R. Williams, *Culture and Society*, xiii. I purposely do not present "mediating," as Wilson employs it in his 1915 speech, as a keyword. Wilson's speech was extensively praised

and quoted, but the phrase "the mediating Nation" was always closely associated with Wilson himself. Thus despite the wide appeal of Wilson's formulation, "mediating" does not exhibit the same contestation over meaning that the other words I am examining in this chapter do.

16. R. Williams, *Keywords*, 22.

17. R. Williams, *Culture and Society*, xix–xx.

18. Dawley, *Changing the World*, 335.

19. Addams, *The Twenty Years at Hull-House*, 285. See also Addams's discussion of Thomas de Quincy's "The Vision of Sudden Death," which she reads as a critique of the limited utility of a literary sensibility in the face of poverty and other social diseases (45–46).

20. Kloppenberg, *Uncertain Victory*, 5, 10. Acknowledged precursors to Kloppenberg and Rodgers include Mann, "British Social Thought and American Reformers of the Progressive Era," 627–92; Morgan, "The Future at Work," 245–71; Stokes, "American Progressives and the European Left," 5–28; Beede, "Foreign Influences on American Progressivism," 529–49; and Coleman, *Progressivism and the World of Reform*.

21. Rodgers, *Atlantic Crossings*, 2–3.

22. Ibid., 4.

23. Bender, *A Nation among Nations*, 246, 250.

24. Ibid., 282.

25. Tyrrell, *Transnational Nation*, 118–19.

26. Ibid., 128. For a more detailed discussion of the rise of the modern passport system, see also Torpey, "The Great War," 256–70.

27. General overviews of the transnational turn in U.S. history that more or less affirm Bender's and Tyrrell's approaches to Progressivism include Guarneri, *America in the World*; Bender, *Rethinking American History*; Reichard and Dickson, *America on the World Stage*; and Geyer and Bright, "World History in a Global Age," 1034–60.

28. Dawley, *Changing the World*, 35, 2.

29. Ibid., 35.

30. Ibid.

31. Hoganson, *Consumer's Imperium*, 11, 14.

32. Ibid., 14.

33. Ibid., 10.

34. Ninkovich, *Global Dawn*, 8, 7.33

35. Ibid., 8.

36. Ibid., 45.

37. Ibid., 54. Although it did not sign the multilateral Berne agreement in 1886, the United States enacted several bilateral copyright agreements with different nations throughout the 1890s. American authors and critics had been pressuring the government for decades to make some sort of arrangement regarding international copyright in order to protect U.S. literary works being circulated abroad. Their lack of success until the 1890s provides yet another example of the increased impetus for state intervention in mediating such international matters at the turn of the twentieth century.

38. Ibid., 3.

39. See Appiah, *Cosmopolitanism*, 130–31. It is worth noting that, of all the quotations Ninkovich provides in his discussion of the rise of internationalism in *Global Dawn*, the

only one that actually contains the word "internationalism" appears in Francis Lieber's pamphlet *Fragments of Political Science on Nationalism and Inter-Nationalism* (1868). The term simply did not become common until the twentieth century. See Ninkovich, *Global Dawn*, 108, 319–20.

40. During the 1910s, for instance, the word "cosmopolitanism" appeared in eleven *Atlantic Monthly* articles, while "internationalism" appeared in twenty-two. Only four articles use both words—the most notable being Randolph Bourne's July 1916 essay "Trans-National America," which I examine in more detail in the fourth chapter. Both "internationalism" and "cosmopolitanism" appear twice in Bourne's essay, and although Bourne uses them interchangeably, their meaning corresponds closely to Faries's definition of "internationalism."

41. Faries, *The Rise of Internationalism*, 29, 14.

42. Herren, Rüesch, and Sibille, *Transcultural History*, 32. Faries is attentive to many of the same historical developments that global theorists have highlighted as crucial to the emergence of globalization, including migration, international conferences, world's fairs, and new technologies of communication.

43. Kant, "Idea for a Universal History with a Cosmopolitan Purpose," 51.

44. Reinsch, *Public International Unions*, 2, 5.

45. Between 1860 and 1899, the word "internationalism" appears only once in the *Atlantic Monthly*. Between 1900 and 1919, by contrast, twenty-six different articles use the word.

46. *The Century Dictionary and Cyclopedia* (1889–91), s.v. "Internationalism."

47. Ibid., s.v. "International," entry 2. See Castronovo, *Beautiful Democracy*, 70–71, 82–87. The first two references to "internationalism" in the *Congressional Record* (June 9, 1874: 4796; and February 14, 1880: 884) unequivocally link the word to "communism," but this meaning disappears altogether by its third appearance (January 26, 1894: 1498), where it is contrasted negatively with the concept of nationalism. By contrast, it appears in ninety-five separate issues of the *Congressional Record* between 1900 and 1919.

48. Howe, "The End of an Economic Cycle," 612.

49. Croly, *The Promise of American Life*, 289.

50. Ibid., 310.

51. Reinsch, *Public International Unions*, 141.

52. Faries, *The Rise of Internationalism*, 120, 122. I discuss the notion of the "melting pot" and the perceived benefits of immigration in the fourth chapter.

53. *Cong. Rec.*, August 12, 1919: 3789.

54. See the entries for "Cosmopolite," "Cosmopolitan," and "Cosmopolitanism" in *American Dictionary* (1828); *The Imperial Dictionary* (1847–50); *The Century Dictionary and Cyclopedia* (1889–91); and the *OED* (1933).

55. Higginson, "The Cant of Cosmopolitanism," 110. See Himmelfarb, "The Illusions of Cosmopolitanism," 72–77. In referring to cosmopolitanism as an "illusion," Himmelfarb means that, in a world made up of nation-states, an individual's lived reality is always structured by a sense of national identity.

56. Reinsch, *Public International Unions*, 141.

57. Roosevelt, "True Americanism," 17, 20.

58. Ibid., 20.

59. Ibid., 22.

60. Ibid., 23.

61. Appiah, *Cosmopolitanism*, 163, and "Cosmopolitan Patriots," 618.

62. Matthews, "Literature in the New Century," 5; Sedgwick, "Literature and Cosmopolitanism," 220.

63. Sedgwick, "Literature and Cosmopolitanism," 219.

64. Peyser, *Utopia and Cosmopolis*, 97.

65. Damrosch, *What Is World Literature?*, 8, 10.

66. Ibid., 123. Damrosch overstates Lodge's opposition to U.S. expansion. At the same time he wrote his introduction to *The Best of the World's Classics* (1909), Lodge, a vocal supporter of the Spanish-American War, was chairing the Senate's Committee on the Philippines.

67. Matthews, "Literature in the New Century," 22–23.

68. Ninkovich, *Global Dawn*, 49.

69. Ibid., 54.

70. Curtis, "Editor's Easy Chair," 309. See also Casanova, *The World Republic of Letters*.

71. Curtis, "Editor's Easy Chair," 309.

72. Alden, *Magazine Writing and the New Literature*, 221.

73. Ibid.

74. Ibid., 230.

75. Ibid., 258–59.

76. Morris, *News from Nowhere*, 129.

77. *OED*, 3rd ed., s.v. "World language." For his discussion of English as a world language, see Whitney, *Language and the Study of Language*, 469–70. Ninkovich points to Ulysses S. Grant's Second Inaugural Address (1873) as evidence for how widespread the hope that English would eventually serve as the world's language had become; see *Global Dawn*, 22.

78. See *OED* (1933), s.v. "world."

79. Harrison, "Musings upon Current Topics," 184. The 2010 *OED* dates this usage back even further, to 1855.

80. Twain, "To the Person Sitting in Darkness," 176.

81. McFadden, "The World's Salvation," 1308.

82. Cable, "Congregational Unity in Georgia," 317.

83. W. James, *Pragmatism*, 125.

84. Coon, "'One Moment in the World's Salvation,'" 73, 87.

85. W. James, *Pragmatism*, 125.

86. Addams, *The Second Twenty Years at Hull-House*, 7, 8.

87. Ibid., 7.

88. Ibid., 6.

89. Bellamy, *Looking Backward*, 241.

90. Ibid., 241.

91. Ibid., 193.

92. In his introduction to the Broadview edition, Alex MacDonald summarizes the influence of Bellamy's novel on literary and political discourse (18–28). In suggesting that "*Looking Backward* may be accurately described as a religious novel," MacDonald also

picks up on the subtle religiosity of Bellamy's use of such phrases as "world's salvation" (11).

93. Peyser, *Utopia and Cosmopolis*, 29.

94. Bellamy, *Looking Backward*, 127, 126.

95. See Kirwan, *Reciprocity (Social and Economic) in the Thirtieth Century*. Like Julian West, Kirwan's narrator also travels to the Boston of the future, where he meets a friendly guide who at one point refers to "the sister Republic of Canada" (137). Furthermore, the U.S. flag still flies over the thirtieth-century "town mansion" in the frontispiece to Kirwan's novel.

96. Quoted in Strong, *Our Country*, 1.

97. LaFeber, *The New Empire*, 73. Strong's influence on such expansionist ideologues as Alfred Thayer Mahan and Frederick Jackson Turner serves as a major theme in most analyses of *Our Country* and turn-of-the-century U.S. imperialism. For a more extensive reading of Strong's rhetoric, see my "America as 'World-Salvation,'" 125–46.

98. Kaplan, *The Anarchy of Empire*, 102.

99. Strong, *Our Country*, 218.

100. Strong, *The New Era*, 265.

101. Ewald, *Commentary on the Prophets of the Old Testament*, 270.

102. *Century Dictionary and Cyclopedia*, s.v. "mediator."

103. Du Bois, "The African Roots of the War," 711.

104. Ibid., 712–13.

105. Ibid., 713. Spivak makes a similarly pragmatic claim in "Poststructuralism, Marginality, Postcoloniality and Value," 219–44. The paradoxical problem of postcolonial identity is to take part in a narrative that has been forced upon one and for which one has no adequate historical point of reference.

106. Du Bois, "The African Roots of the War," 714.

107. Luis-Brown, *Waves of Decolonization*, 126.

108. Du Bois, "The African Roots of the War," 709.

CHAPTER 2

1. Jones, *Strange Talk*, 43. Henry James's tribute to Lowell appears in "James Russell Lowell," 35–51.

2. Howells, "Dialect in Literature," 233–34.

3. In *Cultures of Letters*, Brodhead claims that "virtually every . . . writer of this time who succeeded in establishing himself as a writer did so through the regional form" (116). In *Strange Talk*, Jones calls "the representation of dialect . . . an integral part of a mainstream literature" during the last decades of the nineteenth century (7). See also Brown, *A Sense of Things*, 215, n. 21; and Evans, *Before Cultures*, 83.

4. Toward the end of the 1890s, Henry James expressed amazement at the sheer abundance of dialect fiction that American authors had produced. In his "American Letter," James supposed that "nothing like it, probably—nothing like any such predominance— exists in English, in French, in German work of the same order" (18).

5. Howells, "Dialect in Literature," 241.

6. Ibid., 241.

7. Howells, "Editor's Study," September 1887, 640.

8. In "Sentimental Communities," Cohen calls "the sentimental subgenre" a "*trans-national* literary form" because of its frequent translation and because "it served as a privileged site for the exchange of literary codes and observations concerning national character and difference" (107, original emphasis). The Anglo-French routes of circulation and the emphasis on national contrasts that Cohen identifies at work in the sentimental novel, however, do not fully anticipate the far more widespread use of local color at the end of the nineteenth century.

9. Howells, "Dialect in Literature," 233.

10. Berthoff, *The Ferment of Realism*, 100.

11. Brodhead, *Cultures of Letters*, 116.

12. Kaplan, "Nation, Region, and Empire," 250.

13. Lutz, *Cosmopolitan Vistas*, 26.

14. Ibid., 30; Evans, *Before Cultures*, 111.

15. Bramen, *The Uses of Variety*, 125. In *Reading for Realism*, Glazener makes the similar claim that "regionalism had the potential to swivel in its orientation and serve the periphery" (193).

16. Bramen, *The Uses of Variety*, 128; H. James, preface, 45–46. Howells's review of Dunbar's *Majors and Minors* (1895) appears in "Life and Letters," June 27, 1896, 630.

17. W. James, *Pragmatism*, 65.

18. Howells, "Editor's Study," September 1887, 640.

19. Howells, *Hazard of New Fortunes*, 103. Further quotations are cited parenthetically.

20. Howells, "Bibliographical," v.

21. Martin, *Harvests of Change*, 42. See also Tanner, introduction, x.

22. De Forest, "The Great American Novel," 29, 28.

23. Norris, "The Great American Novelist," 87.

24. Howells's satirizing of Kendricks's interest in local color echoes other satiric treatments of naïve city dwellers' tendency to seek out forms of local color that fit their a priori conceptions. See Woolson, "In Search of the Picturesque"; and Matthews, "In Search of Local Color," 33–40.

25. Lutz summarizes the synecdochical argument in *Cosmopolitan Vistas*, 14.

26. Evans, *Before Cultures*, 111.

27. This passage inspires the title of Bentley's *Frantic Panoramas*, where it emblematizes the rising mass culture that was undermining the cultural authority of high literary forms, such as Howellsian realism. Bentley calls *Hazard* "something of an elegy for realist fiction" because it dramatizes "the breakdown of realist metonymy" (294). By contrast, I read *Hazard*, along with Howells's contemporaneous criticism, as an attempt at revitalizing and internationalizing American literary realism.

28. In *The Capture of Speech*, Certeau describes just this sort of destabilization of identity that immigrants produce: "The questions posed by the interethnic encounter hit the nail on the head: foreigners living among the citizens of a dominant society challenge not only an identity imposed from without but the very idea of identity, especially when they claim the right to be themselves and follow a path of their own in the midst of diversity" (149).

29. Howells, *The Rise of Silas Lapham*, 17, 361.

30. Ibid., 354.

31. Ibid., 44, 193. Handlin reports that, in 1880, the foreign-born population of Boston and Cambridge numbered 114,796 or roughly 20 percent of the total population; see *Boston's Immigrants*, 261.

32. Jones, *Strange Talk*, 135.

33. Barrish, *The Cambridge Introduction to American Literary Realism*, 54. In "The Practice and Promotion of American Literary Realism," Glazener calls free indirect discourse "specially relevant to realism" because of the way it "blurs the character's perspective and the narrator's" (23).

34. Castronovo, *Beautiful Democracy*, 103.

35. Ibid., 100

36. Hsu, *Geography and the Production of Space*, 165; Foote, *Regional Fictions*, 32.

37. Jewett, "The Foreigner," 154.

38. Ibid., 158

39. Ibid., 158–59.

40. Ibid., 159, 166.

41. Ibid., 154, 165.

42. Ibid., 160.

43. Ibid., 159

44. See Howells's "Editor's Study," September 1886, 639–44. The first English translation was published in Britain in 1886. For an overview of the early reception of Russian literature in the United States, see Tall, "English-Russian and American-Russian Literary Relations," 124–26.

45. Damrosch, *What Is World Literature?*, 5.

46. Lukács, *Studies in European Realism*, 242; Casanova, *The World Republic of Letters*, 3.

47. Lukács, *Studies in European Realism*, 244; Casanova, *The World Republic of Letters*, 84; Damrosch, *What Is World Literature?*, 6.

48. Damrosch, *What Is World Literature?*, 3. Marx and Engels mention "world literature" in their *Manifesto of the Communist Party*, 477.

49. Cady, "Armando Palacio Valdés," 31, 33. Although broadened beyond the Howells-Palacio Valdés friendship, Cady's argument remains substantially the same in *The Realist at War*. Cady's work on Howells remains relevant and serves as an important exception to earlier critics' tendency to dismiss Howells as provincial and nationalistic. This tendency can be traced to Norris, *The Responsibilities of the Novelist*; Mencken, "The Dean"; and S. Lewis, *The American Fear of Literature*. Cady's work, by contrast, prefigures such recent reconsiderations of Howells's cosmopolitan attitudes as Lutz, *Cosmopolitan Vistas*; Evans, *Before Cultures*; and Bartel, "Kant's Narrative of Hope in the Gilded Age," 661–88.

50. Howells, "To Thomas S. Perry," 28 January 1886, in *Life in Letters*, 1:378.

51. Howells, "Editor's Study," June 1886, 156.

52. Meyer, "The Changing Cultural Content of the Nation-State," 135.

53. Meyer et al., "World Society and the Nation-State," 173–74. Meyer's concept of "isomorphism," which is central to his larger argument, builds off of neoinstitutional theories of how organizations develop similar structures and processes. See DiMaggio and Powell's "The Iron Cage Revisited," 147–60.

54. B. Anderson, *Imagined Communities*, 139. These ideas also appear in nebulous form in Renan, "What Is a Nation?" Renan categorically rejects each of the popularly believed prehistorical origins of the nation (race, language, religion, royal dynasty, and ethnic character) and argues that each nation-state is the result of "a daily plebiscite" because its citizens find it the most convenient means of maintaining law and order and guaranteeing their own liberty (19). Renan also notes the mutual interdependence of nation-states: "Through their various and often opposed powers, nations participate in the common work of civilization; each sounds a note in the great concert of humanity. . . . Isolated, each has its weak point. . . . Yet all these discordant details disappear in the overall context" (20). Renan's "overall context," I suggest, anticipates Meyer's concept of "world society," and what he views as the complementary nature of different nation-states participating in the "common work of civilization" is the result of each nation-state's embeddedness in a wider global culture. I return to Renan in the third chapter.

55. Meyer et al., "World Society and the Nation-State," 175.

56. For a discussion of the desire of Japan's ruling classes to follow the European model of nationhood, including their willingness to "launch overseas adventures, even if [they were] late to the game," see B. Anderson, *Imagined Communities*, 97–98. I examine the status of Japan in the fourth chapter.

57. Viewed in its entirety, Garland's *Crumbling Idols* follows the same logic by valorizing local color, which Garland calls "the differentiating element" in fiction (57), and by linking the efforts of American local colorists to what "Russia, Norway, Germany, and other of our neighbor nations have done" (173). Like Howells, Garland opposes the idea of "literary centres"; see chapter 10.

58. Howells, "Dialect in Literature," 233, 241.

59. Ibid., 239.

60. Cady, *The Realist at War*, 26.

61. See the advertising matter in Dostoyevsky's *Crime and Punishment* (New York: Thomas Y. Crowell, 1886) and Crowell's advertisement for *Anna Karenina* in *The Nation*, March 25, 1886, iii.

62. Cady makes this claim in "Armando Palacio Valdés," as does Capellán Gonzalo in "William Dean Howells and Armando Palacio Valdés," 451–71.

63. Howells, "Editor's Study," April 1886, 811.

64. Ibid., 812.

65. Howells, "Editor's Study," April 1891, 805.

66. Howells, "To Henry James," 15 Oct. 1911, in *Life in Letters*, 2:306.

67. Howells, "Editor's Study," January 1888, 317.

68. Baxter, "A Great Modern Spaniard," 557.

69. Howells, "Editor's Study," November 1889, 963.

70. Baxter, "A Great Modern Spaniard," 554–55.

71. Palacio Valdés, prologue, *Sister Saint Sulpice*, 8. Further quotations are cited parenthetically. It is worth noting that Howells's quotations of Palacio Valdés were his own translations. They predate and differ slightly from Nathan Haskell Dole's authorized translation.

72. Garland, "Mr. Howells's Latest Novels," 248. Garland uses the word again in *Crumbling Idols* to criticize some of Joaquin Miller's early work (27).

73. Howells, "Editor's Study," November 1889, 966, 965. Indicating that he felt the word was no longer a neologism two years later, Howells removed the italics in *Criticism and Fiction*, 74, 68.

74. Howells, "Editor's Study," November 1889, 966; and *Criticism and Fiction*, 75, 73.

75. See S. T. Williams, *The Spanish Background of American Literature*, 266.

76. Palacio Valdés tended to exaggerate sales of his works abroad, and the numbers cited by Showerman probably originated from Palacio Valdés himself and thus are suspect; see Showerman's "A Spanish Novelist," 385–404. Dendle offers a more nuanced discussion of Palacio Valdés's popularity in Great Britain, France, and the United States; see *Spain's Forgotten Novelist*, 28–31.

77. Rev. of *Sister Saint Sulpice*, 169; Garland, *Crumbling Idols*, 99.

78. Howells, "Editor's Easy Chair," November 1911, 959.

79. Howells wrote an extensive analysis of these historical romances in "The New Historical Romances," 935–49. Recent scholars who largely agree with Howells's conclusions include Glazener, *Reading for Realism*; Kaplan, *The Anarchy of Empire*; and Hebard, *The Poetics of Sovereignty*.

80. Howells, "Editor's Easy Chair," April 1901, 806.

81. Ibid., 805.

82. Ibid.

83. Ibid.

84. See Ocampo, "José Rizal, Father of Filipino Nationalism," 44–51. The sentimental rhetoric and imagery of *Uncle Tom's Cabin* also played an important role in shaping U.S. colonial policies after annexation of the Philippines; see Wesling, *Empire's Proxy*, 69–80. For the publication history of *Noli me tangere*, I rely on Harold Augenbraum's introduction to the Penguin edition (xi–xxiv).

85. Howells, "Editor's Easy Chair" April 1901, 805.

86. Deleuze and Guattari, *Kafka*, 16–17.

87. Ibid., 18.

88. Ibid., 24. For a discussion of the insights and shortcomings of Deleuze and Guattari's interpretation of Kafka, see M. Anderson, *Reading Kafka*, 11.

89. B. Anderson, *Imagined Communities*, 27.

90. Ibid., 36.

91. Rizal, *Noli Me Tangere*, 3.

92. Wesling, *Empire's Proxy*, 94. See also Delmendo, *The Star-Entangled Banner*. In *Frontier Constitutions*, Blanco contends that Rizal's emergence as a father figure for Filipino nationalism and independence "has everything to do . . . with the scholarship of cultural nationalism after World War II" (188). In a reading that suggests Howells's characterization of Rizal's novel as a work of realism may have been a "strategic misreading," too, Blanco examines the "gothic undercurrents" of *Noli me tangere*, which helped Rizal present the Philippines' "colonial history as counterhistory" and thereby provide an alternative to European notions of modernity (232).

93. Craig, *Lineage, Life and Labors of José Rizal*, 13.

94. Mark Twain also inferred Rizal's radical politics while reading *An Eagle Flight*; see Harris, *God's Arbiters*, 154–57. Twain's poem "My Last Thought," a dramatic monologue that recounts a dying U.S. president's regret over annexing overseas territory, borrows its

title from a Rizal poem that was reprinted in the introduction to *An Eagle Flight*. Since Twain's poem is dated May 1901, Twain's reading of Rizal's novel (and poem) may have been prompted and structured by Howells's April 1901 review.

95. Introduction, *An Eagle Flight*, xiii.

96. Ibid., vii.

97. Although this translation also features an altered title, that title does not deemphasize the novel's political content: *The Social Cancer* (1912).

98. See Atkinson, *The Philippine Islands*, 104–5; and Craig, *The Story of José Rizal*, 24

99. Howells, "Editor's Easy Chair," April 1901, 806. In *Shadowing the White Man's Burden*, Murphy offers a more optimistic reading of Rizal's short-term legacy when she notes Rizal's influence upon the father-and-son African American writers T. G. and Frank R. Steward, who appear to have encountered Rizal's novel, under its original title, while serving with the U.S. Army in the Philippines. Murphy claims that the plot of Frank R. Steward's 1903 short story "Starlik: A Tale of Laguna" "echoed that of Rizal's . . . novel" and that both men's encounters with Rizal's fiction helped them draw connections between "the color line at home and abroad" (107, 110). Nevertheless, Murphy acknowledges the comparative obscurity of the Stewards, indicating just how circumscribed this more positive engagement with Rizal's politics was.

CHAPTER 3

1. Howells, *Hazard of New Fortunes*, 303.

2. Hofstadter, *The Age of Reform*, 231.

3. Ibid., 233.

4. Brandeis, *Other People's Money*, 92.

5. Partial accounts of the complicated textual history of *The American*, both as a novel and as a play (which James himself adapted), appear in Cargill, "The First International Novel," 418–25; Edel, *The Complete Plays of Henry James*, 241–52; Tuttleton, "A Note on the Text," 311–17; Parker, "Henry James 'In the Wood,'" 492–513; and Horne's appendix to *Henry James and Revision*, 323–57. For the purposes of my argument, it is important to note that James's revision of *The American* for the New York Edition took place between October or November 1905 and February 1907 and that his work on *The American* overlapped his composition of *The American Scene*, which he began in August 1905. By the time Scribner's sent him copies of *Roderick Hudson* and *The American* in December 1907, James had decided not to write the envisioned second half of *The American Scene*, but he seems to have felt that the revisions themselves and the accompanying prefaces were an adequate trade-off.

6. Edel, *Henry James*, 327. For analyses of James's revision of this novel, see Herrick, "A Visit to Henry James," 724–41; Gettmann, "Henry James's Revision of *The American*," 279–95; Traschen, "An American in Paris," 67–77; Schulz, "The Bellegardes' Feud with Christopher Newman," 42–55; Traschen, "Henry James and the Art of Revision," 39–47; Traschen, "James's Revisions of the Love Affair in *The American*," 43–62; Watkins, "Christopher Newman's Final Instinct," 85–88; Stafford, "The Ending of *The American*," 86–89; Reynolds, "Henry James's New Christopher Newman," 457–68; Horne, "*The American*," 148–83; J. Murphy, "A 'Very Different Dance,'" 231–50; Poole, Appendix 2, 367–84; and

Silver, "Between Communion and Renunciation," 286–96. For broader discussions of James's revisions to the New York edition, see Bosanquet, *Henry James at Work*; Edgar, *Henry James*; Butterfield, "*The American*," 17–35; Parker, *Flawed Texts and Verbal Icons*; Banta, introduction, 1–42; Tintner, *The Twentieth-Century World of Henry James*; J. S. Murphy, "Revision as a 'Living Affair,'" 163–80; and the essays in McWhirter, *Henry James's New York Edition*.

7. H. James, preface, *The American* (1907), 12. As noted in the preceding chapter, discussions about the differences between romance and realism had special political resonance during the early twentieth century. Howells associated romance, particularly historical romance, with the spread of U.S. imperialism and realism with resistance to it. That James's definitions of romance and realism lead him directly into a discussion about economic imperialism suggests that he was at least sympathetic to Howells's more overtly political criticism. Further quotations from James's preface are cited parenthetically.

8. Even a cursory glance at Winston Churchill's family tree confirms this fact. In 1874, Churchill's father Lord Randolph, the third son of the seventh duke of Marlborough, married Jennie Jerome, the daughter of an American millionaire who had made his fortune through stock speculation. Neither Lord Randolph's father (the duke) nor his mother attended the wedding ceremony, perhaps understanding the "cover of night" principle that James envisions a real-life Bellegarde following, but Lord Randolph's marriage carried no stigma as far as his political career was concerned: he eventually served in Lord Salisbury's cabinet.

9. Cargill labels *The American* "The First International Novel," 418–25. Other candidates include Baroness Tautphoeus's *The Initials* (1850), Nathaniel Parker Willis's *Paul Fane* (1857), Nathaniel Hawthorne's *The Marble Faun* (1860), Jules Verne's *Around the World in Eighty Days* (1873), and Howells's *A Foregone Conclusion* (1874). In his November 1882 essay "Henry James, Jr.," Howells claims that James "invented this species of fiction" (27), citing "A Passionate Pilgrim" (1871) as the first example. Robertson lists the rise of the international novel as a distinct genre among the key developments of the "take-off phase" of globalization (1870s–1920s) in *Globalization*, 59. By Robertson's logic, James served as a participant in, as well as an observer of, the emergence of globalization. Howells's conception of the international novel as a genre makes it unwise to dismiss the term altogether. Nevertheless, in *The Old World Journey*, Zetterberg Pettersson rightly observes that "the designation 'international' is actually a misnomer since the genre is not concerned with the encounter with all foreign countries but almost exclusively with the American encounter with Europe. On closer scrutiny, 'international' refers to the particular relationship between America and Europe" (52). Had earlier critics, such as Cargill, included the works of Jules Verne and Rudyard Kipling alongside those of Henry James and Edith Wharton, then our conception of the genre might be broader.

10. For the parallels between Carnegie and Christopher Newman, see Clark, "The Transatlantic Romance of Henry James," 100–114; and Goble, "Media and Communication Technologies," 203–13. There is a significant difference between viewing the two editions of *The American* as early and late "works" rather than early and late "versions" of a single work. Does the 1907 version belong to James's "late" period alongside *The Ambassadors* and "The Jolly Corner"? For a discussion of these issues, see Posnock, "Breaking the Aura of Henry James," 35–38.

11. See Trachtenberg, *The Incorporation of America*. Numerous literary critics have followed Trachtenberg's lead and examined how American authors and intellectuals participated in, contested, or otherwise commented upon the growth of corporate culture at the turn of the twentieth century, including Michaels, *The Gold Standard and the Logic of Naturalism*; Horwitz, *By the Law of Nature*; Banta, *Taylored Lives*; Thomas, *American Literary Realism and the Failed Promise of Contract*; and Leverenz, *Paternalism Incorporated*.

12. Lenin, *Imperialism*, 182.

13. Brandeis, *Other People's Money*, 101.

14. Brandeis discusses the difference between "static" and "dynamic" wealth in ibid., 56–57. His discussion of "dynamic" wealth leads to one of his most famous quotations: "The fetters which bind the people are forged from the people's own gold" (57).

15. Ibid., 64.

16. Ibid., 97, 124.

17. Howells, *Hazard of New Fortunes*, 73.

18. Marx, *Capital*, 779.

19. Lenin, *Imperialism*, 265.

20. Brandeis, *Other People's Money*, 60; Lenin, *Imperialism*, 203.

21. Veblen, *The Theory of Business Enterprise*, 2.

22. Ibid., 44.

23. Ibid., 184–85.

24. Ibid., 269.

25. Lenin, *Imperialism*, 213.

26. Brandeis, *Other People's Money*, 120.

27. "Carnegie Criticizes Congress on Tariff," 1. For an example of Carnegie's earlier arguments against antitrust legislation, see his "The Bugaboo of Trusts," 141–51. Carnegie had never denied that the state could play an important role in ensuring that accumulated wealth was justly redistributed, though. In his famous 1889 essay "Wealth," Carnegie wrote that "men who continue hoarding great sums all their lives, the proper use of which for public ends would work good to the community, should be made to feel that the community, in the form of the state, cannot thus be deprived of its proper share. By taxing estates heavily at death the state marks its condemnation of the selfish millionaire's unworthy life" (659). For Carnegie's complicated views on wealth, philanthropy, and state regulation, see Nasaw, *Andrew Carnegie*, 343–60.

28. Arrighi, *The Long Twentieth Century*, 6.

29. Ibid.

30. Ibid., 59–60.

31. Ibid., 15.

32. Wicker, *Banking Panics of the Gilded Age*, and Sobel, *Panic on Wall Street*, detail the histories of those economic panics. Important studies of literature's relationship to U.S. financial crises of the period include Michaels, *The Gold Standard and the Logic of Naturalism*; and Zimmerman, *Panic!*

33. Sprague, *History of Crises under the National Banking System*, 205.

34. Jameson, "Culture and Finance Capital," 252. For another literary scholar who expands upon Arrighi's work in important ways, see Baucom, *Specters of the Atlantic*.

35. Jameson, "Culture and Finance Capital," 252.

36. Du Gay and Pryke, "Cultural Economy," 5.

37. Brandeis, *Other People's Money*, 70.

38. Ibid., 100.

39. Ibid., 89.

40. Appadurai, *Modernity at Large*, 32.

41. Ibid.

42. Ibid.

43. Brandeis, *Other People's Money*, 142.

44. Ibid., 143.

45. Ibid.

46. Ibid., 144, 146.

47. Sonnichsen, "Consumers' Coöperation," 462.

48. Sprague, *History of Crises under the National Banking System*, 314.

49. Rowe, "Henry James and Globalization," 212.

50. Ibid., 208.

51. Amin and Thrift, introduction, xiv.

52. H. James, *The American* (1877), 33; and *The American* (1907), 35. Subsequent quotations are cited parenthetically, with the abbreviation *AM1* referring to the 1877 edition and *AM2* referring to the 1907 New York edition. (Technically, the 1978 Norton edition is a reprint of the 1879 Macmillan publication, which benefits from minor corrections that James himself authorized.)

53. Veblen discusses "conspicuous leisure," "conspicuous consumption," and "conspicuous waste" in *The Theory of the Leisure Class*. Amin and Thrift cite Veblen's 1898 essay "Why Is Economics Not an Evolutionary Science?" (in which Veblen explicitly refuses to separate culture from economics) as an important antecedent of cultural economy in their introduction, xvi–xvii.

54. In his "Appendix 2," Poole suggests that these latter changes distance Newman from the robber barons and "the stigma associated with the quick fortunes made in the postwar years" (370), but Poole forgets that Cornelius Vanderbilt and Jay Gould made their fortunes before and during the Civil War, respectively.

55. Howells, *Hazard of New Fortunes*, 448. In contrast to Newman's failure, Dryfoos successfully marries off his daughter Christine to a nobleman.

56. Hoganson, *Consumers' Imperium*, 55.

57. Ibid., 9.

58. Schurz, "The Issue of Imperialism," 17. Schurz's biography reads like a more successful version of *Hazard of New Fortune*'s Lindau. As a young man in Bonn, Schurz was involved in the 1848 revolutions. After moving to Wisconsin, he became involved in the abolitionist movement and fought for the Union during the Civil War. Unlike Lindau, however, Schurz went on to distinguished careers in politics and journalism.

59. In light of some of James's other late works, including some he published before he revised *The American*, the implication that Newman may have traveled to Asia is not as farfetched as it might seem. After May Bartram's death in "The Beast in the Jungle" (1903), we are told that John Marcher "visited the depths of Asia" (237).

60. H. James, *The American Scene*, 401. Subsequent quotations of this text are cited parenthetically, with the abbreviation *AS* preceding the page numbers.

61. Renan, "What Is a Nation?," 19.

62. In *Essays in Radical Empiricism*, William James asks, "Is it not time to repeat . . . that to *act like* one is to *be* one? Should we not say here that to be experienced as continuous is to be really continuous, in a world where experience and reality come to the same thing?" (59, original emphasis). In *The Principles of Psychology*, James extends this claim to identity as well: "Whatever . . . things are perceived to be *associated* with this feeling [of bodily existence] are deemed to form part of that me's *experience*; and of them certain ones (which fluctuate more or less) are reckoned to be themselves *constituents* of the me in a larger sense,—such are the clothes, the material possessions, the friends, the honors and esteem which the person receives or may receive" (400, original emphasis).

63. The significance of the title's definite article was not lost on contemporary reviewers, many of whom were displeased by the implications; see Banta, introduction, 23–26.

64. In this revision, James introduces the pseudo-scientific term "race," though he almost certainly uses it as a synonym for "nationality." In his discussion of the word's instability in *Imperial Germany and the Industrial Revolution*, Veblen notes that "it is usual to speak of the several nations of Europe as distinct races" (1). Nevertheless, it is worth keeping in mind Warren's argument in *Black and White Strangers* that "references to race and ethnicity appear as almost 'throwaway' remarks in many of James's fictions" but in fact reveal an ambivalent "contribution to the discourse of race in America" (20, 22). If Newman is the "ideal" example of his nationality, then James's revision serves to code American national identity as white. I discuss the logic of racialism in chapter 5.

65. H. James, *Hawthorne*, 43–44.

CHAPTER 4

1. Stieglitz describes the conditions under which he took the photograph in "How *The Steerage* Happened," 175–78. For discussions of the historical context and significance of the photograph, see Whelan, *Alfred Stieglitz*, 224–26; and Hoffman, *Stieglitz*, 233–38.

2. Kazin, *New York Jew*, 16.

3. This interpretation appears in many descriptions of *The Steerage* at museums where it is on display. See, for example, *Selected Works from the Worcester Art Museum*, 215. Kazin offers this interpretation—without rejecting the personal connection he constructed earlier—in "The Art City Our Fathers Built," 17–26.

4. Whelan, *Alfred Stieglitz*, 225.

5. Unless otherwise specified, the statistics I cite derive from Barde, Carter, and Sutch, *The Historical Statistics of the United States*, 1:523–43. This five-volume work draws together and synthesizes information from various federal institutions, including the U.S. Census Bureau, which published the 1975 edition of this work.

6. Baines summarizes the historical research on return migration in *Emigration from Europe*, 39–42. See also Baines, "European Labor Markets, Emigration and Internal Migration," 35–54; Caroli, *Immigrants Who Returned Home*; Nugent, *Crossings*, 156–62; Wyman, *Round-Trip to America*; and Spellman, *The Global Community*, 75–77. For a list of historians who analyze the rates of return migration by nationality, see Baines's bibliographies.

7. In *Emigration from Europe*, Baines estimates that 2 million Scandinavians moved to the United States before 1914. If his earlier estimate that 20 percent of them eventually

returned is correct, then those return migrants numbered roughly 400,000 (39–40). In *Population Growth and Agrarian Change*, Grigg places the 1910 populations of Norway and Sweden at just under 2.4 and 5.5 million, respectively (208). As many as one in every twenty Scandinavians may have been a return migrant in the 1910s.

8. Yannella, *American Literature in Context*, 42. Yannella dedicates only two paragraphs to the topic of return migration, thereby implying that its impact was insignificant and paradoxically reinscribing the same "core narrative" he questions.

9. See, for example, Lowe, *Immigrant Acts*.

10. Hoganson, *Consumers' Imperium*, 4. Notable exceptions include the historical contextualization of the sojourner mentality of Chinese immigrants to the United States; see Yin, *Chinese American Literature since the 1850s*; and Madsen, "Sexing the Sojourner," 36–49.

11. Sollors, *Beyond Ethnicity*, 5–6.

12. Jacobson, *Barbarian Virtues*, 4.

13. While the two authors I examine inhabited specifically European-oriented migration systems, I suggest that this model of circulation can be extended to include other migration systems as well. For example, José Martí, a contemporary of both Cahan and Hamsun, inhabited a migration system that encompassed Cuba, Spain, New York City, and most of Latin America. My goal, however, is not to establish a canon of return migrant literature that would replace existing exilic and diasporic canons. Rather, I wish to broaden our conception of what constitutes the immigrant experience or an immigrant text. In this respect, I follow Edwards and Gaonkar's suggestion, in their introduction, to focus less on "the enigma of arrival in America" than on the process of "passing through" when considering migrant and diasporic experiences (26).

14. Patterson, "The Emerging West Atlantic System," 228.

15. Foner, *In a New Land*, 85. See also Foner, "What's New about Transnationalism?," 355–76.

16. Gilroy, *The Black Atlantic*, 8.

17. For background on Kürnberger, I draw upon Fluck, "The Man Who Became Weary of America," 171–206.

18. Howells, "New York Low Life in Fiction," 258, 261.

19. Ibid., 261–62.

20. For a discussion of the relationship between Howells and Cahan, see Kirk and Kirk, "Abraham Cahan and William Dean Howells," 27–57.

21. Jones, *Strange Talk*, 10. Jones's fifth chapter explores the late nineteenth-century association of immigrants and urban dialect that Howells's review of *Yekl* exemplifies.

22. Certeau, *The Capture of Speech*, 133–34. Certeau focuses mainly on the dialectical nature of assimilation, and while he complicates our understanding of the process of assimilation in important ways, he is less attentive to the transnational modes of circulation that migration systems enable.

23. H. James, *The American Scene*, 525–26.

24. See Strong, *Our Country*.

25. Previous anti-immigration movements, such as the formation of the American (or Know Nothing) Party in the 1840s and 1850s, resulted as much from religious as racial anxieties; were often directed at very specific groups of immigrants, such as Irish or German Catholics, rather than multiple nationalities; and usually achieved little success.

Shaler brought the debate into a major mainstream magazine and introduced into the equation the more complex terminology of late nineteenth-century race-science, which I discuss in more detail in the next chapter.

26. Shaler, "European Peasants as Immigrants," 647–48.

27. Ibid., 647.

28. Ibid., 655.

29. Since the U.S. Census Bureau began recording the number of foreign-born members of the population in 1850, that number has never accounted for more than 20 percent of the total population. The percentages have, in fact, remained more or less stable over the past 160 years. It would seem that the sheer number and variety of immigrants, rather than the proportion of the population those immigrants made up, caused Shaler's concerns.

30. H. James, *The American Scene*, 400.

31. Ibid., 458.

32. Speranza, "Political Representation of Italo-American Colonies," 521. Although born in Connecticut, Speranza spent his youth in Italy before returning to the United States to obtain a law degree from New York University. During the 1910s and 1920s, Speranza's politics swung to the far right, and he began supporting stricter anti-immigration laws and opposing naturalization for immigrants who had not sufficiently assimilated. For his later views on immigration, see Speranza, *Race or Nation*.

33. United States Congress, Senate, Immigration Commission, *Reports of the Immigration Commission*, 24. For a discussion of the Dillingham Commission's historical significance, see Nugent, *Crossings*, 157–60.

34. Bailey, "The Bird of Passage," 394.

35. Ibid., 395, 392.

36. Faries, *The Rise of Internationalism*, 124.

37. Bourne, "Trans-National America," 258.

38. Ibid., 260.

39. Ibid., 261.

40. Although *The Melting Pot* may be viewed (as it was by contemporary audiences) as an argument in favor of assimilation, even to the point of sacrificing one's own ethnic, cultural, and religious heritage, some critics have suggested that, when read within the context of Zangwill's entire career, the play offers a temporary solution for the particular plight of the Jewish people; see Rochelson, *A Jew in the Public Arena*, 171–204. In other words, the "melting pot" of the United States may serve as a sort of "halfway house" until the establishment of a Jewish state. However one reads it, as a text written by a British-born Jewish activist who waffled between Zionism and territorialism and who contributed an important metaphor to American debates about immigration, *The Melting Pot* is yet another example of the global circulation of U.S. immigrant culture.

41. Bourne, "Trans-National America," 261–62.

42. Ibid., 262.

43. Speranza, "Political Representation of Italo-American Colonies," 521.

44. Bourne, "Trans-National America," 263.

45. I draw primarily upon Current's introduction to *Knut Hamsun Remembers America*, 1–14; and Morgridge's introduction to *The Cultural Life of Modern America*, ix–xxxiv. A

significantly abridged English translation of Ingar Sletten Kolloen's definitive two-volume biography, *Hamsun*, has been published as *Knut Hamsun: Dreamer and Dissenter*. J. Frank provides an in-depth review of Kolloen's original in "In from the Cold," 128–33. See also Ferguson, *Enigma*.

46. See Sollors, *Beyond Ethnicity*, 168–73; Weber, "Outsiders and Greenhorns," 725–45; and von Rosk's "'Go, Make Yourself for a Person,'" 295–335.

47. Cahan, *The Rise of David Levinsky*, 3, 518. Further quotations are cited parenthetically.

48. Certeau, *The Capture of Speech*, 135.

49. Caroli, *Italian Repatriation from the United States*, 75.

50. Cahan wrote *David Levinsky* and many of his other texts in English, while Hamsun wrote almost exclusively in Norwegian or Danish. Thus whereas Cahan's intended audience was American, Hamsun wrote primarily for his fellow Scandinavians. *On the Cultural Life of Modern America* was an outgrowth of a series of lectures Hamsun delivered in Copenhagen in 1888 and 1889 and was therefore not intended for American consumption.

51. See Current, introduction, 7. Hamsun's given name was Knud Pedersen, and he published several works between 1877 and 1885 under that name, Knud Pedersen Hamsund, and variations of the two. (*Hamsund* was the name of his family's farm in Norway.)

52. In this respect, Hamsun followed the example of Frances Trollope, who established her literary reputation in Britain with the publication of *Domestic Manners of the Americas* (1832); however, the expansion of U.S. economic and cultural power in the late nineteenth century leads Hamsun to emphasize the role of migration systems themselves as a means of resisting Americanization in a way that Trollope and other earlier writers do not.

53. Probably the most famous practitioners of this subgenre are the Norwegian American Ole Edvart Rølvaag and the Swedish Vilhelm Moberg. Rølvaag's best-known work, *Giants in the Earth: A Saga of the Prairie* (1927), is a compilation—and translation—of two earlier books that Rølvaag originally wrote in Norwegian. Its lesser-known sequels are *Peder Victorious* (1929) and *Their Father's God* (1931). Moberg published a four-novel cycle known collectively as *The Emigrants* (1949–59).

54. Hamsun, *The Cultural Life of Modern America*, 139. Further quotations from this text are cited parenthetically.

55. For a depiction of Hamsun's late-career Nazi sympathies as an outgrowth of his early views on race, class, ethnicity, and gender, see Zagar, *Knut Hamsun*. Current questions the coupling of Hamsun's early anti-Americanism with his collaborationist activities during the Second World War, noting that Hamsun's attitude toward the United States mellowed with age; see Current, introduction, 10–13. Hamsun's admirers have sought to exonerate him by pointing out that the author was over eighty when Germany invaded Norway in 1940 and that, as a lifelong devotee of German art and culture, he grossly misjudged what the Nazis stood for; see Troell, *Hamsun*, 1996. Since Hamsun wrote most of the texts I examine here before Adolf Hitler was born, I take the view that they have little to do with National Socialism.

56. Morgridge, introduction, xxvi.

57. Hamsun, "Mark Twain," 47, 49.

58. Ibid., 51.

59. Ibid., 52–54.

60. Ibid., 52. Morgridge provides an extensive catalogue of the inaccuracies of *Modern America* in the endnotes to her translation (147–66).

61. Morgridge excerpts several contemporaneous reviews of Hamsun's book and the lectures upon which it was based; see Morgridge, introduction, xx–xxiv, xxix–xxx. Iconoclasm was Hamsun's chief strategy for gaining attention during his early career, and he sometimes wrote just as disparagingly of established Norwegian literary figures, including Bjørnstjerne Bjørnson, who had written a letter of recommendation for Hamsun. In the introduction to his translation of Hamsun's *Pan* (1894), Lyngstad mentions an 1891 lecture in which Hamsun attacked Henrik Ibsen's plays while Ibsen himself sat in the front row. Although neither Ibsen nor Bjørnson seem to have taken these attacks seriously, Lyngstad notes that, on this occasion, several newspaper editors criticized Hamsun for "using Yankee methods to promote his own career" (vii). Thus some of Hamsun's fellow Norwegians were savvy enough to recognize and criticize the values and practices of American culture that were beginning to spread globally through returning migrants like Hamsun.

62. Hamsun, "From America," 17.

63. Ibid., 18–19.

64. Ibid., 18. Hamsun was not free from racial prejudices. After noting that it was "inhumanity [that] stole [Negroes] away from Africa," he goes on to dismiss African Americans as a "nascent human form" and to express distaste at the thought of miscegenation; see *Modern America*, 144.

65. Hamsun, "From America," 21.

66. Ibid.

67. Fluck, "The Man Who Became Weary of America," 174–75.

68. Ibid., 190. I discuss this historical struggle in the introduction. See Wallerstein, "The Three Instances of Hegemony," 100–108; and Arrighi, *The Long Twentieth Century*, 60–63.

69. Quoted in Fluck, "The Man Who Became Weary of America," 183. Kürnberger's acknowledgement of England's displacement of Holland and his vision of Germany's future displacement of England anticipate Arrighi's "successive systemic cycles of accumulation"; see Arrighi, *The Long Twentieth Century*, 6. Blackbourn discusses the efforts to unite the German states throughout the nineteenth century in *History of Germany*.

70. Hamsun, "Mark Twain," 46.

71. Ibid., 54.

72. Ibid.

73. Ibid., 53.

74. Hamsun, "Festina Lente," 134.

75. Ibid., 132.

76. Ibid., 136.

CHAPTER 5

1. Esthus, *Theodore Roosevelt and Japan*, 146.

2. Emmerson chronicles this legislation in *The Eagle and the Rising Sun*, 47.

3. London, "The Unparalleled Invasion," 86.

4. Ibid., 100.

5. For an ironic reading of "The Unparalleled Invasion," see Reesman, *Jack London's Racial Lives*, 101. For a skeptical response to such readings, see Lye, *America's Asia*, 40–41.

6. London, "Unparalleled Invasion," 72–73, 75.

7. Ibid., 87.

8. Stoddard, *The Rising Tide of Color against White World-Supremacy*, 203.

9. In his introduction to Stoddard's book, Madison Grant, whose *The Passing of the Great Race, or the Racial Basis of European History* (1916) was another influential race-science tract of the era, refers to European Russians as "imperfectly Nordicized Alpines" (xv). In the complicated racial hierarchies of the period, Nordics, Alpines, and Mediterraneans comprised the three branches of the Caucasian race.

10. G. Murphy, *Shadowing the White Man's Burden*, 162.

11. That the Japanese public largely resented Roosevelt's involvement, viewing the Treaty of Portsmouth as unfavorable to them despite their victory in the war, demonstrates just how complicated U.S.-Japanese relations could be. For more detailed perspectives on this history, see Dulles, *Yankees and Samurai*; Esthus, *Theodore Roosevelt and Japan*; and the essays collected in Krauss and Nyblade, *Japan and North America*.

12. London, *Jack London Reports*, 106. Unless otherwise indicated, all further quotations of London refer to this collection and are cited parenthetically.

13. A number of Westerners lived in Japan during this period and wrote about the Japanese people and their culture, though none achieved as much fame as either London or Hearn did. The diplomats William George Aston and Sir Ernest Satow and the philologist Basil Hall Chamberlain ranked among the most distinguished British Japanologists. Both Chamberlain and the American art historian Ernest Fenollosa were friends with Hearn in Tokyo. Fenollosa's efforts to popularize Chinese and Japanese visual art in the West influenced both Ezra Pound and William Butler Yeats after his death. For an introduction to Fenollosa's biography and work, see Chisolm, *Fenollosa*.

14. G. Murphy, *Shadowing the White Man's Burden*, 181; Lye, *America's Asia*, 10.

15. Appiah, *In My Father's House*, 13. Appiah traces a much longer and more involved history of racialism in "Race," 274–87.

16. Appiah, *In My Father's House*, 13.

17. Du Bois, "The Conservation of Races," 22. Appiah discusses Du Bois's evolving views on race in "The Uncompleted Argument," 21–37; and *In My Father's House*, 28–46.

18. Taylor, "Two Theories of Modernity," 20–21.

19. Ibid., 21, 25.

20. Arguably, Taylor's two most important essays on this subject are "The Self in Moral Space," 25–52; and "The Politics of Recognition," in *Multiculturalism*, 25–73. Not coincidentally, *Multiculturalism* contains a response to Taylor by Appiah entitled "Identity, Authenticity, Survival: Multicultural Societies and Social Reproduction" in which Appiah outlines several dangers that result from using forms of collective identity to guide ethical or political action, including most notably what Appiah calls the "politics of compulsion" (163). It is worth noting that Taylor ran for the Canadian House of Commons on four occasions during the 1960s, the same decade that Canadian politics brought the word "multiculturalism" into common parlance. In the latter volume, however, both Taylor and Appiah level several pointed criticisms at certain simplistic tendencies in contemporary discussions of multiculturalism.

21. I stop short of suggesting that, in tracing the genealogies of racialism and of multiculturalism, we might find that they converge, though such a historical study might be productive.

22. Said, *Orientalism*, 204.

23. See, for example, Goebel, "Japan as Western Text," 188–205. Despite acknowledging that "Japan continues to resist our urge to attribute universal validity to Western sociopolitical, philosophical, and aesthetic discourse" (191), Goebel ultimately reaffirms Said's Orientalist model. For notable critical responses to Said, see B. Lewis, "The Question of Orientalism," and Ahmad, "Between Orientalism and Historicism." Lewis, one of the modern orientalists whose work Said examines, criticizes Said for a number of omissions and inaccuracies that, Lewis claims, slant Said's evidence in favor of a predetermined set of beliefs and prejudices. Ahmad criticizes Said for not properly historicizing his argument and for what Ahmad views as Said's opportunistic use of certain European thinkers, such as Marx, in support of his claims, despite the fact that many of those thinkers dismissed or ignored non-Western history and culture.

24. Said, *Orientalism*, 7. Said's original text focuses on nineteenth-century *European* discursive practices, with Said himself claiming that "to speak of Orientalism . . . is to speak mainly, although not exclusively, of a British and French cultural enterprise" (4). In his 2003 preface to the twenty-fifth anniversary edition, however, Said pinpoints continued Orientalist thinking as the cause of the U.S. military intervention in Iraq; see Said, *Orientalism*, xx.

25. Lye, *America's Asia*, 3.

26. Howells, "Editor's Study," September 1890, 641–42. Shigemi's given name is misspelled "Shinkichi" in Howells's review.

27. Lye, *America's Asia*, 12.

28. Reesman, "Marching with 'the Censor,'" 138. This essay is incorporated into the third chapter of Reesman's *Jack London's Racial Lives*.

29. For fuller histories of the war and its political, social, and cultural dimensions, see Connaughton, *The War of the Rising Sun and the Tumbling Bear*; Warner and Warner, *The Tide at Sunrise*; and Steinberg et al., *The Russo-Japanese War in Global Perspective*. When referring to place names, I follow London's or Hearn's usage and spelling. In those instances where confusion may ensue, I place the current name in brackets.

30. Wells and Wilson, foreword, ix.

31. Japan's military leaders worried that foreign correspondents would reveal information useful to Russia or dangerous to Japanese morale. Hendricks and Shepard include a copy of the regulations London had to abide by in *Jack London Reports*, 25–26. See also Slattery, *Reporting the Russo-Japanese War*, 61–69; and Sweeney, "'Delays and Vexation,'" 548–59.

32. Davis, "The Japanese-Russian War," 220. In contrast to London's "freedom amongst aliens," Davis concludes this chapter by referring to what he viewed as his wasted time in Korea as a period of "bondage" (235).

33. See Davis, "Honoring the Heroes and the Dead," 107.

34. For the purposes of clarity in this chapter, I do *not* follow the Japanese custom of placing family name (in this case, Koizumi) first. Moreover, I still refer to him as Lafcadio Hearn because he continued to use this name when publishing in English.

35. See Bisland, *The Life and Letters of Lafcadio Hearn*, and Cowley, introduction, *The Selected Writings of Lafcadio Hearn*. For Hearn's early critical reception, see Guo, "Interpreting Japan's Interpreters," 106–18; and Bronner, Introduction, 1–33.

36. Howells, "Editor's Study," September 1890, 642.

37. Hearn, *Japan: An Attempt at Interpretation*, 6.

38. Ibid., 16.

39. Hearn's full name was Patricio Lafcadio Tessima Carlos Hearn.

40. Hearn, "Cincinnati Salamanders," 109.

41. Lears, *No Place of Grace*, 175, xv.

42. Ibid., 149.

43. Hearn, *Glimpses of Unfamiliar Japan*, 7.

44. Ibid., xii, xiii, xv.

45. Hearn, *Kokoro*, 1. Further quotations of this text are cited parenthetically.

46. See Hishida, "Formosa," 267–81. This appellation elides the complex history of Okinawa, which was invaded by Japan in the seventeenth century and became a Japanese prefecture in 1879. Comprehensive accounts of the Sino-Japanese War available in English include Lone, *Japan's First Modern War*, and Paine, *The Sino-Japanese War of 1894–1895*. This war is sometimes called the First Sino-Japanese War in order to distinguish it from the conflict between China and Japan (1937–45) that overlapped World War II.

47. The classic English-language study of this period in Japanese history is Beasley, *The Meiji Restoration*.

48. See Bender, *A Nation among Nations*, 246–47, 249–50, 282–83.

49. Bronner, introduction, 29. Bronner provides an overview of Hearn's life, particularly of the years he spent in the United States.

50. Hearn, "Les Chiffonniers," 97.

51. Hearn, "The Roar of the City," 229.

52. Hearn, "Growth of Population in America," 210.

53. Ibid., 210.

54. Daniel Stempel, "Lafcadio Hearn," 15.

55. Hearn, *Japan*, 8–9.

56. Despite the celebratory tone of much of Hearn's writing about Japan, his personal correspondence reveals feelings of ambivalence about his life there. See, for example, Murray, *A Fantastic Journey*, 145–46, 191–93, 206–07, 270. Hearn seems to have been a rather cantankerous man in private life, and these expressions of ambivalence generally correspond to unhappy periods in his life, such as his resignation from Tokyo Imperial University in 1903 following an argument over his salary.

57. Esthus covers the 1907 crisis extensively in *Theodore Roosevelt and Japan*. See also Neumann, *America Encounters Japan*, 123–28.

58. Esthus, *Theodore Roosevelt and Japan*, 146.

59. Others include Homer Lea, whose *The Valor of Ignorance* (1909) predicted that the United States would lose a war with Japan; Jesse Steiner, who wrote *The Japanese Invasion* (1917); and Stoddard. Perhaps the most famous prophet of war was General Billy Mitchell.

60. Flowers, *The Japanese Conquest of American Opinion*, 10–11.

61. I note Strong's significance in my first chapter. Hishida earned his Ph.D. at Columbia University and often wrote in English. Much like Nitobe Inazō, a Japanese diplomat

whose influential study of samurai culture *Bushido, the Soul of Japan* (1899) was part of the growing Japanese discourse on military ethics but was originally published in English in the United States, Hishida clearly intended to address an international audience. For a discussion of how Japanese intellectuals shaped domestic political discourse in Japan by publishing their work internationally, see Benesch, "Bushido: The Creation of a Martial Ethic in Late Meiji Japan."

62. Hishida, *The International Position of Japan as a Great Power*, 261. Further quotations are cited parenthetically. Kaiser Wilhelm II is usually credited with coining the phrase "yellow peril" in 1895.

63. Hearn, *Japan*, 383.

64. Ibid.

65. Ibid.

66. Ibid., 391, 390.

CODA

1. Brooks, *The Pilgrimage of Henry James*, 160.

2. Mencken, "Henry James," 500–501.

3. Parrington, *The Beginnings of Critical Realism in America*, 240.

4. Michaels, *Our America*, 2–3.

5. Bender, *A Nation among Nations*, 245.

6. Stein, *The Autobiography of Alice B. Toklas*, 78. Several major scholars of American modernism have rejected Michaels's argument outright. For example, Perloff criticizes him for largely ignoring poets and some of the more avant-garde writers of the period in "Modernism without the Modernists," 99–105.

7. See Rosenberg, *Spreading the American Dream*, 138–60.

8. E. Wilson, *A Prelude*, 276.

9. For detailed analyses of these statistics, see Barry, *The Great Influenza*, 396–98; and Crosby, *Epidemic and Peace*, 205–07. The most conservative estimates initially placed the worldwide death toll at 21 million, though recent studies suggest that the disease claimed that many lives in the Indian subcontinent alone. Current estimates range between 50 and 100 million (roughly 2.5–5 percent of the world's total population at the time). The classic account of the pandemic is Jordan, *Epidemic Influenza*. For a historiographical overview of literature written on the pandemic, see Phillips and Killingray, Introduction, 12–21.

10. E. Wilson, *A Prelude*, 276.

11. Ibid., 277.

12. Ibid.

13. Ibid.

14. Ibid., 278.

15. "The Death of a Soldier" first appeared in *The Undertaker's Garland* (1922), which Wilson coauthored with the poet John Peale Bishop. Wilson's story follows the last days in the life of a young AEF soldier named Henry, who succumbs to influenza before seeing any military action.

16. See E. Wilson, *The Shores of Light*. "A Nation of Foreigners" originally appeared unsigned in *New Republic* 5 Oct. 1927, 161–62. To be fair, Wilson collected some of his

writings about marginalized Americans as early as *The American Jitters* (1932). Dabney notes Wilson's regret over not engaging the Harlem Renaissance more productively in *Edmund Wilson*, 419.

17. Pease, introduction, 14.

18. Ibid., 15.

19. In their introduction to *States of Emergency*, Castronovo and Gillman suggest that Americanists prioritize "comparability" as a methodology and thereby make "visible both the global and the local routes that bring the objects of American studies—race, slavery, immigration, *the state*—into circulation" (4, 7; emphasis added). Pease's own recent work builds on Giorgio Agamben's notion of the state of exception and calls for viewing U.S. history as a series of states of exception. In his introduction to *Re-Framing the Transnational Turn in American Studies*, Pease argues that Americanists should examine how "U.S. state apparatuses . . . set the rules of the newly globalized world order [and thus enabled] the invasive introduction of neoliberal market values in regions that adhered to values that were incompatible with the assumptions of the global marketplace" (24). See also Pease, *The New American Exceptionalism*; and Pease, "American Studies after American Exceptionalism?" 47–83.

20. Pease, introduction, 38.

21. E. Wilson, "The Ambiguity of Henry James," 105.

22. For this account of James's naturalization, see Edel, *Henry James*, 528–32.

23. E. Wilson, *The Shores of Light*, 227.

Bibliography

Addams, Jane. *The Second Twenty Years at Hull-House, September 1909 to September 1929: With a Record of a Growing World Consciousness.* New York: Macmillan, 1930.

———. *Twenty Years at Hull-House.* 1910. New York: Signet, 1961.

Ahmad, Aijaz. "Between Orientalism and Historicism." In *Orientalism: A Reader*, ed. Alexander Lyon Macfie. New York: New York University Press, 2001. 285–97.

Alden, Henry Mills. *Magazine Writing and the New Literature.* New York: Harper and Brothers, 1908.

Althusser, Louis. "Ideology and the Ideological State Apparatuses (Notes towards an Investigation)." In *Lenin and Philosophy and Other Essays*, trans. Ben Brewster. New York: Monthly Review, 1971. 127–86.

"America First." *New York Times*, April 21, 1915: 12.

"'America First,' Wilson's Slogan." *New York Times*, April 21, 1915: 1.

American Dictionary of the English Language. 1828.

Amin, Ash, and Nigel Thrift, eds. Introduction. *The Blackwell Cultural Economy Reader.* Oxford: Blackwell, 2004. x–xxx.

Anderson, Amanda. "Cosmopolitanism, Universalism, and the Divided Legacies of Modernity." In *Cosmopolitics: Thinking and Feeling beyond the Nation*, ed. Pheng Cheah and Bruce Robbins. Minneapolis: University of Minnesota Press, 1998. 265–89.

Anderson, Benedict. *Imagined Communities: Reflections on the Origin and Spread of Nationalism.* Rev. ed. London: Verso, 1991.

Anderson, Mark, ed. *Reading Kafka: Prague, Politics, and the Fin de Siècle.* New York: Schocken, 1989.

Appadurai, Arjun. *Modernity at Large: Cultural Dimensions of Globalization.* Minneapolis: University of Minnesota Press, 1996.

Appiah, Kwame Anthony. *Cosmopolitanism: Ethics in a World of Strangers.* New York: W. W. Norton, 2006.

———. "Cosmopolitan Patriots." *Critical Inquiry* 23.3 (1997): 617–39.

———. "Identity, Authenticity, Survival: Multicultural Societies and Social Reproduction." In *Multiculturalism: Examining the Politics of Recognition*, ed. Amy Gutmann. Princeton: Princeton University Press, 1994. 149–64.

———. *In My Father's House: Africa in the Philosophy of Culture.* Oxford: Oxford University Press, 1993.

———. "Race." In *Critical Terms for Literary Study*, ed. Frank Lentricchia and Thomas McLaughlin. 2nd ed. Chicago: University of Chicago Press, 1995. 274–87.

———. "The Uncompleted Argument: Du Bois and the Illusion of Race." *Critical Inquiry* 12.1 (1985): 21–37.

Arrighi, Giovanni. *The Long Twentieth Century: Money, Power and the Origins of Our Times.* Rev. ed. London: Verso, 2010.

Atkinson, Fred W. *The Philippine Islands.* Boston: Ginn, 1905.

Bailey, W. B. "The Bird of Passage." *American Journal of Sociology* 18.3 (1912): 391–97.

Baines, Dudley. *Emigration from Europe, 1815–1930.* London: Macmillan, 1991.

———. "European Labor Markets, Emigration and Internal Migration, 1850–1913." In *Migration and the International Labor Market, 1850–1939,* ed. Timothy J. Hatton and Jeffrey G. Williamson. New York: Routledge, 1994. 35–54.

Banta, Martha. *Taylored Lives: Narrative Productions in the Age of Taylor, Veblen, and Ford.* Chicago: University of Chicago Press, 1993.

———, ed. Introduction. *New Essays on "The American."* Cambridge: Cambridge University Press, 1987. 1–42.

Barde, Robert, Susan B. Carter, and Richard Sutch, eds. *The Historical Statistics of the United States: Earliest Times to the Present.* Millennial edition. Cambridge: Cambridge University Press, 2006.

Barrish, Phillip J. *The Cambridge Introduction to American Literary Realism.* Cambridge: Cambridge University Press, 2011.

Barrows, Adam. *The Cosmic Time of Empire: Modern Britain and World Literature.* Berkeley: University of California Press, 2010.

Barry, John M. *The Great Influenza: The Epic Story of the Deadliest Plague in History.* New York: Penguin, 2005.

Bartel, Kim. "Kant's Narrative of Hope in the Gilded Age." *American Literary History* 19.3 (2007): 661–88.

Baucom, Ian. *Specters of the Atlantic: Finance Capital, Slavery, and the Philosophy of History.* Durham, N.C.: Duke University Press, 2005.

Baxter, Sylvester. "A Great Modern Spaniard." *Atlantic Monthly,* April 1900: 546–60.

Beasley, William G. *The Meiji Restoration.* Stanford, Calif.: Stanford University Press, 1972.

Beede, Benjamin R. "Foreign Influences on American Progressivism." *Historian* 45.4 (1983): 529–49.

Bellamy, Edward. *Looking Backward, 2000–1887.* Ed. Alex MacDonald. 1888. Peterborough, Ont.: Broadview, 2003.

Bender, Thomas. *A Nation among Nations: America's Place in World History.* New York: Hill and Wang, 2006.

———, ed. *Rethinking American History in a Global Age.* Berkeley: University of California Press, 2002.

Benesch, Oleg. "Bushido: The Creation of a Martial Ethic in Late Meiji Japan." Ph.D. diss., U. of British Columbia, 2011.

Bentley, Nancy. *Frantic Panoramas: American Literature and Mass Culture, 1870–1920.* Philadelphia: University of Pennsylvania Press, 2009.

Berthoff, Warner. *The Ferment of Realism: American Literature, 1884–1919.* 1965. Cambridge: Cambridge University Press, 1981.

Bhabha, Homi, ed. *Nation and Narration.* London: Routledge, 1990.

Bisland, Elizabeth. *The Life and Letters of Lafcadio Hearn.* 2 vols. Boston: Houghton Mifflin, 1906.

Blackbourn, David. *History of Germany, 1780–1918: The Long Nineteenth Century*. 2nd ed. Malden, Mass.: Blackwell, 2003.

Blanco, John D. *Frontier Constitutions: Christianity and Colonial Empire in the Nineteenth-Century Philippines*. Berkeley: University of California Press, 2009.

Bosanquet, Theodora. *Henry James at Work*. 2nd ed. London: Hogarth, 1927.

Bourne, Randolph. "Trans-National America." In *The Radical Will: Selected Writings, 1911–1918*. Ed. Olaf Hansen. New York: Urizen, 1977. 248–64.

Boynton, H. W. "Books New and Old." *Atlantic Monthly*, April 1904: 560–72.

Bramen, Carrie Tirado. *The Uses of Variety: Modern Americanism and the Quest for National Distinctiveness*. Cambridge, Mass.: Harvard University Press, 2000.

Brandeis, Louis D. *Other People's Money and How the Bankers Use It*. 1914. Ed. Melvin I. Urofsky. Boston: Bedford/St. Martin's, 1995.

Brodhead, Richard H. *Cultures of Letters: Scenes of Reading and Writing in Nineteenth-Century America*. Chicago: University of Chicago Press, 1993.

Bronner, Simon J., ed. Introduction. *Lafcadio Hearn's America: Ethnographic Sketches and Editorials*. Lexington: University Press of Kentucky, 2002. 1–33.

Brooks, Van Wyck. *The Pilgrimage of Henry James*. New York: E. P. Dutton, 1925.

Brown, Bill. *A Sense of Things: The Object Matter of American Literature*. Chicago: University of Chicago Press, 2003.

Brownell, W. C. "Henry James." *Atlantic Monthly*, April 1905: 496–519.

Butterfield, R. W. "*The American*." In *The Air of Reality: New Essays on Henry James*, ed. John Goode. London: Methuen, 1972. 17–35.

Cable, George Washington. "Congregational Unity in Georgia." *Congregationalist*, September 26, 1889: 317.

Cadle, Nathaniel. "America as 'World-Salvation': Josiah Strong, W. E. B. Du Bois, and the Global Rhetoric of American Exceptionalism." In *American Exceptionalisms: From Winthrop to Winfrey*, ed. Sylvia Söderlind and James Taylor Carson. Albany: State University of New York Press, 2011. 125–46.

Cady, Edwin H. "Armando Palacio Valdés Writes to William Dean Howells." *Symposium* 2.1 (1948): 19–37.

———. *The Realist at War: The Mature Years of William Dean Howells, 1885–1920*. Syracuse, N.Y.: Syracuse University Press, 1958.

Cahan, Abraham. *The Rise of David Levinsky*. 1917. New York: Modern Library, 2001.

Capellán Gonzalo, Angel. "William Dean Howells and Armando Palacio Valdés: A Literary Friendship." *Revista de Estudios Hispanicos* 10.3 (1976): 451–71.

Cargill, Oscar. "The First International Novel." *PMLA* 73.4 (1958): 418–25.

Carnegie, Andrew. "The Bugaboo of Trusts." *North American Review*, February 1889: 141–51.

———. "Wealth." *North American Review*, June 1889: 653–65.

"Carnegie Criticizes Congress on Tariff." *New York Times*, February 13, 1909: 1.

Caroli, Betty Boyd. *Immigrants Who Returned Home*. New York: Chelsea, 1990.

———. *Italian Repatriation from the United States, 1900–1914*. New York: Center for Migration Studies, 1973.

Casanova, Pascale. *The World Republic of Letters*. 1999. Trans. M. B. DeBevoise. Cambridge, Mass.: Harvard University Press, 2004.

Castronovo, Russ. *Beautiful Democracy: Aesthetics and Anarchy in a Global Era*. Chicago: University of Chicago Press, 2007.

Castronovo, Russ, and Susan Gillman, eds. Introduction. "The Study of the American Problems." *States of Emergency: The Object of American Studies*. Chapel Hill: University of North Carolina Press, 2009. 1–16.

Cazdyn, Eric, and Imre Szeman. *After Globalization*. Hoboken, N.J.: Wiley-Blackwell, 2011.

The Century Dictionary and Cyclopedia. New York: Century, 1889–91.

Certeau, Michel de. *The Capture of Speech and Other Political Writings*. 1994. Ed. Luce Giard. Trans. Tom Conley. Minneapolis: University of Minnesota Press, 1997.

Chisolm, Lawrence W. *Fenollosa: The Far East and American Culture*. New Haven, Conn.: Yale University Press, 1963.

Chua, Amy. *World on Fire: How Exporting Free Market Democracy Breeds Ethnic Hatred and Global Instability*. New York: Doubleday, 2003.

Clark, Robert. "The Transatlantic Romance of Henry James." In *American Fiction: New Readings*, ed. Richard Gray. London: Vision, 1983. 100–114.

Cohen, Margaret. "Sentimental Communities." In *The Literary Channel: The Inter-National Invention of the Novel*, ed. Margaret Cohen and Carolyn Dever. Princeton, N.J.: Princeton University Press, 2002. 106–32.

Coit, Stanton. *The Soul of America: A Constructive Essay in the Sociology of Religion*. New York: Macmillan, 1914.

Coleman, Peter J. *Progressivism and the World of Reform: New Zealand and the Origins of the American Welfare State*. Lawrence: University Press of Kansas, 1987.

Connaughton, R. M. *The War of the Rising Sun and the Tumbling Bear: A Military History of the Russo-Japanese War, 1904–5*. London: Routledge, 1988.

Cook, James W., and Lawrence B. Glickman. "Part 1: Introduction: Twelve Propositions for a History of U.S. Cultural History." In *The Cultural Turn in U.S. History: Past, Present, and Future*, ed. J. W. Cook, L. B. Glickman, and Michael O'Malley. Chicago: University of Chicago Press, 2008. 3–57.

Coon, Deborah J. "'One Moment in the World's Salvation': Anarchism and the Radicalization of William James." *Journal of American History* 83.1 (1996): 70–99.

Cowley, Malcolm. Introduction. *The Selected Writings of Lafcadio Hearn*. Ed. Henry Goodman. New York: Citadel, 1949. 1–15.

Craig, Austin. *Lineage, Life and Labors of José Rizal*. Manila: Philippine Education Co., 1913.

———. *The Story of José Rizal, the Greatest Man of the Brown Race*. Manila: Philippine Education Co., 1909.

Croly, Herbert. *The Promise of American Life*. 1909. New York: Macmillan, 1914.

Crosby, Alfred W., Jr. *Epidemic and Peace, 1918*. Westport, Conn.: Greenwood, 1976.

Current, Richard Nelson. Introduction. *Knut Hamsun Remembers America: Essays and Stories, 1885–1949*. Columbia: University of Missouri Press, 2003. 1–14.

Curtis, George William. "Editor's Easy Chair." *Harper's New Monthly Magazine*, July 1885: 308–13.

Damrosch, David. *What Is World Literature?* Princeton, N.J.: Princeton University Press, 2003.

Davis, Richard Harding. "Honoring the Heroes and the Dead." In *The Russo-Japanese War: A Photographic and Descriptive Review of the Great Conflict in the Far East*. New York: P. F. Collier and Son, 1905. 107.

———. "The Japanese-Russian War: Battles I Did Not See." In *Notes of a War Correspondent*. New York: Charles Scribner's Sons, 1910. 213–35.

Dawley, Alan. *Changing the World: American Progressives in War and Revolution*. Princeton, N.J.: Princeton University Press, 2003.

De Forest, John William. "The Great American Novel." *Nation*, January 9, 1868: 27–29.

Deleuze, Gilles, and Félix Guattari. *Kafka: Toward a Minor Literature*. 1975. Trans. Dana Polan. Minneapolis: University of Minnesota Press, 1986.

Delmendo, Sharon. *The Star-Entangled Banner: One Hundred Years of America in the Philippines*. New Brunswick, N.J.: Rutgers University Press, 2004.

Dendle, Brain J. *Spain's Forgotten Novelist: Armando Palacio Valdés (1853–1938)*. Lewisburg, Pa.: Bucknell University Press, 1995.

Derbyshire, Charles, trans. *The Social Cancer: A Complete English Version of "Noli Me Tangere" from the Spanish of José Rizal*. Manila: Philippine Education Co., 1912.

"Dernburg Asserts Press Is Partial." *New York Times*, April 28, 1915: 3.

Dewey, John. *Reconstruction in Philosophy*. New York: Henry Holt, 1920.

DiMaggio, Paul J., and Walter W. Powell. "The Iron Cage Revisited: Institutional Isomorphism and Collective Rationality in Organizational Fields." *American Sociological Review* 48.2 (1983): 147–60.

Du Bois, W. E. B. "The African Roots of the War." *Atlantic Monthly*, May 1915: 707–14.

———. "The Conservation of Races." In *W. E. B. Du Bois: A Reader*, ed. David Levering Lewis. New York: Henry Holt, 1995. 20–27.

Du Gay, Paul, and Michael Pryke, eds. "Cultural Economy: An Introduction." In *Cultural Economy: Cultural Analysis and Commercial Life*. London: Sage, 2002. 1–19.

Dulles, Foster Rhea. *Yankees and Samurai: America's Role in the Emergence of Modern Japan, 1791–1900*. New York: Harper and Row, 1965.

Edel, Leon. *Henry James: The Master, 1901–1916*. Philadelphia: J. B. Lippincott, 1972.

———, ed. *The Complete Plays of Henry James*. Philadelphia: J. B. Lippincott, 1949.

Edgar, Pelham. *Henry James: Man and Author*. Boston: Houghton Mifflin, 1927.

Edwards, Brian T., and Dilip Parameshwar Gaonkar, eds. Introduction. *Globalizing American Studies*. Chicago: University of Chicago Press, 2010. 1–44.

Emmerson, John K. *The Eagle and the Rising Sun: America and Japan in the Twentieth Century*. Reading, Mass.: Addison-Wesley, 1988.

Esthus, Raymond A. *Theodore Roosevelt and Japan*. Seattle: University of Washington Press, 1966.

Evans, Brad. *Before Cultures: The Ethnographic Imagination in American Literature, 1865–1920*. Chicago: University of Chicago Press, 2005.

Ewald, Georg Heinrich August von. *Commentary on the Prophets of the Old Testament*. Trans. J. Frederick Smith. Vol. 4. London: Williams and Norgate, 1880.

Faries, John Culbert. *The Rise of Internationalism*. New York: W. D. Gray, 1915.

Ferguson, Robert. *Enigma: The Life of Knut Hamsun*. New York: Farrar, Straus, and Giroux, 1987.

Fisher, Philip. Introduction. "The New American Studies." In *The New American Studies: Essays from Representations*. Berkeley: University of California Press, 1991. vii–xxii.

Flowers, Montaville. *The Japanese Conquest of American Opinion*. New York: George H. Doran, 1917.

Fluck, Winfried. "The Man Who Became Weary of America: Ferdinand Kürnberger's Novel *Der Amerika-Müde* (1855)." In *German? American? Literature?: New Directions in German-American Studies*, ed. Winfried Fluck and Werner Sollors. New York: P. Lang, 2002. 171–206.

———. "A New Beginning? Transnationalisms." *New Literary History* 42.3 (2011): 365–84.

Foner, Nancy. *In a New Land: A Comparative View of Immigration*. New York: New York University Press, 2005.

———. "What's New about Transnationalism? New York Immigrants Today and at the Turn of the Century." *Diaspora* 6.3 (1997): 355–76.

Foote, Stephanie. *Regional Fictions: Culture and Identity in Nineteenth-Century American Literature*. Madison: University of Wisconsin Press, 2001.

Frank, Andre Gunder. *Reorient: Global Economy in the Asian Age*. Berkeley: University of California Press, 1998.

Frank, Andre Gunder, and Barry K. Gills, eds. *The World System: Five Hundred Years or Five Thousand?* London: Routledge, 1993.

Frank, Jeffrey. "In from the Cold: The Return of Knut Hamsun." *New Yorker*, December 26, 2005–January 2, 2006: 128–33.

"French Look to Us." *New York Times*, April 24, 1915: 2.

Fry, Joseph A. "From Open Door to World Systems: Economic Interpretations of Late Nineteenth Century American Foreign Relations." *Pacific Historical Review* 65.2 (1996): 277–303.

Garland, Hamlin. *Crumbling Idols: Twelve Essays on Art Dealing Chiefly with Literature, Painting, and the Drama*. Chicago: Stone and Kimball, 1894.

———. "Mr. Howells's Latest Novels." *New England Magazine*, May 1890: 243–50.

Gettmann, Royal A. "Henry James's Revision of *The American*." *American Literature* 16.4 (1945): 279–95.

Geyer, Michael, and Charles Bright. "World History in a Global Age." *American Historical Review* 100.4 (1995): 1034–60.

Giddens, Anthony. *The Consequences of Modernity*. Stanford, Calif.: Stanford University Press, 1990.

Gilroy, Paul. *The Black Atlantic: Modernity and Double Consciousness*. Cambridge, Mass.: Harvard University Press, 1993.

Glazener, Nancy. "The Practice and Promotion of American Literary Realism." In *A Companion to American Fiction, 1865–1914*, ed. Robert Paul Lamb and G. R. Thompson. Malden, Mass.: Blackwell, 2005. 15–34.

———. *Reading for Realism: The History of a U.S. Literary Institution, 1850–1910*. Durham, N.C.: Duke University Press, 1997.

Goble, Mark. "Media and Communication Technologies." In *Henry James in Context: The Construction of Authorship*, ed. David McWhirter. Cambridge: Cambridge University Press, 2010. 203–13.

Goebel, Rolf J. "Japan as Western Text: Roland Barthes, Richard Gordon Smith, and Lafcadio Hearn." *Comparative Literary Studies* 30.2 (1993): 188–205.

Grigg, D. B. *Population Growth and Agrarian Change: An Historical Perspective.* Cambridge: Cambridge University Press, 1980.

Guarneri, Carl. *America in the World: United States History in Global Context.* New York: McGraw-Hill, 2007.

Guo, Nanyan. "Interpreting Japan's Interpreters: The Problem of Lafcadio Hearn." *New Zealand Journal of Asian Studies* 3.2 (2001): 106–18.

Hamsun, Knut. *The Cultural Life of Modern America.* 1889. Ed. and trans. Barbara Gordon Morgridge. Cambridge, Mass.: Harvard University Press, 1969.

———. "Festina Lente." In *Knut Hamsun Remembers America,* 131–38.

———. "From America." Reprinted as "The American Character." In *Knut Hamsun Remembers America,* 17–23.

———. *Knut Hamsun Remembers America: Essays and Stories, 1885–1949.* Ed. Richard Nelson Current. Columbia: University of Missouri Press, 2003.

———. "Mark Twain." In *Knut Hamsun Remembers America,* 45–56.

Handlin, Oscar. *Boston's Immigrants, 1790–1880.* 50th anniversary edition. Cambridge, Mass.: Harvard University Press, 1991.

Hannerz, Ulf. "Cosmopolitans and Locals in World Culture." *Theory, Culture and Society* 7.2 (1990): 237–51.

Harris, Susan K. *God's Arbiters: Americans and the Philippines, 1898–1902.* Oxford: Oxford University Press, 2011.

Harrison, Benjamin. "Musings upon Current Topics." *North American Review,* February 1901: 177–90.

Hart, Albert Bushnell, ed. *Selected Addresses and Public Papers of Woodrow Wilson.* New York: Modern Library, 1918.

Harvey, David. *Justice, Nature and the Geography of Difference.* Oxford: Blackwell, 1996.

Hearn, Lafcadio. "Cincinnati Salamanders: A Confederation of Twenty Little Communities." In *Lafcadio Hearn's America,* 109–14.

———. *Glimpses of Unfamiliar Japan.* 1894. Rutland, Vt.: Charles E. Tuttle, 1976.

———. "Growth of Population in America." In *Lafcadio Hearn's America,* 209–10.

———. *Japan: An Attempt at Interpretation.* 1904. New York: ICG Muse, 2001.

———. *Kokoro: Hints and Echoes of Japanese Inner Life.* 1896. New York: ICG Muse, 2001.

———. *Lafcadio Hearn's America: Ethnographic Sketches and Editorials.* Ed. Simon J. Bronner. Lexington: University Press of Kentucky, 2002.

———. "Les Chiffonniers: How They Live, Work, and Have Their Being." In *Lafcadio Hearn's America,* 97–102.

———. "The Roar of the City." In *Lafcadio Hearn's America,* 229.

Hebard, Andrew. *The Poetics of Sovereignty in American Literature, 1885–1910.* Cambridge: Cambridge University Press, 2013.

Herren, Madeleine, Martin Rüesch, and Christiane Sibille. *Transcultural History: Theories, Methods, Sources.* Berlin: Springer, 2012.

Herrick, Robert. "A Visit to Henry James." *Yale Review* 12.4 (1923): 724–41.

Higginson, Thomas Wentworth. "The Cant of Cosmopolitanism." In *Book and Heart: Essays on Literature and Life.* New York: Harper and Brothers, 1897. 110–15.

Himmelfarb, Gertrude. "The Illusions of Cosmopolitanism." In *For Love of Country*, ed. Joshua Cohen. Boston: Beacon Press, 1996. 72–77.

Hishida, Seiji. "Formosa: Japan's First Colony." *Political Science Quarterly* 22.2 (1907): 267–81.

———. *The International Position of Japan as a Great Power*. Studies in History, Economics, and Public Law 24. New York: Columbia University Press, 1905.

Hobsbawm, Eric. *The Age of Capital, 1848–1875*. 1975. New York: Vintage, 1996.

———. *The Age of Empire, 1875–1914*. New York: Pantheon, 1987.

———. *The Age of Revolution, 1789–1848*. London: Weidenfeld and Nicolson, 1962.

Hoffman, Katherine. *Stieglitz: A Beginning Light*. New Haven, Conn.: Yale University Press, 2004.

Hofstadter, Richard. *The Age of Reform: From Bryan to F.D.R.* New York: Vintage, 1955.

Hoganson, Kristin L. *Consumers' Imperium: The Global Production of American Domesticity, 1865–1920*. Chapel Hill: University of North Carolina Press, 2007.

Horne, Philip. *Henry James and Revision: The New York Edition*. Oxford: Oxford University Press, 1990.

Horwitz, Howard. *By the Law of Nature: Form and Value in Nineteenth-Century America*. New York: Oxford University Press, 1991.

Howe, Frederic C. "The End of an Economic Cycle." *Atlantic Monthly*, November 1902: 611–13.

Howells, William Dean. "Bibliographical." In *A Hazard of New Fortunes*. New York: Harper and Brothers, 1911. v–ix.

———. *Criticism and Fiction*. New York: Harper and Brothers, 1891.

———. "Editor's Easy Chair." *Harper's Monthly*, April 1901: 802–6.

———. "Editor's Easy Chair." *Harper's Monthly*, November 1911: 958–61.

———. "Editor's Study." *Harper's Monthly*, April 1886: 808–12.

———. "Editor's Study." *Harper's Monthly*, June 1886: 153–57.

———. "Editor's Study." *Harper's Monthly*, September 1886: 639–44.

———. "Editor's Study." *Harper's Monthly*, September 1887: 638–43.

———. "Editor's Study." *Harper's Monthly*, January 1888: 316–22.

———. "Editor's Study." *Harper's Magazine*, September 1890: 638–44.

———. "Editor's Study." *Harper's Monthly*, November 1889: 962–67.

———. "Editor's Study." *Harper's Monthly*, April 1891: 802–7.

———. *A Hazard of New Fortunes*. 1890. Oxford: Oxford University Press, 1990.

———. "Henry James, Jr." *Century*, November 1882: 25–29.

———. "Life and Letters." *Harper's Weekly*, June 8 and 22, 1895. Reprinted as "Dialect in Literature" in *W. D. Howells as Critic*, 231–42.

———. "Life and Letters." *Harper's Weekly*, June 27, 1896: 630.

———. *Life in Letters of William Dean Howells*. Ed. Mildred Howells. 2 vols. Garden City, N.Y.: Doubleday, Doran, 1928.

———. *My Mark Twain: Reminiscences and Criticism*. New York: Harper and Brothers, 1910.

———. "The New Historical Romances." *North American Review*, December 1900: 935–49.

———. "New York Low Life in Fiction," *New York World*, July 26, 1896. Reprinted in *W. D. Howells as Critic*, 256–62.

———. *The Rise of Silas Lapham*. 1885. New York: Penguin, 1983.

——. *W. D. Howells as Critic*. Ed. Edwin H. Cady. London: Routledge and Kegan Paul, 1973.

Hsu, Hsuan L. *Geography and the Production of Space in Nineteenth-Century American Literature*. Cambridge: Cambridge University Press, 2010.

Hunt, Michael H. *Ideology and U.S. Foreign Policy*. New Haven, Conn.: Yale University Press, 1987.

The Imperial Dictionary. Glasgow: Blackie and Son, 1847–50.

Introduction. *An Eagle Flight: A Filipino Novel Adapted from "Noli Me Tangere" by Dr. José Rizal*. New York: McClure, Phillips, 1900. v–xiv.

Jacobson, Matthew Frye. *Barbarian Virtues: The United States Encounters Foreign Peoples at Home and Abroad, 1876–1917*. New York: Hill and Wang, 2000.

James, Henry. *The American*. 1877. Ed. James W. Tuttleton. New York: W. W. Norton, 1978.

——. *The American*. 1907. Ed. Adrian Poole. Oxford: Oxford University Press, 1999.

——. "American Letter." *Literature*, July 9, 1898: 17–19.

——. *The American Scene*. 1907. In *Collected Travel Writings: Great Britain and America*. New York: Library of America, 1993. 351–736.

——. "The Art of Fiction." *Longman's Magazine*, September 1884: 502–21.

——. "The Beast in the Jungle." In *The Better Sort*. New York: Charles Scribner's Sons, 1903. 189–244

——. *Hawthorne*. London: Macmillan, 1879.

——. "James Russell Lowell." *Atlantic Monthly*, January 1892: 35–51.

——. Preface. *The Portrait of a Lady*. 1908. New York: Penguin, 1986. 41–55.

James, William. *Essays in Radical Empiricism*. New York: Longmans, Green, 1912.

——. *Pragmatism: A New Name for Some Old Ways of Thinking*. In *Pragmatism and Other Writings*, ed. Giles Gunn. 1907. London: Penguin, 2000. 5–132.

——. *The Principles of Psychology*. Vol. 1. New York: Henry Holt, 1890.

Jameson, Fredric. "Culture and Finance Capital." *Critical Inquiry* 24.1 (1997): 246–65.

Jewett, Sarah Orne. "The Foreigner." *Atlantic Monthly*, August 1900: 152–67.

Jones, Gavin. *Strange Talk: The Politics of Dialect Literature in Gilded Age America*. Berkeley: University of California Press, 1999.

Jordan, Edwin O. *Epidemic Influenza: A Survey*. Chicago: American Medical Association, 1927.

Kallen, Horace. *The Structure of Lasting Peace: An Inquiry into the Motives of War and Peace*. Boston: Marshall Jones, 1918.

Kant, Immanuel. "Idea for a Universal History with a Cosmopolitan Purpose." 1784. In *Political Writings*, ed. H. S. Reiss. 2nd ed. Cambridge: Cambridge University Press, 1991. 41–53.

Kaplan, Amy. *The Anarchy of Empire in the Making of U.S. Culture*. Cambridge, Mass.: Harvard University Press, 2002.

——. "Nation, Region, and Empire." In *The Columbia History of the American Novel*, ed. Emory Elliott. New York: Columbia University Press, 1991. 240–66.

——. *The Social Construction of American Realism*. Chicago: University of Chicago Press, 1988.

Kazin, Alfred. "The Art City Our Fathers Built." *American Scholar* 67.2 (1998): 17–26.

——. *New York Jew*. 1978. Syracuse, N.Y.: Syracuse University Press, 1996.

———. *On Native Grounds: An Interpretation of Modern American Prose Literature.* 1942. New York: Harcourt, Brace, 1995.

Kirk, Rudolf, and Clara M. Kirk. "Abraham Cahan and William Dean Howells: The Story of a Friendship." *American Jewish Historical Quarterly* 52.1 (September 1962): 27–57.

Kirwan, Thomas. *Reciprocity (Social and Economic) in the Thirtieth Century: The Coming Co-operative Age.* New York: Cochrane, 1909.

Kloppenberg, James T. *Uncertain Victory: Social Democracy and Progressivism in European and American Thought, 1870–1920.* Oxford: Oxford University Press, 1986.

Koebner, Richard, and Helmut Dan Schmidt. *Imperialism: The Story and Significance of a Political World, 1840–1960.* London: Cambridge University Press, 1964.

Kolloen, Ingar Sletten. *Hamsun.* 2 vols. Oslo: Gyldendal Norsk Forlag, 2003–4. Reprinted as *Knut Hamsun: Dreamer and Dissenter.* Trans. Deborah Dawkin and Erik Skuggevik. New Haven, Conn.: Yale University Press, 2009.

Krauss, Ellis, and Benjamin Nyblade, eds. *Japan and North America: First Contacts to the Pacific War.* Routledge Curzon Library of Modern Japan. Vol. 1. New York: Routledge, 2004.

LaFeber, Walter. *The New Empire: An Interpretation of American Expansion, 1869–1898.* Ithaca: Cornell University Press, 1963.

Lears, T. J. Jackson. *No Place of Grace: Antimodernism and the Transformation of American Culture, 1880–1920.* 1981. Chicago: University of Chicago Press, 1994.

Legrain, Philippe. "Cultural Globalization Is Not Americanization." *Chronicle Review* 49.35 (May 9, 2003): B7.

Lenin, Vladimir Ilyich. *Imperialism, the Highest Stage of Capitalism.* 1916. In *Essential Works of Lenin*, ed. Henry M. Christman. New York: Bantam, 1966. 177–270.

Leverenz, David. *Paternalism Incorporated: Fables of American Fatherhood, 1865–1940.* Ithaca, N.Y.: Cornell University Press, 2003.

Lewis, Bernard. "The Question of Orientalism." In *Orientalism: A Reader*, ed. Alexander Lyon Macfie. New York: New York University Press, 2001. 249–70.

Lewis, Sinclair. *The American Fear of Literature.* Stockholm: P. A. Norstedt and Söner, 1931.

Lieber, Francis. *Fragments of Political Science on Nationalism and Inter-Nationalism.* New York: Charles Scribner, 1868.

Lloyd, David, and Paul Thomas. *Culture and the State.* New York: Routledge, 1998.

London, Jack. *Jack London Reports: War Correspondence, Sports Articles, and Miscellaneous Writings.* Ed. King Hendricks and Irving Shepard. Garden City, N.Y.: Doubleday and Doubleday, 1970.

———. "The Unparalleled Invasion." In *The Strength of the Strong.* New York: Macmillan, 1914. 71–100.

Lone, Stewart. *Japan's First Modern War: Army and Society in the Conflict with China, 1894–1895.* New York: St. Martin's, 1994.

Lowe, Lisa. "Globalization." In *Keywords for American Cultural Studies*, ed. Bruce Burgett and Glenn Hendler. New York: New York University Press, 2007. 120–23.

———. *Immigrant Acts: On Asian American Cultural Politics.* Durham, N.C.: Duke University Press, 1996.

Luis-Brown, David. *Waves of Decolonization: Discourses of Race and Hemispheric Citizenship in Cuba, Mexico, and the United States.* Durham, N.C.: Duke University Press, 2008.

Lukács, Georg. *Studies in European Realism: A Sociological Survey of the Writings of Balzac, Stendhal, Zola, Tolstoy, Gorki and Others*. 1950. Trans. Edith Bone. New York: Howard Fertig, 2002.

Lutz, Tom. *Cosmopolitan Vistas: American Regionalism and Literary Value*. Ithaca, N.Y.: Cornell University Press, 2004.

Lye, Colleen. *America's Asia: Racial Form and American Literature, 1893–1945*. Princeton: Princeton University Press, 2005.

Lyngstad, Sverre, trans. Introduction. *Pan*. By Knut Hamsun. New York: Penguin, 1998. vii–xxiv.

MacDonald, Alex. Introduction. *Looking Backward, 2000–1887*. By Edward Bellamy. Peterborough, Ont.: Broadview, 2003. 11–38.

Madsen, Deborah L. "Sexing the Sojourner: Imagining Nation/Writing Women in the Global Chinese Diaspora." *Contemporary Women's Writing* 2.1 (2008): 36–49.

Mann, Arthur. "British Social Thought and American Reformers of the Progressive Era." *Mississippi Valley Historical Review* 42.4 (1956): 627–92.

Martin, Jay. *Harvests of Change: American Literature, 1865–1914*. Englewood Cliffs, N.J.: Prentice-Hall, 1967.

Marx, Karl. *Capital: A Critique of Political Economy*. Trans. Samuel Moore and Edward Aveling. Vol. 1. London: Swan Sonnenschein, 1906.

———. "Introduction to a Critique of Political Economy." 1857. In *The German Ideology: Part One, with Selections from Parts Two and Three and Supplementary Texts*, ed. C. J. Arthur. New York: International, 1970. 124–52.

Marx, Karl, and Friedrich Engels. *Manifesto of the Communist Party*. In *The Marx-Engels Reader*, ed. Robert C. Tucker. 2nd ed. New York: W. W. Norton, 1978. 469–500.

Matthews, Brander. "In Search of Local Color." *Harper's Monthly*, June 1894: 33–40.

———. "Literature in the New Century." In *Inquiries and Opinions*. New York: Charles Scribner's Sons, 1907. 1–25.

McFadden, John Duke. "The World's Salvation." In *The World's Parliament of Religions*, ed. John Henry Barrows. Vol. 2. Chicago: Parliament, 1893. 1308.

McGowan, John. "Literature as Equipment for Living: A Pragmatist Project." *Soundings: An Interdisciplinary Journal* 86.1–2 (2003): 119–48.

McWhirter, David, ed. *Henry James's New York Edition: The Construction of Authorship*. Stanford: Stanford University Press, 1995.

Mencken, H. L. "The Dean." *Smart Set*, January 1917: 266–68.

———. "Henry James." In *A Mencken Chrestomathy*. 1920. New York: Vintage, 1982. 500–501.

Meyer, John W. "The Changing Cultural Content of the Nation-State: A World Society Perspective." In *State/Culture: State Formation after the Cultural Turn*, ed. George Steinmetz. Ithaca, N.Y.: Cornell University Press, 1999. 123–41.

Meyer, John W., John Boli, George M. Thomas, and Francisco O. Ramirez. "World Society and the Nation-State." *American Journal of Sociology* 103.1 (1997). Reprinted in *World Society: The Writings of John W. Meyer*, ed. Georg Krücken and Gili S. Drori. Oxford: Oxford University Press, 2009. 173–74.

Michaels, Walter Benn. *The Gold Standard and the Logic of Naturalism: American Literature at the Turn of the Century*. Berkeley: University of California Press, 1987.

————. *Our America: Nativism, Modernism, and Pluralism*. Durham, N.C.: Duke University Press, 1995.

Morgan, Kenneth O. "The Future at Work: Anglo-American Progressivism, 1890–1917." In *Contrast and Connection: Bicentennial Essays in Anglo-American History*, ed. H. C. Allen and Roger Thompson. Athens: Ohio University Press, 1976. 245–71.

Morgridge, Barbara Gordon. Introduction. *The Cultural Life of Modern America*. By Knut Hamsun. Cambridge, Mass.: Harvard University Press, 1969. ix–xxxiv.

Morris, William. *News from Nowhere*. Boston: Roberts Brothers, 1891.

Murphy, Gretchen. *Shadowing the White Man's Burden: U.S. Imperialism and the Problem of the Color Line*. New York: New York University Press, 2010.

Murphy, J. Stephen. "Revision as a 'Living Affair' in Henry James's New York Edition." *Henry James Review* 29.2 (2008): 163–80.

Murphy, James. "A 'Very Different Dance': Intention, Technique, and Revision in Henry James's New York Edition." *Resources for American Literary Study* 20.2 (1994): 231–50.

Murray, Paul. *A Fantastic Journey: The Life and Literature of Lafcadio Hearn*. Folkestone, UK: Japan Library, 1993.

Nasaw, David. *Andrew Carnegie*. London: Penguin, 2006.

Neumann, William L. *America Encounters Japan: From Perry to MacArthur*. Baltimore: Johns Hopkins University Press, 1963.

The New York Times Current History: The European War, July–September 1917. Vol. 12. New York: New York Times Company, 1917.

Ninkovich, Frank. *Global Dawn: The Cultural Foundations of American Internationalism, 1865–1890*. Cambridge, Mass.: Harvard University Press, 2009.

Norris, Frank. "The Great American Novelist." In *The Responsibilities of the Novelist and Other Literary Essays*. New York: Doubleday, Page, 1903. 85–89.

Nugent, Walter. *Crossings: The Great Transatlantic Migrations, 1870–1914*. Bloomington: Indiana University Press, 1992.

Nussbaum, Martha, et al. *For Love of Country: Debating the Limits of Patriotism*. Ed. Joshua Cohen. Boston: Beacon Press, 1996.

Ocampo, Esteban A. de. "José Rizal, Father of Filipino Nationalism." *Journal of Southeast Asian History* 3.1 (1962): 44–51.

O'Loughlin, John, Lynn Staeheli, and Edward Greenberg, eds. Introduction. *Globalization and Its Outcomes*. New York: Guilford, 2004.

Ong, Aihwa. *Flexible Citizenships: The Cultural Logics of Transnationality*. Durham, N.C.: Duke University Press, 1999.

O'Rourke, Kevin H., and Jeffrey G. Williamson. *Globalization and History: The Evolution of a Nineteenth-Century Atlantic Economy*. Cambridge, Mass.: MIT Press, 1999.

Paine, S. C. M. *The Sino-Japanese War of 1894–1895: Perceptions, Power, and Primacy*. Cambridge: Cambridge University Press, 2003.

Palacio Valdés, Armando. *Sister Saint Sulpice*. Trans. Nathan Haskell Dole. New York: Thomas Y. Crowell, 1890.

Parker, Hershel. *Flawed Texts and Verbal Icons: Literary Authority in American Fiction*. Evanston, Ill.: Northwestern University Press, 1984.

————. "Henry James 'In the Wood': Sequence and Significances of His Literary Labors, 1905–1907." *Nineteenth-Century Fiction* 38.4 (1984): 492–513.

Parrington, Vernon Louis. *The Beginnings of Critical Realism in America, 1860–1920*. Main Currents in American Thought: An Interpretation of American Literature from the Beginnings to 1920. Vol. 3. 1930. New York: Harcourt, Brace, 1958.

Patler, Nicholas. *Jim Crow and the Wilson Administration: Protesting Federal Segregation in the Early Twentieth Century*. Boulder: University Press of Colorado, 2004.

Patterson, Orlando. "The Emerging West Atlantic System: Migration, Culture, and Underdevelopment in the United States and Circum-Caribbean Region." In *Population in an Interacting World*, ed. William Alonso. Cambridge, Mass.: Harvard University Press, 1987. 227–60.

Pease, Donald E. "American Studies after American Exceptionalism?: Toward a Comparative Analysis of Imperial State Exceptionalisms." In *Globalizing American Studies*, ed. Brian T. Edwards and Dilip Parameshwar Gaonkar. Chicago: University of Chicago Press, 2010. 47–83.

———. "Introduction: Re-Mapping the Transnational Turn." In *Re-Framing the Transnational Turn in American Studies*, ed. Winfried Fluck, Donald E. Pease, and John Carlos Rowe. Hannover, N.H.: University Press of New England, 2011. 1–46.

———. *The New American Exceptionalism*. Minneapolis: University of Minnesota Press, 2009.

Perloff, Marjorie. "Modernism without the Modernists: A Response to Walter Benn Michaels." *Modernism/Modernity* 3.3 (1996): 99–105.

Perry, Bliss. "Number 4 Park Street." *Atlantic Monthly*, January 1903: 1–5.

Peyser, Thomas. *Utopia and Cosmopolis: Globalization in the Era of American Literary Realism*. Durham, N.C.: Duke University Press, 1998.

Phillips, Howard, and David Killingray, eds. Introduction. *The Spanish Influenza Pandemic of 1918–19: New Perspectives*. New York: Routledge, 2003. 1–25.

Poole, Adrian, ed. Appendix 2. "The Revised Version for the New York Edition." In *The American*. By Henry James. Oxford: Oxford University Press, 1999. 367–84.

Posnock, Ross. "Breaking the Aura of Henry James." In *Henry James's New York Edition: The Construction of Authorship*. Stanford: Stanford University Press, 1995. 23–38.

Pratt, Lloyd. *Archives of American Time: Literature and Modernity in the Nineteenth Century*. Philadelphia: University of Pennsylvania Press, 2010.

Renan, Ernst. "What Is a Nation?" 1882. Trans. Martin Thom. In *Nation and Narration*, ed. Homi K. Bhabha. London: Routledge, 1990. 8–22.

Reesman, Jeanne Campbell. *Jack London's Racial Lives: A Critical Biography*. Athens: University of Georgia Press, 2009.

———. "Marching with 'the Censor': The Japanese Army and Jack London, Author." *Jack London Journal* 6 (1999): 135–74.

Reichard, Gary W., and Ted Dickson, eds. *America on the World Stage: A Global Approach to U.S. History*. Urbana: University of Illinois Press, 2008.

Reinsch, Paul Samuel. *Public International Unions: Their Work and Organization*. Boston: Ginn, 1911.

Rev. of *Sister Saint Sulpice*. By Armando Palacio Valdés. *Literary World*, 24 May 1890: 168–69.

Reynolds, Larry J. "Henry James's New Christopher Newman." *Studies in the Novel* 5 (1973): 457–68.

Rizal, José. *Noli Me Tangere*. 1887. Trans. Harold Augenbraum. London: Penguin, 2006.

Robbins, Bruce. "Comparative Cosmopolitanisms." In *Cosmopolitics: Thinking and Feeling beyond the Nation*, ed. Pheng Cheah and Bruce Robbins. Minneapolis: University of Minnesota Press, 1998. 246–64.

Robertson, Roland. *Globalization: Social Theory and Global Culture*. London: Sage, 1992.

Robinson, Edgar E., and Victor J. West. *The Foreign Policy of Woodrow Wilson, 1913–1917*. New York: Macmillan, 1918.

Rochelson, Meri-Jane. *A Jew in the Public Arena: The Career of Israel Zangwill*. Detroit: Wayne State University Press, 2008.

Rodgers, Daniel T. *Atlantic Crossings: Social Politics in a Progressive Age*. Cambridge, Mass.: Belknap Press, 1998.

Roosevelt, Theodore. "True Americanism." In *American Ideals and Other Essays, Social and Political*. New York: G. P. Putnam's Sons, 1897. 14–32.

Rosenberg, Emily S. *Spreading the American Dream: American Economic and Cultural Expansion, 1890–1945*. New York: Hill and Wang, 1982.

Rosk, Nancy von. "'Go, Make Yourself for a Person': Urbanity and the Construction of an American Identity in the Novels of Abraham Cahan and Anzia Yezierska." *Prospects* 26 (October 2001): 295–335.

Rowe, John Carlos. "Henry James and Globalization." *Henry James Review* 24.3 (2003): 205–14.

Said, Edward. *Orientalism*. New York: Vintage, 1979.

Schulz, Max F. "The Bellegardes' Feud with Christopher Newman: A Study of Henry James's Revision of *The American*." *American Literature* 27.1 (1955): 42–55.

Schurz, Carl. "The Issue of Imperialism." In *Speeches, Correspondence, and Political Papers of Carl Schurz*, ed. Frederic Bancroft. 1899. New York: G. P. Putnam's Sons, 1913. 1–36.

Sedgwick, Henry Dwight. "Literature and Cosmopolitanism." *Atlantic Monthly*, February 1915: 215–21.

Selected Works from the Worcester Art Museum. Worcester, Mass.: Worcester Art Museum, 1994.

Shaler, Nathaniel S. "European Peasants as Immigrants." *Atlantic Monthly*, May 1893: 646–55.

Showerman, Grant. "A Spanish Novelist." *Sewanee Review* 22.4 (1914): 385–404.

Silver, Naomi E. "Between Communion and Renunciation: Revising *The American*." *Henry James Review* 22.3 (2001): 286–96.

Slattery, Peter. *Reporting the Russo-Japanese War, 1904–5: Lionel James's First Wireless Transmissions to "The Times."* Folkestone, UK: Global Oriental, 2004.

Sobel, Robert. *Panic on Wall Street: A History of America's Financial Disasters*. London: Macmillan, 1968.

Sollors, Werner. *Beyond Ethnicity: Consent and Descent in American Culture*. Oxford: Oxford University Press, 1986.

Sonnichsen, Albert. "Consumers' Coöperation: The New Mass Movement." *American Review of Reviews*, April 1913: 455–64.

Spellman, W. M. *The Global Community: Migration and the Making of the Modern World*. Stroud, UK: Sutton, 2002.

Speranza, Gino C. "Political Representation of Italo-American Colonies in the Italian Parliament." *Charities and the Commons*, January 20, 1906: 521–22.

———. *Race or Nation: A Conflict of Divided Loyalties.* Indianapolis: Bobbs-Merrill, 1925.

Spivak, Gayatri Chakravorty. "Poststructuralism, Marginality, Postcoloniality and Value." In *Literary Theory Today*, ed. Peter Collier and Helga Geyer-Ryan. Ithaca, N.Y.: Cornell University Press, 1990. 219–44.

Sprague, O. M. W. *History of Crises under the National Banking System.* Washington, D.C.: Government Printing Office, 1910.

Stafford, William T. "The Ending of *The American*: A Defense of the Early Version." *Nineteenth-Century Fiction* 18.1 (1963): 86–89.

Stieglitz, Alfred. "How *The Steerage* Happened." *Twice a Year*, 8–9 (Spring/Summer and Fall/Winter 1942): 175–78.

Stein, Gertrude. *The Autobiography of Alice B. Toklas.* 1933. New York: Vintage, 1990.

Steinberg, John W., Bruce W. Menning, David Schimmelpenninck van der Oye, David Wolff, and Shinji Yokote, eds. *The Russo-Japanese War in Global Perspective: World War Zero.* Lenden, Neth.: Brill, 2005.

Stempel, Daniel. "Lafcadio Hearn: Interpreter of Japan." *American Literature* 20.1 (1948): 1–19.

Stoddard, Lothrop. *The Rising Tide of Color against White World-Supremacy.* New York: Charles Scribner's Sons, 1920.

Stokes, Melvyn. "American Progressives and the European Left." *Journal of American Studies* 17.1 (1983): 5–28.

Streeby, Shelley. "Empire." In *Keywords for American Cultural Studies*, ed. Bruce Burgett and Glenn Hendler. New York: New York University Press, 2007. 95–101.

Strong, Josiah. *The New Era; or, The Coming Kingdom.* New York: Baker and Taylor, 1893.

———. *Our Country: Its Possible Future and Its Present Crisis.* New York: Baker and Taylor, 1885.

Sweeney, Michael S. "'Delays and Vexation': Jack London and the Russo-Japanese War." *Journalism and Mass Communication Quarterly* 75.3 (1998): 548–59.

Tall, Emily. "English-Russian and American-Russian Literary Relations." In *Handbook of Russian Literature*, ed. Victor Terras. New Haven, Conn.: Yale University Press, 1985. 124–26.

Tanner, Tony. Introduction. *A Hazard of New Fortunes.* By William Dean Howells. 1965. Oxford: Oxford University Press, 1990. vii–xxxv.

Taylor, Charles. "The Politics of Recognition." In *Multiculturalism: Examining the Politics of Recognition*, ed. Amy Gutmann. Princeton: Princeton University Press, 1994. 25–73.

———. "The Self in Moral Space." In *Sources of the Self: The Making of the Modern Identity.* Cambridge, Mass.: Harvard University Press, 1989. 25–52.

———. "Two Theories of Modernity." *The Responsive Community: Rights and Responsibilities* 6.3 (1996): 16–25.

Thomas, Brook. *American Literary Realism and the Failed Promise of Contract.* Berkeley: University of California Press, 1997.

Tintner, Adeline R. *The Twentieth-Century World of Henry James: Changes in His Work after 1900.* Baton Rouge: Louisiana State University Press, 2002.

Torpey, John. "The Great War and the Birth of the Modern Passport System." In *Documenting Individual Identity: The Development of State Practices in the Modern*

World, ed. Jane Caplan and John Torpey. Princeton: Princeton University Press, 2001. 256–70.

Trachtenberg, Alan. *The Incorporation of America: Culture and Society in the Gilded Age*. New York: Hill and Wang, 1982.

Traschen, Isadore. "An American in Paris." *American Literature* 26.1 (1954): 67–77.

———. "Henry James and the Art of Revision." *Philological Quarterly* 35.1 (1956): 39–47.

———. "James's Revisions of the Love Affair in *The American*." *New England Quarterly* 29.1 (1956): 43–62.

Trent, William P. "Cosmopolitanism and Partisanship." In *War and Civilization*. New York: Thomas Y. Crowell, 1901. 25–52.

Troell, Jan, dir. *Hamsun*. Starring Max von Sydow. Bayerischer Rundfunk et al., 1996.

Tucker, William Jewett. "The Crux of the Peace Problem." *Atlantic Monthly*, April 1916: 451–60.

Tuttleton, James, ed. "A Note on the Text." In *The American*. By Henry James. New York: W. W. Norton, 1978. 311–17.

Twain, Mark. *Tom Sawyer Abroad*. 1894. In *Tom Sawyer Abroad and Tom Sawyer, Detective*. Berkeley: University of California Press, 1982. 1–104.

———. "To the Person Sitting in Darkness." *North American Review*, February 1901: 161–76.

Tyrrell, Ian. *Transnational Nation: United States History in Global Perspective since 1789*. New York: Palgrave Macmillan, 2007.

United States Congress. Senate. Immigration Commission. *Reports of the Immigration Commission*. 61st Cong. 3rd sess. S. Doc. 749/1. Vol. 1. Washington: GPO, 1911.

Veblen, Thorstein. *Imperial Germany and the Industrial Revolution*. New York: Macmillan, 1915.

———. *The Theory of Business Enterprise*. New York: Charles Scribner's Sons, 1904.

———. *The Theory of the Leisure Class*. New York: Macmillan, 1899.

Wald, Priscilla. *Constituting Americans: Cultural Anxiety and Narrative Form*. Durham, N.C.: Duke University Press, 1995.

Wallerstein, Immanuel. *The Modern World-System*. New York: Academic Press, 1974–89.

———. "The Three Instances of Hegemony in the History of the Capitalist World-Economy." *International Journal of Comparative Sociology* 24.1–2 (1983): 100–108.

———. "World-System Analysis." In *The Essential Wallerstein*. New York: Free Press, 2000. 129–48.

Warner, Denis, and Peggy Warner. *The Tide at Sunrise: A History of the Russo-Japanese War, 1904–1905*. 2nd ed. London: Frank Cass, 2002.

Warren, Kenneth W. *Black and White Strangers: Race and American Literary Realism*. Chicago: University of Chicago Press, 1993.

Waters, Malcolm. *Globalization*. 2nd ed. London: Routledge, 2001.

Watkins, Floyd C. "Christopher Newman's Final Instinct." *Nineteenth-Century Fiction* 12.1 (1957): 85–88.

Weber, Donald. "Outsiders and Greenhorns: Christopher Newman in the Old World, David Levinsky in the New." *American Literature* 67.4 (1995): 725–45.

Weisbuch, Robert. *Atlantic Double-Cross: American Literature and British Influence in the Age of Emerson*. Chicago: University of Chicago Press, 1986.

Wells, David, and Sandra Wilson, eds. Foreword. *The Russo-Japanese War in Cultural Perspective, 1904–05*. New York: St. Martin's, 1999. ix–xiii.

Wells, David A. *Recent Economic Changes, and Their Effect on the Production and Distribution of Wealth and the Well-Being of Society.* 1889. New York: Appleton, 1899.

Wesling, Meg. *Empire's Proxy: American Literature and U.S. Imperialism in the Philippines.* New York: New York University Press, 2011.

Whelan, Richard. *Alfred Stieglitz: A Biography.* Boston: Little, Brown, 1995.

Whitney, William Dwight. *Language and the Study of Language.* New York: Charles Scribner, 1867.

Wicker, Elmus. *Banking Panics of the Gilded Age.* Cambridge: Cambridge University Press, 2000.

Williams, Raymond. *Culture and Society: 1780–1950.* New York: Columbia University Press, 1983.

———. *Keywords: A Vocabulary of Culture and Society.* Rev. ed. New York: Oxford University Press, 1983.

Williams, Stanley T. *The Spanish Background of American Literature.* Vol. 2. New Haven, Conn.: Yale University Press, 1955.

Williams, William Appleman. *The Tragedy of American Diplomacy.* 1959. New York: W. W. Norton, 1988.

Wilson, Edmund, Jr. "The Ambiguity of Henry James." In *The Triple Thinkers: Twelve Essays on Literary Subjects.* 1948. New York: Noonday, 1976. 88–132.

———. *The American Jitters: A Year of the Slump.* New York: Charles Scribner's Sons, 1932.

———. "The Death of a Soldier." In *The Undertaker's Garland.* By John Peale Bishop and Edmund Wilson Jr. New York: Alfred K. Knopf, 1922. 99–120.

———. "A Nation of Foreigners." *New Republic,* October 5, 1927: 161–62.

———. *A Prelude: Landscapes, Characters and Conversations from the Early Years of My Life.* New York: Farrar, Straus and Giroux, 1967.

———. *The Shores of Light: A Literary Chronicle of the 1920s and 1930s.* New York: Farrar, Straus and Young, 1952.

Wilson, Woodrow. *The Papers of Woodrow Wilson.* Ed. Arthur S. Link et al. Vol. 33. Princeton: Princeton University Press, 1980.

Woolson, Constance Fenimore. "In Search of the Picturesque." *Harper's Monthly,* July 1872: 161–68.

Wyman, Mark. *Round-Trip to America: The Immigrants Return to Europe, 1880–1930.* Ithaca, N.Y.: Cornell University Press, 1993.

Yannella, Philip R. *American Literature in Context from 1865–1929.* Chichester: Wiley-Blackwell, 2011.

Yin, Xiao-huang. *Chinese American Literature since the 1850s.* Urbana: University of Illinois Press, 2000.

Zagar, Monika. *Knut Hamsun: The Dark Side of Literary Brilliance.* Seattle: University of Washington Press, 2009.

Zetterberg Pettersson, Eva. *The Old World Journey: National Identity in Four American Novels from 1960 to 1973.* Uppsala: Uppsala University Press, 2005.

Ziff, Larzer. *The American 1890s: Life and Times of a Lost Generation.* 1966. New York: Viking, 1968.

Zimmerman, David A. *Panic!: Markets, Crises, and Crowds in American Fiction.* Chapel Hill: University of North Carolina Press, 2006.

Index

Hannerz, Ulf, 32

Harper's Monthly, 30, 46–47, 65, 77, 86, 177, 192

Harper's Weekly, 58–59, 100

Harriman, E. H., 101

Harrison, Benjamin, 48

Harte, Bret, 58

Harvey, David, 10, 23, 202 (n. 34)

Hayashi, Tadasu, 186

Hearn, Lafcadio, 4, 25, 28, 60, 165, 177–78, 187, 225 (n. 56); on modernity, 167–68, 179, 181–83, 190–91; *Youma*, 169, 177–78; *Japan: An Attempt at Interpretation*, 178, 184–85, 190–91; *Glimpses of Unfamiliar Japan*, 179; *Kokoro: Hints and Echoes of Japanese Inner Life*, 179–86

Hearst, William Randolph, 164

Heath Anthology of American Literature, 127

Higginson, Thomas Wentworth, 43

Himmelfarb, Gertrude, 43, 207 (n. 55)

Hishida, Seiji, 188–90, 225–26 (n. 61)

Hobsbawm, Eric, 13–14

Hofstadter, Richard, 21, 96–97, 203–4 (n. 48)

Hoganson, Kristin L., 37–38, 114, 130

Howe, Frederic C., 41–42, 48

Howells, William Dean, 4, 22, 25, 27, 46–47, 192, 194, 205 (n. 1); relocation to New York, 18, 30, 65, 77; *A Hazard of New Fortunes*, 18, 60, 62–78, 85, 94, 96–97, 101, 113, 146, 175; *The Rise of Silas Lapham*, 18, 67–68, 110–11; and Haymarket Affair, 18, 77; reviews of other authors' works, 18–19, 58–63, 81–95, 133, 169, 177–78, 215 (n. 9); *Criticism and Fiction*, 60, 62, 64, 79, 85–87; critical legacy of, 211 (n. 49)

Hsu, Hsuan, 75

Immigration, 6–7, 14, 27, 62, 67–68, 76, 220 (n. 29); and return migration, 27, 127–31, 137–44, 150–51, 156, 158–60, 218–19 (n. 7); and Americanization, 35, 37, 44, 117–18, 127–31, 134–35, 139–40, 143–44, 146–47, 150, 154–56, 195–98;

as impetus for state regulation, 72–73, 135, 138; and immigrant literature, 127, 133, 141, 144, 152; from Europe, 129, 136, 138; and migration systems, 132, 137, 140–50, 156–57, 221 (n. 52); and anti-immigrant sentiments, 135–36, 154, 167, 219–20 (n. 25); from Asia, 161–62, 170, 186–88

Imperialism, 10, 13–14, 26, 52–53, 57, 158, 168; and anti-imperialism, 20, 48, 88, 94; as territorial expansion, 27–28, 45, 54–55, 89–90, 122–25, 171, 176; as consolidation of economic power, 101–2, 114–15, 182, 190, 215 (n. 7). *See also* Japan: imperial expansion of

Indigenization, 26, 107

Influenza pandemic (1918–19), 194–96, 198, 226 (n. 9)

International copyright, 7, 38–39, 46, 206 (n. 37)

Internationalism, 6, 27, 34–35, 48–49, 54–55, 57, 139–40, 189, 207 (n. 40); as synonym for communism, 14, 41, 43, 92, 207 (n. 47); as neologism, 31–33, 37–41; and individual nation-states, 40–44, 52; utopian impulses of, 52, 141. *See also* Cosmopolitanism; State formation

Interstate Commerce Act, 96–97

Investment bankers, 12, 27, 100–103, 105

Jacobson, Matthew Frye, 130–31

James, Henry, 4, 6, 21–22, 25, 38, 60, 83; cosmopolitan reputation of, 4, 29–32, 44, 46–47, 129, 192; *The Portrait of a Lady*, 18, 29, 63, 85, 99; *The Tragic Muse*, 18, 169; "The Art of Fiction," 19; *The American Scene*, 20, 27, 100, 109, 116–25, 134–37, 144, 183, 214 (n. 5); *The American*, 27, 29, 97–100, 107, 109–20, 124–26, 214 (n. 5); and international novel, 29, 98–99, 119–20, 215 (n. 9); on local color, 58, 209 (n. 4); and New York Edition, 97, 116; *Hawthorne*, 120, 154; posthumous reception of, 192–94, 198–99; "The Beast in the Jungle," 217 (n. 59)

Napoleon III (emperor of France), 116
Neoliberalism, 10, 14–15, 23, 203 (n. 38)
New York City, as economic and cultural
    center, 18, 29–30, 46, 65–67, 101, 142–43,
    146–48
New York Times, 1, 8
Ninkovich, Frank, 16, 31, 38–39, 46, 206–7
    (n. 39)
Norris, Frank, 17–18, 66, 170
North American Review, 48

O'Rourke, Kevin H., 14
Oxford English Dictionary (1933), 43, 47–48

Palacio Valdés, Armando, 60, 79, 81–83,
    88–90, 94; Sister Saint Sulpice, 84–87
Pan-Africanism, 34, 55–56
Pardo Bazán, Emilia, 83
Paris Commune, 41, 116
Parrington, Vernon, 18, 19–20, 192–94, 198,
    203 (n. 44)
Patterson, Orlando, 132, 137
Pease, Donald, 23, 26, 197–98, 227 (n. 19)
Perry, Bliss, 29–31, 35, 39, 47
Perry, Matthew, 163, 180
Perry, Thomas Sergeant, 79
Peyser, Thomas, 24–26, 45, 204 (n. 60), 205
    (n. 63)
Phelps, Austin, 52
Pond, Enoch, 49
Postcolonial subjectivity, 209 (n. 105)
Progressive movement, 9, 19–22, 26, 32,
    34–35, 41–42, 49, 51, 53; transnational
    aspects of, 5–6, 36–39, 181; and state
    regulation of monopolies, 73, 96–97,
    99, 101–5; and immigration, 138–39;
    decline of, 193. See also Late realism: and
    Progressive movement
Pryke, Michael, 106

Quota Acts (1920s), 135, 193, 196–97

Racialism, 163, 165, 168, 173–74, 184,
    187, 190, 218 (n. 64), 223 (n. 9); as
    distinct from racism, 165–66; and

multiculturalism, 167, 223 (n. 20), 224
    (n. 21)
Realism: and free indirect discourse, 69–71,
    211 (n. 33); in opposition to romance, 86,
    88–89, 94, 97–98, 215 (n. 7); and multi-
    culturalism, 194. See also Late realism;
    Local color
Red Scare (1919–20), 193, 196–97
Reesman, Jeanne Campbell, 170
Reinsch, Paul Samuel, 40–44, 57
Renan, Ernst, 117, 125, 212 (n. 54)
Rizal, José, 25, 60; Noli me tangere, 79, 82,
    88–93; posthumous reception of, 93–94,
    213 (n. 92), 214 (n. 99)
Robertson, Roland, 11, 13–16, 202 (n. 31),
    215 (n. 9)
Rockefeller, John D., 108
Rodgers, Daniel T., 21, 36
Roosevelt, Theodore, 20–21, 53, 89, 163,
    186–87; "True Americanism," 44
Rosenberg, Emily S., 193
Rowe, John Carlos, 109
Ruskin, John, 85, 114
Russo-Japanese War, 162–64, 170–71, 179,
    186, 188. See also Battle of the Yalu River

Said, Edward, 168, 224 (n. 24); responses to,
    224 (n. 23)
St. Louis Post-Dispatch, 159
San Francisco Examiner, 164
Schurz, Carl, 115, 123, 217 (n. 58)
Sedgwick, Henry Dwight, 45, 60
Sentimentalism, 60, 210 (n. 8), 213 (n. 84)
Shaler, Nathaniel, 135–36, 141, 154, 167
Sherman Antitrust Act, 96–97, 103
Shigemi, Shiukichi, 169
Sino-Japanese War (1894–95), 179–80
Social gospel, 20, 49–50
Sollors, Werner, 130–31
Sonnichsen, Albert, 108
Spanish-American War, 45, 62, 88–89, 208
    (n. 66)
Speranza, Gino C., 138, 141, 220 (n. 32)
Sprague, O. M. W., 105, 108
Standard Oil Company, 96, 101

World literature, 27, 31, 45, 47–48, 59–63, 77–79, 81–83, 88, 90–91, 94–95, 189
World-salvation, 27, 32–35, 37, 48–57
World time, 14, 16–17, 203 (n. 42)
World War I, 1–2, 14, 37, 40, 54–55, 139, 188, 192–96, 198

Yannella, Philip R., 130

Zangwill, Israel: *The Melting Pot*, 140, 220 (n. 40)
Zetterberg Pettersson, Eva, 215 (n. 9)
Ziff, Larzer, 18, 203 (n. 44)